THE GIRL WHO WOULD BE MARILYN MONROE

Also by Tony Castro

MICKEY & BILLY
The Glory and Tragedy of a Yankee Friendship

THE BOOK OF MARILYN
A Novel

MARIS & MANTLE
Two Yankees, Immortality, and the Age of Camelot

MANTLE
The Best There Ever Was

GEHRIG & THE BABE
The Friendship and The Feud

LOOKING FOR HEMINGWAY
Spain, the Bullfights & A Final Rite of Passage

DIMAG & MICK
Sibling Rivals, Yankee Blood Brothers

THE PRINCE OF SOUTH WACO
American Dreams and Great Expectations

MICKEY MANTLE
America's Prodigal Son

CHICANO POWER
The Emergence of Mexican America

THE GIRL WHO WOULD BE MARILYN MONROE

An Intimate Portrait of the Young Norma Jeane

TONY CASTRO

BLOOMSBURY ACADEMIC
NEW YORK • LONDON • OXFORD • NEW DELHI • SYDNEY

BLOOMSBURY ACADEMIC
Bloomsbury Publishing Inc, 1359 Broadway, New York, NY 10018, USA
Bloomsbury Publishing Plc, 50 Bedford Square, London, WC1B 3DP, UK
Bloomsbury Publishing Ireland, 29 Earlsfort Terrace, Dublin 2, D02 AY28, Ireland

BLOOMSBURY, BLOOMSBURY ACADEMIC and the Diana logo are trademarks of Bloomsbury Publishing Plc

First published in the United States of America 2026

Cover images:

Cover image Twentieth Century-Fox Film Corporation/Photofest, inset of young Marilyn Monroe/Photofest. Cover design by Diana Nuhn

Library of Congress Cataloging-in-Publication Data
Names: Castro, Tony author
Title: The girl who would be Marilyn Monroe : an intimate portrait of the young Norma Jeane / by Tony Castro.
Identifiers: LCCN 2026007906 (print) | LCCN 2026007907 (ebook) | ISBN 9798216448648 hardback | ISBN 9798216448655 epub | ISBN 9798216448662 pdf
Subjects: LCSH: Monroe, Marilyn,1926–1962—Childhood and youth | Motion picture actors and actresses—United States | LCGFT: Biographies
Classification: LCC PN2287.M69 C395 2026 (print) | LCC PN2287.M69 (ebook)
LC record available at https://lccn.loc.gov/2026007906
LC ebook record available at https://lccn.loc.gov/2026007907

ISBN: HB: 979-8-216-44864-8
ePDF: 979-8-216-44866-2
eBook: 979-8-216-44865-5

Typeset by Deanta Global Publishing Services, Chennai, India
Printed and bound in the United States of America

For product safety related questions contact productsafety@bloomsbury.com.

To find out more about our authors and books visit www.bloomsbury.com and sign up for our newsletters

For Renee

CONTENTS

PREFACE

THE CENTENNIAL

In 2026, the world will pause to remember a woman who never really left. Marilyn Monroe, born Norma Jeane Mortenson in 1926, would have turned one hundred. The number feels impossible. She belongs to the eternal youth of celluloid and flashbulbs, a face forever in her twenties, her laugh forever mid-flight. And yet the calendar insists: a century.

It is a milestone that asks us to reckon not just with Marilyn's life, but with her myth. She was never simply an actress, never only a starlet, never merely the blonde bombshell of tabloid shorthand. Marilyn was invention layered upon invention—a child who learned to survive with a smile, a young woman who turned vulnerability into magnetism, an artist who carried wounds into performance and made them shimmer. Her story is not nostalgia. It is prophecy.

For a hundred years her name has circled the globe like a refrain. It sells perfume and diamonds, posters and T-shirts, streaming marathons and academic symposia. But behind that name, the girl still waits—the girl in second-hand shoes, in orphanage dormitories, in front of cracked mirrors rehearsing the smile that would become her passport. This book seeks her out. Not to dismantle the icon, but to braid her myth back into the marrow of her beginnings.

The centennial is not only commemoration; it is confrontation. To stand at this threshold is to admit that Marilyn still unsettles us. She embodies contradictions that America has never resolved—innocence and desire, glamour and ruin, adoration and abandonment. She is both the dream and the cost of dreaming. To look at her now is to look at ourselves, and at the century that shaped us.

And she is not alone in this rare company. Cleopatra's face—painted in mosaics, reimagined in Shakespeare, revived by Elizabeth Taylor—became shorthand for beauty and power so intoxicating it toppled empires. Greta Garbo withdrew from the screen and yet remains eternal in her silence, her aloof mystery making her more present in absence than many who stayed.

Princess Diana, gone in an instant of shattered glass, still walks with us as the "people's princess," a modern saint for an age of paparazzi and fractured fairy tales.

These women, like Marilyn, became more than themselves. They became a language through which the world speaks of longing, of desire, of grief. They remind us that myth is not ancient—it is ongoing. Cleopatra's Egypt, Garbo's Hollywood, Diana's Kensington Gardens, Marilyn's Los Angeles: all are shrines where memory still flickers like votive flames.

To place Marilyn in their company is not exaggeration but recognition. She is the American Cleopatra, the Garbo of vulnerability, the Diana of the silver screen—claimed too soon, immortalized too young, carried forward by the ache of what might have been. Her centennial is therefore not only an American event but a global reckoning.

This, then, is not a backward glance. It is a centennial reckoning, a chance to place Marilyn Monroe back in time and out of it, in history and above it. She was not only a star of the twentieth century; she is a mirror held up to the twenty-first. Her image lives in pixels and holograms, in artificial resurrections that prove her body may be gone, but her presence still commands.

One hundred years since her birth, Marilyn remains America's unfinished sentence. This book is an attempt to complete it—or at least to trace its shape.

ACKNOWLEDGMENTS

Any writer foolhardy enough to take on a new biography of Marilyn Monroe, more than half a century after her death, probably ought to pause and reconsider what he's about to do. I certainly did. It was never my intention to be "Marilyn's biographer." When I set out in 1978, newly arrived as a columnist at the *Los Angeles Herald Examiner*, the book I imagined writing someday was the life of my father's hero, Joe DiMaggio. That was the north star.

It is a long story how I was sidetracked, and an even longer one how DiMaggio led me to Marilyn. Eventually I did profile Joltin' Joe in the dual biography *DiMag & Mick*, and I still hope to return to him in a definitive way. But when I came to Los Angeles, the plan was simple: spend as much time as possible in San Francisco, in Joe's shadow.

My deepest thanks go first to the people who gently—and sometimes not so gently—redirected me. At the top of that list is my colleague and longtime desk mate, James Bacon. Jim knew DiMaggio from the period of his brief marriage to Marilyn and from the long, haunted years after her death. He was the first to insist that it would be impossible to understand DiMaggio without understanding the role Marilyn had played in his life. He was also the first to suggest that I consider them not just as characters in each other's story but as separate subjects, worthy of separate biographies.

Perhaps that is why he was so generous. Jim shared with me not only his memories but his files: clippings, magazine pieces, book excerpts, studio gossip, old call sheets—an improvised Marilyn archive that had grown on his desk and in his home over decades. The files he left me made the early research easier; the stories he told made it impossible to look away from the girl who had been Norma Jeane.

By the time we became neighbors in the newsroom, Jim was already in his mid-sixties, a legendary Hollywood columnist and instrumental in my soft landing as a Los Angeles writer. He was full of mischief and ideas, including what he thought would be a completely unexpected debut column: a profile of Marilyn's last home. It might have been, except the editor killed it. I resigned in protest; the publisher promptly offered me a newer, better deal. That, too, is a story for another book.

Jim also possessed an expense account unmatched in the newsroom and used it as a kind of informal fellowship. He treated himself—and often me—to lunches at the Polo Lounge at the Beverly Hills Hotel and dinners at Patrick Terrail's Ma Maison. There, at Jim's prompting, early financial backer Gene Kelly told behind-the-scenes stories about childish hijinks on the set of *Let's Make Love*, his 1960 collaboration with Marilyn. Jim arranged a complimentary membership for me at The Daisy, Jack Hanson's private Rodeo Drive discotheque, where the owner—an ex–minor league shortstop—became both friend and source. He also ushered me into Hugh Hefner and Stan Herman's Pips, the Beverly Hills disco and backgammon club where you could sit in a corner, listen, and have column material for a lifetime. In all of those places, Marilyn was strangely present: in the way people lowered their voices when her name came up, in the unfinished stories, in the long silences.

Like all biographers, I have built on and argued with the work that came before me. Most books about Marilyn rightly focus on the screen goddess. *The Girl Who Would Be Marilyn* turns its gaze backward, toward the child and adolescent who became that woman. For that reason, the early chapters in previous biographies—often skimpy out of necessity—were both invaluable and insufficient. I leaned on them where they offered solid footing; I departed from them where new documents or a different emphasis demanded it.

A large part of this book rests on Norma Jeane's family history. I have drawn on records that shed light on the identity of her biological father and a previously unknown half-brother. These materials also offer a more detailed view of her mother, Gladys Baker, and her struggle with paranoid schizophrenia—a struggle that left deep marks on her daughter. Because Marilyn's own mental health is central to her story, I consulted doctors' files and correspondence where accessible. Those records helped trace her psychological deterioration and the borderline paranoid schizophrenia diagnosis that, in many ways, mirrored her mother's condition.

Research is a relay race of kindnesses. At the institutional level, my thanks to the staff and archivists at the JFK Library (for contextual family papers that intersect with the era), the Margaret Herrick Library of the Academy of Motion Picture Arts and Sciences, UCLA Library Special Collections, the USC Cinematic Arts Library, the UCLA Film & Television Archive, the Paley Center for Media, the Los Angeles Public Library history desk, and the New York Public Library for the Performing Arts.

At the local level, the Los Angeles County Registrar-Recorder/County Clerk, the California State Archives, the California Department of State Hospitals reference staff, and the custodians of records for Rockhaven Sanitarium and the Los Angeles Orphans Home Society (Hollygrove) assisted with guidance about what exists, what is restricted, and how to read between the lines when the silences in a record say more than the entries.

Closer to Marilyn's first geographies, I am indebted to volunteers and librarians at Santa Monica, Hawthorne, Van Nuys, and West Los Angeles historical collections; to parish secretaries and church archivists who checked registers patiently even when the answer was "no, not here"; and to the few remaining neighbors who remembered the Bolender house and the North Second Street years better than they remembered what they had for lunch. You gave me place.

Photographers and their estates were crucial guides. My thanks to the representatives of André de Dienes, Bruno Bernard (Bernard of Hollywood), Milton Greene, and George Barris for permissions, conversations and for clarity about what a contact sheet shows and what it never could. To the team at Authentic Brands Group, who manage the Marilyn Monroe Estate, for fielding licensing questions; and to picture editors at Getty, Bettmann/Corbis, AP, and MPTV, who steered me toward images that illuminated an argument rather than merely burnished a legend.

Many writers have come before me. Acknowledging them is both courtesy and method. The full list belongs in the bibliography; here I single out a few whose work served as scaffolding or as sparring partner: Fred Lawrence Guiles, Donald Spoto, Anthony Summers, Lois Banner, Gary Vitacco-Robles, Sarah Churchwell, J. Randy Taraborrelli, and the editors of *Fragments* (Marilyn's own notebooks and jottings). Agreeing or disagreeing is less important than understanding how they reasoned from their sources. When I part company with a predecessor, the argument lives in the notes, not as flourish here.

Several people shared private recollections of encounters with Marilyn or with those closest to her—memories offered quietly and, at times, with ambivalence. Where a source requested anonymity, I honored it. Where a story could not be independently corroborated, I weighed it against contemporaneous documents and used it, if at all, to illuminate mood or context rather than to establish fact. To those friends, assistants, neighbors, and studio hands who said, "I'm not sure this helps," and then spoke anyway: it did.

I am grateful to working physicians and medical historians who helped me translate mid-century diagnoses into plain English and who reminded me what is knowable and what is conjecture when reading old charts. My thanks as well to legal counsel who explained what privacy survives a death certificate and to FOIA officers at local and federal agencies who returned calls even when the message was "records not found."

Finally, to the early readers who lived with rough pages and circled the sentences that felt too certain: thank you. A special note of appreciation to Deni Remsberg, my editor at Bloomsbury, for her belief in the book and her support in its acquisition; and the kind assistance in its production of Jenna Dutton and Arun Kumar Selvam. And, as always, to my family—who endured my wall of timelines and my habit of rereading notes and old studio call sheets at dinner—your patience and love made it possible to carry this to the end. Any book worth its ink owes more than it can repay. This one is no exception.

AUTHOR'S NOTE

From the time Marilyn Monroe was a child—when she first began to form consciousness of the world around her—she was enchanted by everything she saw, heard, or even imagined. A voice's inflection, the way light fell across a window, the sudden flapping of wings from a bird overhead that no one else would notice—these details stayed with her.

Her friend Susan Strasberg once told me this was Marilyn's gift: the ability to hold a moment as if it were eternal. Susan remembered long nights when Marilyn stayed at her apartment and they would watch old movies until the TV channel signed off, laughing and giggling like the schoolgirls they no longer were. Marilyn would launch into stories—sometimes for half an hour—about a single instant from her childhood that had branded itself into her memory. Often, she returned to the same ones. Susan never minded. She was spellbound, as I would later be, by the way Marilyn turned recollection into reverie.

If only Marilyn had written those recollections down, Susan would say. Maybe she herself might have told the story. But neither of them did. Perhaps it was because our culture prefers memories to come wrapped in neat packages, tied off like cellophane candies at a McCrory's store of the 1950s. What Marilyn carried within her could never be so easily boxed. Her stream of consciousness, her looping return to images that haunted her, defied the tidy expectations of autobiography.

That is the spirit in which *The Girl Who Would Be Marilyn Monroe* has been written: not as a straight chronology, but as a work of remembrance, woven from the stories Marilyn told—sometimes to Susan Strasberg, sometimes to Jim Bacon, sometimes to others. They were often delivered in what outsiders dismissed as rambling. But I came to believe those "ramblings" revealed a truer self than any polished narrative ever could.

I came to see myself less as an author than as a listener, a witness. My task was not to impose order on her memories, but to honor their texture—the way they circled back, overlapped, and sometimes contradicted themselves. Memory does not move in straight lines, and neither did Marilyn. Her past lived in her like a chorus, voices rising and fading, always returning with new inflections.

In the end, this book is not about Marilyn Monroe the myth, nor Norma Jeane the child, but about the fragile thread between them—the remembering voice that never stopped reaching backward while the world kept pushing her forward. These chapters attempt to let her speak again, in the way she once spoke late at night to those few who had the patience to listen.

At the *Los Angeles Herald Examiner*, I sat beside Jim Bacon, the old Hollywood wire-service man whose desk was sometimes surrounded with cartons of booze from grateful publicists. On long afternoons he would refill our coffee cups with whiskey, and the newsroom blurred into a theater of memory. Bacon never cared for rules—he cared for stories. He told Marilyn's with a detail and cadence that betrayed their origin in her own words. Younger reporters dismissed them as embellishment. But Bacon wasn't one to invent; if anything, he had too much truth at his disposal. Many nights I crashed on a couch in the women's lounge or in some darkened cubbyhole rather than drive home. Those nights I learned that Marilyn's voice, as Bacon carried it, was circular, persistent, urgent—never letting a listener forget what she could not forget herself.

Susan Strasberg reinforced that impression. In the late 1970s and early 1980s, when she was teaching at her father's school on Santa Monica Boulevard, we often met nearby, and talk inevitably turned to Marilyn. Susan described how Marilyn could fixate on one flicker of memory: the angle of light on a foster-home wall, the smell of mothballs in a borrowed dress, the coo of pigeons outside a window. She spoke of Marilyn's endless circling back, the way she told the same story as if repetition might finally grant it permanence. Susan recognized it not as madness but as a child's insistence that her story mattered.

I have often thought that Marilyn's real autobiography was hidden in those late-night conversations, in the fragments she entrusted to friends when she felt safe enough to let the walls fall. They were not polished accounts, but raw impressions—the kind a child carries in her pocket like pebbles, long after others would have let them slip away. A piece of sky glimpsed through a window at the orphanage. The sound of her mother's laughter turning suddenly into sobs. The feel of shoes that pinched because they had belonged to someone else first. These details were not trivia to her; they were the essence of how she understood the world.

To hear her describe them was to feel that you were being handed something fragile, luminous, and fleeting. You couldn't capture it all, any more than you could catch light in your hands. But you could carry its glow. That glow is what

I have tried to preserve here—not the official history, not the studio publicity myths, but the pulse of memory that animated her being.

Hollywood itself provided other keepers of her memory. One of them was Edwin H. Blum, a screenwriter of the golden era—co-writer of *Stalag 17*, creator of Basil Rathbone's *Sherlock Holmes* adventures, veteran of the Writers Guild wars, neighbor in the North Rodeo Drive house where Joseph P. Kennedy and Gloria Swanson once carried on their affair. At a memorial gathering next door, whiskey flowing and conversation loose, Blum bent my ear about Kennedy, Swanson, and Marilyn. His recollections were precise, colored with the authority of a man who had lived in the rooms where power and myth intertwined. Listening to him, I realized again that Marilyn's story had always been passed hand to hand, voice to voice, never entirely captured by the written record.

This book, then, is not a definitive ledger of her life, nor an attempt to tame her into tidy chapters, but an echo of the way Marilyn remembered herself—messy, lyrical, unfinished, yet charged with wonder. It honors the way Marilyn told her own childhood stories—not polished into conventional narrative, but confessional, haunting, alive in their repetitions. I first heard them not from her directly, but in the voices of those who had listened closely: Jim Bacon, Susan Strasberg, and others who had the patience to absorb her fragmented remembrances and recognize them for what they were.

If I have done my work well, the reader may glimpse what Susan Strasberg once glimpsed, what Jim Bacon once heard: a girl at the edge of stardom, still Norma Jeane in her heart, chasing fragments of memory like fireflies. To follow her story is to follow her voice, and to hold, if only for a moment, the light she carried through the shadows.

What is written here, then, is not an academic chronology but a confessional chorus: Marilyn telling and retelling the girl she once was, through the voices of those who listened when she most needed to be heard.

NOTES ON SOURCES AND METHOD

This book is about Norma Jeane becoming Marilyn Monroe—the childhood, adolescence, and early adulthood that most biographies treat as prelude. Writing about an origin rather than a reign shifts the evidentiary center: fewer press agents and polished interviews; more school records, case files, neighborhood papers, studio memos, and photographs that capture a face before it learned to pose. What follows is a brief accounting of how I built the narrative, what I counted as reliable, and where reasonable people may differ.

1. Primary records

I prioritized contemporaneous documents over retrospective memoir: birth and hospital records where available; school enrollment and transfer slips; guardianship and foster-care paperwork; city directories; property deeds and leases; employment cards; Social Security applications; and studio contracts and call sheets from the period when Norma Jeane began modeling and acting. Some categories are restricted or incomplete. Mid-century medical records are often fragmentary; mental health files are frequently sealed. In those cases, I leaned on published summaries, court minutes, and the testimony of attending physicians as quoted in reputable sources, making clear when an assertion rests on indirect rather than direct inspection.

2. Archival and institutional sources

I worked in, or drew from, finding aids at the Margaret Herrick Library (studio and personal papers; fan magazines), UCLA Special Collections, the USC Cinematic Arts Library, the UCLA Film & Television Archive (broadcast appearances, news footage), the Los Angeles Public Library (local newspapers), and community historical societies in Santa Monica, Hawthorne, Van Nuys, and West Los Angeles. For the cultural weather of the time, I read Hedda Hopper and Louella Parsons with gloves on: invaluable as barometers of gossip and perception, unreliable as fact unless corroborated. Where FBI or agency files have been cited by others, I attempted to obtain or verify them; when I could not, I treat the secondary citation as a claim, not a document.

3. Oral histories and interviews

Memories are primary sources of feeling and secondary sources of fact. I conducted interviews with individuals who knew Marilyn or her early circle, and I read or listened to prior oral histories held by institutions. In each case, I note the date, the format (recording, transcript, notes), and the proximity of the witness to the events described. When accounts conflict, I ask: whose memory is closer in time; whose interest is at stake; what do contemporaneous documents say; and, if the event remains irreducibly contested, whether the disagreement itself reveals something about how Marilyn was seen. I avoid conflating a pattern (for instance, a long-standing reputation for lateness) with a specific ("on this call sheet, she arrived at 10:17 a.m.") without documentation.

4. Published biographies and studies

The secondary literature on Marilyn Monroe is vast. I used earlier books for three purposes: to locate leads (documents, names, dates); to map areas of consensus and dissent; and to test my own emphasis. Where a prior author's interpretation seems persuasive, I say so. Where I part ways, I show my work: the documents relied on, the countervailing evidence, and why I weighed one stack of receipts more heavily than another. This book is neither a rebuttal brief nor a coronation; it is an attempt to rearrange what we know in order to better see the human being beneath the image.

5. Photographs as documents

Still images are not proof of motive, but they can establish sequence, setting, and social proximity. A contact sheet may tell you who was in the room and what happened before and after the "iconic" frame. I relied on photographers' session notes when available and reached out to estates to clarify dates. When an image serves primarily as illustration, I treat it as such; when a caption bears argumentative weight (e.g., identifying a location or companion), I source it.

6. Medical and psychological claims

Writing about Marilyn's health—and about her mother's—requires care. I use the vocabulary of diagnoses and symptoms as it appears in the records available to me and in the best medical histories, with the caveat that mid-century labels often bundled phenomena we would separate now. Where I discuss mental health, I do so to illuminate constraint and consequence, not to pathologize character. I avoid retrofitting a modern diagnosis onto a past life; instead, I anchor statements to documents, physicians' notes, and consistent accounts across sources. When certainty is not possible, I say so.

7. Religion, class, and community

Norma Jeane's early life touched Pentecostal congregations, boardinghouses, foster homes, and working-class Los Angeles neighborhoods that rarely leave rich paper trails. Church minutes, if they survive, are uneven; municipal records miss what happens in kitchens and on porches. To reconstruct community, I read neighborhood newspapers, city directories, and census schedules and, when appropriate, employed the historian's "thick description": carefully inferring texture from a mosaic of small receipts rather than claiming what cannot be known.

8. Studio system context

The leap from Norma Jeane to Marilyn is not only personal; it is institutional. I relied on studio memos, casting sheets, contract clauses, publicity releases, and trade press to track how a young woman was turned into a marketable idea. The chapter notes point to the records behind each step—who changed a hairstyle and why, when a name appeared in a column, how a photographer's portfolio guided a test shoot. Reading those materials with a cold eye helps separate wishful origin stories from how things actually happened.

9. Quotations, permissions, and fair use

Direct quotations are cited in the bibliography and, where necessary, cleared. Short quotations used for critique, comment, or scholarship generally fall under fair use; I nevertheless sought permission when the excerpt's extent or the rights holder's position warranted it. Lyrics are trimmed or paraphrased unless permission has been granted.

10. Credibility and composites

I do not invent scenes. Where dialogue appears, it comes from letters, transcripts, recorded interviews, court records, or contemporaneous reporting, and the note for that passage identifies the source. In rare cases where a living person's privacy could be compromised by a trivial identifying detail, I have muted or shifted that detail without altering the substance; I do not combine multiple people into a single "composite" character. If an anecdote survives only as a story without documents, I may use it to color context, but I do not let it bear the full weight of fact.

11. What this book does not attempt

This is not a book about the circumstances of Marilyn's death, nor an inventory of theories that cannot be finally proved. It is not a catalog of lovers or a ledger of scandals. Those topics appear where they intersect with the formation of a person—the making of Marilyn from Norma Jeane—but they are not this book's claim. My interest is in how a bright, vulnerable, determined young woman learned to survive, improvise, and at times transcend the constraints of her body, her family history, her industry, and her era.

12. A word about DiMaggio

Joe DiMaggio appears in these pages not as a subject but as part of the narrative weather—one of the relationships that shaped how Marilyn understood loyalty, sanctuary, and cost. In researching him, I gained entry points into her world I would not otherwise have found. The debts there are acknowledged in earlier books; the benefit here is context, not possession.

13. How to read the sources

The bibliography records the shelf of works that informed the book—monographs, articles, documentaries, and archival collections—and points readers toward further exploration.

If there is a principle under all this, it is simple: treat Marilyn not as an emblem but as a person. Respect the limits of what can be known; be explicit about what is inferred; set rumor aside unless it earns its way in; and let the surviving paper speak first. Myth can be beautiful, but the human being who lived beneath it is more interesting. That is the story I have tried to write.

PROLOGUE

When he first arrived on the set of *The Misfits*, Jim Bacon couldn't immediately understand the disillusionment on the face of his longtime drinking pal, Clark Gable. There had always been a charming, roguish quality to Gable. Even now, the look of a cowhand in jeans, work shirt, and sweat-stained Stetson suited the aging actor who had enchanted moviegoers with his screen appearances for three decades.

He was standing next to the pickup truck in which he and co-star Marilyn Monroe would drive through the desert in the film's last scene—shot on November 4, 1960, 12 miles east of Dayton, Nevada, a place later known as Misfits Flat. The truck itself looked like it had been through two lives already—its blue paint sun-bleached to a dusty gray, its chrome dulled, its tailgate hanging slightly askew. Rust streaked down from the wheel wells like tears in a funeral suit. The Nevada wind kicked up fine desert sand that clung to every bolt and surface, settling into the creases of canvas chairs and the corners of the crew's eyes.

Now 59, Gable didn't look old as much as he did tired and worn. But in that cool late afternoon light, the sun reflecting off his tanned face painted a vivid, glistening image of health—as deceptive as the best of any Hollywood magic. The dry air shimmered, humming with the faint metallic whine of insects and power cables, the way deserts do when they're listening in on secrets.

Bacon, the veteran entertainment writer for the Associated Press, had just arrived as part of a promotional junket for Hollywood journalists. It was the last day of shooting for a highly anticipated film starring the two biggest names in the industry: Gable and Monroe. Filming would wrap with their final scene together. So why would Gable—whose $750,000 payday still had him at the top of the box office draws—be looking so unhappy and increasingly grumpy?

Was it because of the film's well-known delays or the gossip and rumors about Marilyn's increasingly erratic behavior on and off the set? Or was this just a sign of Gable's declining health? The lifelong drinker and smoker had suffered a heart attack in 1959, and he remained almost in denial of his recovery. Plus, *The Misfits* was physically demanding. Gable still insisted on performing his own stunts, even in the heat, the dust, and the thinning air of high desert plains.

But the moment Bacon arrived on the set, something shifted. It seemed to reset the smile on Gable's face. He motioned the writer over to his side against the truck, putting an arm around him like someone reuniting with a wartime buddy. On film sets, Bacon often seemed more at ease than the biggest mogul strolling his own studio lot. Gable, John Wayne, Marilyn—all of them saw in Jim Bacon, this cherubic man in his mid-forties whose smile never faded, not a snooping reporter but a friend. A friend who had been more instrumental in making their careers than any high-priced publicist in the business.

"When I started at Universal," actress Mamie Van Doren often said, "it was James Bacon who put the publicity out that my name was Mamie Van Doren and I was Universal's answer to Marilyn Monroe."

That day, hanging out with Gable in the desert, Bacon and the movie star retreated to a folding table propped in the shade of a sagging canvas tent. They chatted over drinks, a silver thermos of coffee that might've been something else entirely, and waited for Marilyn to show up.

At one point, Gable turned to Bacon, shaking his head.

"What is it with this girl?" he said. "She's always late on the set."

Bacon learned that Gable didn't really know much about Marilyn, beyond her bombshell image and whatever had trickled down through gossip columns. He didn't know anything about her childhood, about the chain of troubled years that had carried over into her teens and affected every fiber of her life. Bacon would later say he wished, in that moment, that he had the time to explain it all. And to his surprise, he *was* given the time.

Jim had known her since their earliest days in Hollywood. He'd written the first feature article about the young actress then known as Norma Jeane Baker—and later there had been more. In 1949, he had crossed the line forbidden to poor, conscientious reporters: for about three months, he and Marilyn had become romantically involved.

"She had a child's fascination with people and life," Jim told me once. "When she touched you, she was like a child who had been cautioned about breaking things. So her touch had the lightest feel. She touched so tenderly, as if to be sure she didn't break you—which, of course, was how she wished people had touched her."

She was 22, luminous and hungry, still fighting for every glimmer of attention in a town that didn't yet know her name. At the time, Marilyn had just filmed *Ladies of the Chorus*, her first starring role, and a fleeting part in the Marx Brothers' *Love Happy*. She'd been in half a dozen forgettable pictures by then—blink-and-you-miss-her roles—but nothing guaranteed her a future.

Stardom was still a whisper, not a promise. That same year, out of financial desperation, she posed nude for a pin-up calendar—fifty dollars she needed and would later regret. The photos would resurface years later in the debut issue of *Playboy*, long after the world had fallen in love with her.

During that precarious chapter, Marilyn took dance lessons from Nico Charisse, the ex-husband of Cyd Charisse. She studied acting under the watchful gaze of Natasha Lytess and took singing lessons with Phil Moore at the Mocambo, where jazz and smoke wrapped around every note. That was when she met Jim—handsome in a boy-next-door sort of way, with a Notre Dame charm that clung to him like old leather. He'd spent three years at Notre Dame before dropping out to help his family after a flood claimed their home, later finishing his degree in journalism at Syracuse and serving in the Navy during the war. Bacon arrived in Hollywood with the Associated Press in the late 1940s, and when he met Marilyn, he was the AP's lead entertainment reporter—well-liked, well-connected, and one of the few men in town who treated her like she might become more than a footnote.

They never made it a big romance—no studio lot love affair, no headlines—but in those few months, they shared something warm, private, and real. "She was more Norma Jeane Baker than she was Marilyn Monroe in those days," Jim would later say.

Jim told me this in one of our long, wandering conversations about Marilyn, the kind we began having in 1978. More famously, he retold the story to Larry King and Mamie Van Doren on *Larry King Live* in 2005:

KING: . . . you were sexually intimate. Were you?
BACON: Yes.
KING: OK, Jim.
BACON: Yes. Yes.
VAN DOREN: Good for you, James.
KING: Still living, and they can't wipe the smile off your face.
BACON: I had a fling for about three months with her.
VAN DOREN: He never got it off.
KING: You had a three-month fling?
BACON: Yes.
KING: Between what marriage and what marriage?
BACON: Well, it was 1949. She was more Norma Jeane Baker than she was Marilyn Monroe in those days, yes.
KING: All right. Do you . . .

BACON: I'm still smiling, yes.

KING: She got a bad rap?

BACON: Yes. In a way she did, yes. She got a bad rap. She was not a dumb blonde. She was a very smart blonde. She read a lot.

But it was about Marilyn's *traumatic early years* that Bacon wanted to discuss with Clark Gable on that breezy, cool November afternoon in the Nevada desert. And Gable, perhaps seeing something in Bacon's tone that went deeper than gossip, gave him the grace of five uninterrupted hours.

"We waited five hours for Marilyn to show up," Bacon recalled. "And I told him all about her insecurities and foster homes and everything. So he understood."

Later, as the sun slipped behind the Sierra Nevadas, Bacon stood in the dust and watched Gable climb into that old truck for the final take. He remembered thinking how symbolic it all felt—Gable driving off into the desert with Marilyn, just as the film demanded, just as fate was already arranging. Within days, Gable would be gone. And within two years, so would she.

But in that hour, in that golden hour before the end, two men sat and spoke about a woman who was still trying to outrun the shadows of her girlhood.

And for a moment, she was not a legend or a scandal or a ghost.

She was just Norma Jeane.

1

A Star Is Born

Before she was Marilyn Monroe, before the glimmer of her name lit up theater marquees and whispered through the smoky lounges of Hollywood, she was Norma Jeane Mortenson—a child born not to fame, but to fracture. She arrived in a world that hadn't made room for her. She was not a star then, but already torn—between truth and myth, between the mother who birthed her and the fathers she would never know. She was born at 9:30 in the morning on Tuesday, June 1, 1926, in the charity ward of Los Angeles County Hospital—a public facility often confused with the later Los Angeles General but already serving the city's poorest families under various names and incarnations. Seven years later, the hospital would be rebuilt as a gleaming art-deco monolith, but in 1926 it was a patchwork of crowded wards and overworked nurses. One of those beds held a baby girl blinking into the soft light of early summer...

Los Angeles at the time was surging into its second act. The city's population had more than doubled since 1920, swollen by dreamers from the Midwest and Mexico. Oil derricks pumped wealth from Huntington Beach northward toward the city. Real estate fever fueled the rise of neighborhoods stretching from downtown to Santa Monica. Broadway thrummed with theaters and retail stores. And just a few blocks east, on the outskirts of Boyle Heights—then a predominantly Jewish neighborhood—a baby was born. The name on her birth certificate might have been equally part of the anonymity.

Her mother, Gladys Pearl Baker (née Monroe), carried her daughter into that world alone. Gladys had once been a dreamy girl born in Piedras Negras, Coahuila, Mexico, to a poor Midwestern family chasing work and hope in foreign lands. Her father, Otis Monroe, a house painter from Indianapolis, had crossed the border with his wife Della Hogan in search of a livelihood, working for the railroad in that Mexican town just across from Eagle Pass, Texas. Otis's trade—transient, humble—would carry the Monroes as far west as Los Angeles, where they settled in 1903. Yet their American dream had a way of slipping through paint-chipped fingers. Otis died in 1909, and his daughter Gladys, fatherless at an early age, would echo that loss down through the generations.

Otis himself had known loss. As a five-year-old in Indianapolis, he lived with his parents, Jacob and Mary Monroe. Jacob was a farmer, born in Indiana, who would later leave his plowshare to enlist in the 70th Indiana Regiment of the Union Army in 1862. Under the command of Colonel Benjamin Harrison, a future president, Jacob was wounded during the bloody Battle of Resaca in Sherman's Atlanta Campaign. He survived the carnage but died not long after returning home, leaving behind his widow, Mary, and their children. He was scarcely forty. Marilyn Monroe's bloodline, it seemed, was stamped with premature farewells.

The Monroes were pioneer stock—tenacious and tragic. Jacob's father, William Monroe, died in 1831, just as Indianapolis was becoming the state capital. William left behind six children, all minors, and land in Switzerland County, Indiana. The Monroe men were builders and fighters, seekers and sufferers. They moved westward with each generation, into Kansas, then Mexico, and finally California—riding the same currents of hope and hardship that carried so many Americans in the post–Civil War years.

The Monroe women had been widows, wanderers, and warriors in their own quiet way. Della Monroe, Gladys's mother, had moved from Arkansas to Mexico and back again, burying a husband and raising children on borrowed time. Mary Monroe, Marilyn's great-grandmother, had seen her husband Jacob return from war only to die young. These women knew sorrow like an old friend. They wore it as quietly as their Sunday dresses. Norma Jeane was their heir—not only to their pain, but to their perseverance.

From Switzerland County to Kansas, from Piedras Negras to Los Angeles, the Monroe story had followed the arc of America itself: migration, war, hardship, reinvention. And now, in 1926, in a hospital where no cameras flashed, another chapter began. A child born in chaos, a future carved from myth. A girl without a father. A mother already slipping away. And a name that would one day belong to the most famous woman in the world.

But not yet. For now, she was Norma Jeane.

And she was already torn.

For all their wandering, the Monroes never seemed to find rest. The men in the family died young. The women bore the burden of memory.

Gladys Monroe was one of those women. Her beauty—pale, fine-boned, with thick auburn hair—belied the chaos she carried. At fourteen, she married John Newton ("Jasper" or "Jap") Baker, a Kentucky man sixteen years her senior. They were married on May 17, 1917, with her mother Della's permission and a signed affidavit that Gladys was 18, the legal age to marry in that state. Gladys, however, would not turn fifteen for another ten days. Baker was a businessman who owned the Kentucky apartment building that Della once managed. He was also violent and volatile. They had two children, Berniece Inez Gladys and Robert Kermit, known as "Jackie." In 1923, Gladys finally left him, gaining sole custody. But Baker kidnapped the children and fled to Kentucky, leaving Gladys shattered. The wound from that loss would never fully close, and it bled into her later years, into her parenting of Norma Jeane, into every quiet moment of instability that followed.

Two years after divorcing Baker, Gladys married Martin Edward Mortensen in Los Angeles. It was a brief, unhappy union. They separated within months and never formally divorced until years later. Yet when she gave birth to Norma Jeane in 1926, she listed Mortensen (misspelled "Mortenson") on the birth certificate as the father. Most biographers agree this was almost certainly a fiction. Gladys had been involved with Charles Stanley Gifford, her boss at RKO Studios—a tall, charismatic man with a strong jaw and a quick wit. In 2022, DNA analysis confirmed what Gladys had never admitted aloud: Gifford was the biological father of Norma Jeane.

Stranger still, Gladys insisted to her toddler Norma Jeane that her real father was none other than Clark Gable—the biggest box office draw in Hollywood. She even gave her daughter a fan magazine photo of the actor, which the child carried for years, staring at it longingly. It was a lie, but it was the only story that made her feel beautiful.

In 1959, on the set of *The Misfits*, which she starred in opposite Gable, she reflected, "I don't think he would mind me saying this. OK. Clark Gable. I always pretended he was my father. I was just seven years old. And he was a very young man. That was how I wanted my father to look."

Gifford never acknowledged his daughter. He vanished from her life like a vanishing father in a silent film. No visit, no note, no picture. Just a blank space where a man should have stood. That erasure—that refusal—would haunt Marilyn for the rest of her life. Her origin was a lie typed on a government form. Her story began in absence. Gifford slipped back into the Los Angeles fog. Gladys never spoke of him to her daughter, not really. She just wrote his name once, in an old address book, in the same shaky script she used when she started to lose track of what was real.

What was real was the baby. Norma Jeane. A quiet child with wide eyes that drank the world in. The hospital staff noted her stillness. She didn't cry. She observed. The air around her already seemed tinged with future grief. She was born with absence folded into her skin.

The newborn was only days old when Gladys brought her home, wrapped in a borrowed blanket. The dresser was chipped. The window faced west. But there was a crib. And for a moment, there was hope. Not the kind written in baby books—the kind whispered to the walls when no one else is listening. The kind that starts not with a cradle, but with a crack.

Two weeks after her birth, on June 13, 1926, Norma Jeane was dropped off by her mother at the foster home of Ida E. Masheeco and Albert Wayne Bolender in Hawthorne, California, just south of Los Angeles. The foster home arrangement had been made by the baby girl's grandmother, Della Monroe, though she had at least arranged things with the Bolenders before running off to India.

In Los Angeles, Gladys had first been employed at Consolidated Film Industries at Seward and Romaine, a film lab tucked inside Hollywood's backlot underworld. Wearing white gloves, she spliced and repaired celluloid, helping shape dreams frame by frame. She handled the negatives of *The Covered Wagon*, *The Hunchback of Notre Dame*, and *Ben-Hur*. Gloria Swanson. Ramon Novarro. Joan Crawford. She trimmed their reels, fixed their flaws, breathed life into illusions. And then she went home.

At the lab, she met Grace McKee—a spirited woman with movie-star hair and sweeping declarations. Grace became her closest friend, perhaps the only person who understood Gladys's hunger for glamour, her longing to be part of something luminous. They moved in together that summer, into a small apartment at 1211 Hyperion Avenue in Silver Lake. The walls were thin and the windows crooked, but the air was filled with laughter, cigarettes, and movie talk. Gladys floated through her days. She danced at parties. She read *Photoplay*. She took drives up into the hills. There were men, but none who stayed. She was charming. She was lonely. She was beautiful in a way that was already starting to fade.

Gladys and Grace embraced the freedom of the Roaring Twenties, becoming flappers who, according to biographer Donald Spoto, "chose to extend the recent women's suffrage amendment to include the various social and sexual autonomies long claimed by men." Under Grace's guidance, Gladys transformed from a brown-haired "plain jane" to an attractive red-headed woman who wore stylish clothing—and was soon described by coworkers at RKO as "beautiful, having twinkling green eyes and a lively spirit, delightful, and funny."

In 1925, Grace McKee married actor Ervin Silliman "Doc" Goddard. Gladys also found romance. In the summer of 1924, she met Martin Edward Mortensen, the 27-year-old divorced son of a Norwegian immigrant and a meterman for the Southern California Gas Company. They married on October 11, 1924, but she soon grew bored of him. She left him around early 1925 and moved in with Grace. Mortensen tried to win his wife back, but gave up, filing for divorce on May 26, 1925, citing desertion. Their divorce was not finalized until August 15, 1928.

By then, Gladys was already unraveling. But the disintegration had begun years earlier. In 1923, three years before Norma Jeane's birth, she had finalized her divorce from John Baker and effectively surrendered custody to him of their two children. She later visited them once in Kentucky, a brief reunion visit that ended in disappointment. She boarded a train back to California. Alone.

After her breakup with Mortenson, Gladys had fallen into the ill-fated romance with her RKO coworker, the newly divorced Charles Stanley Gifford. In late 1925, when Gladys discovered she was pregnant, Gifford took her to meet his family—who disapproved of him marrying a pregnant woman who was not raising her existing children.

That rejection seemed like the fatal blow to any romantic happiness. When Gladys gave birth to Norma Jeane, she did not allow Gifford to visit her in the hospital. She wanted nothing more to do with him. He later remarried and kept his parentage of Norma Jeane a secret from his wife. So, because Gladys was still married to Mortensen, he was legally Norma Jeane's father.

But the real victim throughout was Norma Jeane, who grew up in the fragile shadow of Gladys's unraveling mind. Mental illness hung over her like a fog, creeping closer with every year. She spoke in riddles, cried over invisible wounds, and sometimes disappeared for days at a time. When Norma was still a toddler, Gladys would leave her in the care of neighbors or near-strangers, retreating into depressive episodes or the arms of dangerous men.

Still, Gladys Baker tried. She tried harder than history remembers. Yet for all her demons, Gladys adored Norma Jeane. She bought her dolls and read to her, showed her baby pictures, told her she was special. For fleeting moments, they were a mother and daughter like any other. But the darkness was never far behind.

She was a woman carrying ghosts, working in an industry built on illusion, holding too much grief to cradle a child without trembling.

Gladys floated again—new jobs, new addresses. The voices came and went. So did the furniture. A string of half-furnished rooms linked by second-hand hope. Meanwhile, Norma Jeane was passed between neighbors. No crib lasted. No picture frame stayed filled.

And yet, oddly, her early years with the Bolenders were the most stable of her young life. The Bolenders were strict Christians. Ida, the religious extremist; Albert, the soft-spoken husband. Ida was in her late 30s and her husband in his mid-40s when they began fostering Norma Jeane. The foster father, on the contrary, was remembered as a quiet, soft-spirited, good-hearted man, submissive to his wife in the raising of their foster kids. Norma Jeane later recalled often chatting with her foster father while he shaved in the bathroom. There, she would sit on the stool next to the bathtub and ask him questions. Each night the Bolenders had a ritual they would practice with each of their foster children. Among their prayers, they would have them recite: "I promise God helping me, not to buy, drink, sell or give alcohol while I live. From all tobacco I'll abstain, and never take God's name in vain."

For a while, Gladys Baker also appeared the most devoted she ever would be to Norma Jeane. She would often stop by the Bolender home to visit her daughter. All she had left was Norma Jeane, and she was now determined not to lose her as well. When she was old enough, Norma Jeane would occasionally join her mother for sleepovers at her apartment in Hollywood, or she would be taken out to the picture palaces in Hollywood to see matinee movies.

But Gladys soon showed increased signs of the mental instability that was plaguing her own mother as well—and making both women dangerous to be around. As detailed in *The Secret Life of Marilyn Monroe* by J. Randy Taraborrelli, an agitated Gladys Baker one day showed up at the Bolenders' foster home, demanding to take her three-year-old daughter home. She even locked Ida out of her own back door and attempted to abscond with Norma Jeane stuffed in a duffel bag, before the foster mom succeeded in thwarting the attempt.

Then Gladys Baker's mental state hit rock bottom. In the fall of 1933, she learned that her thirteen-year-old son Jackie, while living with his father in Kentucky, had died of kidney disease. Her reaction was a sign of how unwell she was; Gladys lashed out at Norma Jeane, resentful that she had lived while Jackie had died. Shortly after that, Gladys was hit with two additional shocking developments. She discovered that her grandfather had hanged himself and learned that her studio was going on strike. It was too much. Her mind cracked.

Unfortunately for Norma Jeane, she became an unwitting witness to her mother's emotional collapse. In 1934, barely eight years of age, the child watched her mother kick and scream wildly before being taken into police custody. Gladys Baker was diagnosed as suffering from paranoid schizophrenia and institutionalized for the first time at the state hospital in Norwalk.

For the next few years, Norma Jeane saw her mother on an intermittent basis as she shuttled between the residences of her new legal guardian: Gladys's close friend Grace Goddard; her mom's sister-in-law; and the Los Angeles Orphans' Home.

Things stabilized again for the teenager when she landed in the home of "Aunt Ana"—Grace Goddard's family friend Edith Ana Lower—an older divorcee who managed to impress on both Norma Jeane and Gladys the teachings of her Christian Science faith.

Around this time, Gladys made Norma Jeane aware she had an older half-sister, Berniece. Thrilled to know she wasn't so alone, she began corresponding with Berniece in Kentucky, sparking an important relationship that would carry through Marilyn's final days. And even while in and out of foster care, Norma Jeane struggled to understand her mother's absence, the chasm between them. Gladys hovered like a ghost—present, then gone. Sometimes lucid, sometimes not. Sometimes kind, sometimes terrifying. The longing for her mother's love would become a wound she carried into every relationship that followed.

She would learn early that monsters didn't just live under beds. Sometimes they tucked you in. Sometimes they kissed your cheek. Sometimes they were the silence that followed the slam of a door.

Trauma doesn't vanish—it burrows. So deep, in fact, that it can alter the very script of our genes, inscribing sorrow into the body's memory. Sometimes, that coded ache travels forward, winding its way into the bloodlines of children not yet born. If the wounds of our parents, our grandparents—of generations lost in fog—can ripple forward into our marrow, then what are we? Ghost stories wrapped in skin? Are we destined to inherit the heartbreak we never lived, to bleed from invisible wounds passed down like heirlooms?

Marilyn Monroe never knew her maternal grandfather, Otis Elmer Monroe, but a dive into what shaped her mother, and by extension Marilyn, inevitably leads to him. Born in Indiana, Otis moved to Missouri and, in 1899, married Marilyn's maternal grandmother, Della Mae Hogan. Della remembered Otis as a "gentleman's gentleman," with a scar on his left cheek that gave him the look of a dashing, world-weary romantic. He was fair-skinned, red-haired, hazel-eyed—a dreamer who spoke of painting watercolors from a houseboat on the

Seine. But the dream soured. The honeymoon brought them not to Paris, but to the Mexican border town of Piedras Negras, overlooking the Rio Grande and Eagle Pass, Texas.

There, Otis traded paintbrushes for a position with the Mexican National Railway. Della, now a reluctant newlywed in an alien world, filled her time midwifing and attempting to teach local women. She soon became pregnant, and on May 27, 1902, gave birth to a daughter named Gladys Pearl. A Mexican judge certified the birth. Within a year, the young family moved to Los Angeles, and Otis began working for the Pacific Electric Railway.

But the move brought no salvation. Otis unraveled. Between 1903 and 1909, he moved his family through at least eleven homes. He drank heavily. He forgot where he was. He suffered from debilitating headaches and violent rages. Della, pregnant again, gave birth to a son in 1905, but their home life collapsed into chaos. Otis's moods turned terrifying. The children were shuffled off to neighbors. There were nights they didn't know if their father would return—or who he'd be if he did. His remorse was real, but fleeting. His hands trembled. Seizures seized him. He wept. Della fought to hold the pieces together until, in 1908, Otis was committed to the Southern California State Hospital.

There, doctors diagnosed general paresis—the final stage of neurosyphilis, a cruel and irreversible deterioration of the brain. He was forty-three when he died on July 22, 1909. One physician insisted the illness came not from sexual transmission but from unsanitary working conditions in Mexico, where syphilis was rampant. But the truth may never be known. What is certain is that Otis left behind more than a death certificate. He left behind a legacy of instability, silence, and the cracked lens through which Della—and later Gladys—would view the world.

Across the Atlantic, that same day Marilyn was born, Princess Elizabeth of England was being christened in the private chapel of Buckingham Palace. Two girls, worlds apart. One swaddled in silk and certainty. The other in confusion and need. One born into a destiny of crowns. The other, into a destiny no one saw coming.

2

The Baby Nobody Kept

Hawthorne was a town of low houses and long shadows, a place where the sky pressed down like the palm of a stern hand and the streets were a loose lattice of dust and discipline. In the mornings the hymns rang first, before the trucks, before the sparrows. The Bolenders began each day with prayer, and so did the neighbors who minded their children like Bibles that could be lost. In this neighborhood the air kept a tally of every sound—the squeak of a back door, the strike of a match, the soft, practiced sigh of a mother who had run out of questions. Into this ledger of small noises came the infant who would become a woman with a name brighter than glass. She arrived in the way a comet arrives in someone's dream—brief, unbelievable, and destined to be told later with the certainty of folklore.

At two weeks old, the baby was delivered to a house where love was measured in clean hands and exact bedtimes. Albert and Ida received her as if she had been prayed into their arms, a fragile answer whose question they would never fully learn. Ida counted the diapers like rosary beads, folded the blanket to the width of a ruler, warmed the milk to the modest temperature a righteous soul might favor. Order, they believed, was a form of care. They had a cradle that made a cage of its lace shadow on the wall and a song about Jesus that knew how to keep a baby from crying by reminding her that heaven had a schedule.

The child's name on Ida's lips was a soft thing, a truce between syllables, and yet it filled the room like a candle does, quietly deciding where everyone will look. When she slept, she clenched one fist as if she held a secret. When she woke, her blue eyes drank the light and repeated it back. The neighbors said she looked serious for a baby, and serious babies are like solemn houses—something in them has already chosen a future shape.

In that early season of her life the Bolender house made a bargain with time. Days were domesticated: breakfast, chores, a midday nap, evening prayers, blue dusk at the kitchen window like the inside of a chapel. But time is an animal only so long as it is fed, and there were other hungers circling.

Sometimes a hawk rode the air above the sycamores and Ida would shiver as if the bird's orbit carried a message for those who were paying attention. The baby watched it too, tracking the silent circle the way a person studies a word she almost recognizes. In the yard, ants made caravans of the smallest dreams. There were oranges that sweetened slowly and a fence that knew how to refuse without cruelty. The Bolenders were good people. Even their sternness had a careful skin on it, like pudding that refuses to spill.

But love offered on conditions teaches a child to listen for the latch. She learned the distance between the door and the prayer. She learned that the clink of a teacup could sound like agreement and that repentance had a smell—soap, starch, a curl of cold ironed hair. At night Ida knelt by her bed and asked the Lord to keep this little one safe, to keep all little ones safe, and in the spaces between those petitions, the girl learned silence, that brittle kindness adults use when the truth would be rude to God. When Ida kissed her forehead the kiss felt like an oath, binding as any promise spoken in a chapel, and also like the end of a sentence that had been long coming. The infant breathed and the house sighed with her, a ship riding out its own destiny at the curb.

The mother came like weather. She might arrive with perfume still arguing on her wrists or with the pale, exhausted triumph of someone who had outrun a lie. She had eyes that seemed to be trying to decide whether to be blue or gray, and she wore her hair as if it had been told a secret in sleep. Gladys could be tender in a way that frightened the room, as if tenderness were an edge you could fall from. She brought little things—a ribbon, a picture that had been bent at the corner twice, a story about a film where the lovers never met when they were supposed to and were therefore doomed to meet forever. She would lift the baby and begin talking to her as though the child had asked a question that flourished like a tree between them.

"Do you know, baby," she would whisper, "there are houses in this city that remember you from before you were born? There are rooms where your laughter has already happened. Sometimes I hear it in the walls at night, like a radio in the apartment next door."

She would rock and hum an off-duty hymn, something that remembered church without submitting to it. "You were an idea first," she'd say. "You were somebody's beautiful mistake of light."

Sometimes baby Norma Jeane would go perfectly still and her face would lose the plot. A stillness like the last page of a book. In those moments, Ida stepped forward, arms out, a modest wall of virtue to collect the child without accusation.

They had an agreement, in theory—that Gladys could visit, could take the baby for a walk under a California sky that liked to flirt with its citizens, could kiss the tiny ear that already seemed to be trying to overhear the future. But agreements for people like them were paper boats; lovely, earnest, and always drifting toward the one element they could not survive.

The Bolenders' street had no time for gossip out loud, but it hoarded suspicion the way good housewives save twine in a drawer. They said Gladys worked at the studio sometimes and that movies make a person think she is immune to the ordinary gravity of days. They said she laughed too quickly or cried without a reason or stood at the bus stop smiling at a thought that was not the one available to the rest of them.

Ida, who believed in the mercy at the center of things, told herself that a woman may carry a family like a clock inside her and also carry a small thunderstorm no one else can see. She told herself that a person cannot always decide which story in her blood will speak up first.

There was an afternoon—there is always an afternoon that becomes the paragraph that keeps a whole book alive—when Gladys arrived with a certainty lodged behind her ribs. The sun fell through the kitchen in slanted sentences, and the radio was explaining somebody else's misfortune in a voice that sounded like moderation.

Gladys walked in the way a gambler walks into a room where the table recognizes her, and Ida felt the air divide into a before and an after. The baby on the linoleum with a red wooden block in her fist looked up at the kind of smile that means rescue and catastrophe at once.

"I'm taking her," Gladys said, but she said it to the world and not to Ida. "I'm taking what's mine."

Ida tried a reasonable voice, the kind that believes in pencils, in checks cashed, in the county clerk who put his hand on the Bible as if he were closing a lid over a jar of bees.

"Gladys," she said, "the Lord knows your heart, and we know you love her. But she is settled here. You can take her Sunday, once we've—"

Sunday had never been less interesting. Gladys had already folded her love into a duffel bag, the kind men used to pretend war was a sport. The bag was clean and awful on the chair, an animal that had decided to hold its breath until it got what it wanted. She moved with that efficient hurry grief gives a person and Ida watched a scene assemble itself in front of her, like the God of this particular story had a taste for neat metaphors—the child to be packed like laundry, delivered like a sin to be confessed later.

When Ida tried to step between them, she found herself pleading with a version of history that was unavoidable.

"Not like this," she said, and her mouth dried out. "You can't keep a child in a sack, Gladys. You can't. Someone will see. Someone will stop you."

But no one likes to interrupt a bad miracle in progress; the neighbors' windows practiced the ancient art of being open and pretending to be closed. The duffel yawed. There was just enough space for a promise.

For years after, the child remembered the air between her mother and Ida as a specific temperature. She remembered the smell of canvas. She remembered the way the light sat on the kitchen table like an audience that couldn't believe what it was witnessing. In that moment she learned that a body has more than one exit and that a life can be folded in half without permission. She made a sound that was not quite a word and not quite a cry, something like an oath a saint might make if she realized her God had other appointments.

The bag happened anyway—let us admit the truth of that—and also failed to happen all the way, because there are angels whose job is simply to drop a pan loudly on the other side of the house at the right second so that a tragedy can change its mind.

The baby was lifted, then set down, then lifted again; her mother's hands were a nervous boat. Ida spoke a dozen versions of the same sentence, a rosary of reasons. The fact of how it ended—whether the bag was zipped fully or not, whether the street saw or the street merely imagined it had—matters less than the law that was written that day on the child's skin: she was claimable in the abstract and disclaimable in practice, a parcel with too many addresses, a note that fit into too many pockets. She belonged so much she ended up belonging to the air. The air, at least, was consistent.

After that day the Bolenders prayed harder and Gladys visited as if she were sneaking into a dream. She would stand at the fence sometimes and rest her head against the wood, listening as though the boards kept a diary. When she did come inside she brought a picture of a beach from a magazine. She held it up to the child and said, "Look, this is where the ocean keeps the things it doesn't know what to do with."

The girl reached out and patted the glossy water like a pet. Gladys laughed, and then the laugh cut itself short in her throat. She looked at Ida with a soft, terrified authority.

"When she is older, don't forbid mirrors," she said. "A girl like this needs to learn early that her reflection is a collaborator and not a witness."

At night the house gathered itself around the crib. Ida's hand on the child's belly, counting the breaths. Albert's boots by the door, a grammar of labor.

Somewhere the hawk wrote another loop above the sycamores, and each loop meant the same thing in a language no one wanted to admit existed. The prayers that had once felt like blankets now had the texture of ropes. The child slept with her fist unclenching slowly, a daisy after rain.

It is easier to talk about God than madness in any town small enough to know everyone's washing. So madness kept to the alleys; it wore a hat and said excuse me. In this story it came down the family line with the punctuality of an heirloom. Della, the grandmother, had not died but had withdrawn into a room so small it fit behind her eyes. They said she had a music in her head that was not for dancing. They said she could sit at a kitchen table and listen to the sugar bowl tell a story about a winter that had not happened.

Della's absence had the quality of a porch light left on by someone who cannot remember who she is waiting for. Her name hung in the air like the last slice of a shadow. The child did not know her, but the blood knew. Blood is an archivist with a strict filing system and an exquisite sense of irony. In the evenings when the wind made the curtains behave like old ladies' gossip, Ida would think of Della, and her hands would steady themselves around the bowl of peas as if steadiness itself were a prayer.

Gladys's visits grew thinner, thinner, like a skirt worn through at the hem. Sometimes she came smiling in a way that suggested the joke had chosen her specifically for its intimacy. Sometimes she stayed away long enough to let the house relax. The city was full of late shifts and longer dreams. Studios that pretended to be churches of light. Churches that tried to be studios of forgiveness. Men who swore they loved the truth, women who knew how to stand beside the truth and look more interesting. Somewhere not far enough away, a boulevard learned how to purr. The baby learned to recognize the scent of menthol and the shape of a lie.

One afternoon Gladys took the baby for a walk and returned with sand on her shoes.

"She likes the ocean," she said. "The ocean likes her."

Ida smiled in the careful way of a woman who will not reward audacity but cannot help admiring it.

"She should like the bathtub too," Ida said, and they both laughed, and in the laughter was a brief sweetness that felt borrowed from a better family.

Later, when the child sat in the tub and kicked the water until it threw up its small hands, Ida saw a look on her face that made her think of what a prophet looks like before anyone has given her a god to work for.

The neighbors told a story—Hawthorne liked to keep itself amused—that Gladys sometimes stood on the sidewalk and addressed an invisible audience.

"Ladies and gentlemen," she would say, "tonight you will see a miracle disguised as a mistake."

Or: "A woman can be a church with no congregation and still keep the candles lit."

Or, simply, to no one and to everyone, "You have no idea what a girl like that can do with a room full of light."

The neighbors shook their heads because shaking your head is a way to keep your own story from wobbling.

The doctor wrote notes in a precise script that looked like it belonged to a violinist. Words like "episode" and "unstable" sat beside the name like dogs pretending to be statues. It would be convenient to say that on a particular date the door closed—an admission, a diagnosis, a set of iron bars explained to a child as a kind of quiet vacation—but lives seldom respect paperwork.

What is true is that the precipice became a hallway, and Gladys walked down it. What is true is that men in coats took on the ridiculous job of naming an ocean, and the ocean refused to cooperate. What is true is that a girl in a crib learned to hum to herself when the house had gone to sleep, and that the hum was in a key that good people associate with endurance.

In the middle of that winter the Bolenders' kitchen developed a sympathy for the past. Bread rose the way hope rises in the stories told to children who have already figured out that hope is a currency adults use when they're short on coins. The child's first words came out shy and literal, devoted to the objects that could not betray her. Cup. Cat. Light. She learned the difference between the light in the morning and the light in the evening. She knew which light made Ida's hands softer and which light made Albert sigh. When she laughed, it was like a drawer opening.

One day a photograph arrived in an envelope that did not include a letter. In it, Gladys stood with a smile that had the temperature of glass and a haircut that looked like the idea of a wave. Behind her, Hollywood posed with its chin in its hand. On the back of the photograph, in a tidy script that had been taught by a strict woman to an eager schoolgirl, was written, "for my girl who will not be kept by anyone but herself."

Ida looked at the picture and at the child and felt a strange crackling—fear trying to change places with pride and failing. She tucked the photograph into the Bible the way a person hides a confession in a hymn.

There are stories that insist every life announces itself with a visible sign. A comet. A breath held by the whole town without agreement. A hawk that refuses to abandon its circle. A river that runs backward for an hour. If anyone asked Hawthorne what sign it had been given, it would laugh and point at the obvious—the beautiful child being kept by people who did not make her. But a more honest sign was the one the child carried inside: the knowledge that all doors are temporary, that love is a room with many windows and some of them are painted shut, that a person can be an answer nobody has thought to ask.

Once, when Ida believed the child old enough to endure a certain form of honesty, she took her to visit the place where Gladys was trying to remember how to be herself. The room had the brutal cleanliness of a bowl that has decided never to be used again. The nurse spoke in the sing-song we reserve for those whose minds have begun to retire without notice. Gladys sat with her hands folded in the posture of a schoolgirl who has practiced obedience until it became a talent. She looked at her daughter and the look traveled across three different weathers before it arrived at recognition.

"You've grown into your eyes," she said, and then she laughed softly at the strangeness of her own sentence. "Do they show you different things, both of them? Mine do. One shows me the world as it is on Tuesdays, the other shows me what it looks like when the angels are tired."

She leaned forward.

"When the angels are tired," she repeated, "it's the best time for beauty. Beauty doesn't like to be chaperoned."

Ida wanted to say that the child knew beauty in the ordinary ways—sun on a dish, a dog too clumsy to be wicked, the afterglow of a good woman's work—but she kept quiet. Gladys lifted a strand of her daughter's hair and let it fall, as if measuring the weight of future crowns.

"Do you hear the ocean?" she whispered. "I hear it in the pipes at night. It says we are all sailors whether or not we own boats."

On the way home, the child watched the telephone wires draw straight lines against the sky and understood that most straight lines are rough drafts. Her hand in Ida's felt like a lesson in belonging. The hawk above the road performed its ordinary miracle, and no one in the car mentioned it. Albert drove with the authority of a man who trusts maps. Ida hummed under her breath. The girl rested her head against the window and watched the world slide by in a rehearsal of cinema—the first cuts, the first dissolves, the first knowledge that the heart is a projector that will play whatever film you feed it.

Norma Jeane learned early that people can be honest by accident and dishonest with exquisite sincerity. In church, she listened to the way God's name made mouths behave themselves. In the marketplace, she learned that sugar can pretend to be salt if you only look at it. She learned the economy of glances. She learned that if you stand very still, the world will reveal its favorite magic trick: pretending to be simple. Sometimes, when no one was watching, she stood on a chair and addressed an invisible audience the way she had seen her mother do at the fence.

"Ladies and gentlemen," she whispered, "tonight we will attempt the impossible and ask a child to survive her childhood with grace." She bowed then, the way a girl bows when she knows the floor approves of her.

Ida, who had not asked for a prophet and did not trust prophecy, continued to teach the child useful things: how to scrub a stain until its memory surrendered, how to fold a sheet alone by using your whole body as a second pair of hands, how to apologize before you are fully sure you were the one who did the damage. Ida believed in the holiness of competence. It is a good belief. It does not save anyone, but it gives them a clean place to stand while they are drowning.

Sometimes at night the child dreamed of a duffel bag large enough to hold the moon. In the dream, the moon was calm about it; it knew it would be taken and returned, taken and returned, a practice run for an affection that would follow her into rooms with better chandeliers. She would wake and find her hand clenched again, an old habit returning the way birds return to the exact edge of the roof. She would unclench it and find nothing, and this, too, became knowledge helpful in later years, when she learned to close her hands around applause without trying to keep any.

In the spring, a woman in the neighborhood hung a dress on the line that caught the wind like a surrender flag. The child reached for it and laughed when the hem kissed her face.

"Careful," Ida said, "you'll think it loves you."

The child did not argue. She already knew that anything that moved beautifully could be mistaken for affection. She knew, too, that affection could be taught, like prayers, until the person offering it believed entirely in the sincerity of what she had learned to say.

When people spoke about the girl they used phrases that were meant to be compliments and were really confessions. She's so good, they said, meaning she does not ask us to rearrange ourselves. She's so pretty, they said, meaning we would like to put her in a story that redeems us. She's so quiet, they said, meaning we hope never to hear the verdict she is silently composing. The girl accepted their words the way a cat accepts a name: as one more piece of furniture in a house that has never properly belonged to her.

The day came when the Bolenders could not keep her any longer, not in the way the county counts keeping. Papers required signatures. Signatures required strangers. The world made that shuffling sound it makes when it is about to move a child for the good of everyone else. The house was cleaner than usual for a week, as if scrubbing could persuade history to revise its plans. Ida packed small things—the blanket that smelled of the story of sleep, a wooden lamb whose paint had taken on the digressions of years, a hair ribbon that would not hold any hair of consequence but might hold a morning together.

"Be obedient," Ida said, and then winced at herself, because obedience is a word you should hand to a child only if you are entirely sure of the person who will be using it on her. "Be kind," she amended, "even to the people who have not received their kindness yet."

She kissed the child's forehead and left a little more of her soul there than she intended. Albert shook the girl's hand, because a man like him shakes hands with any serious creature, and then he patted her shoulder as if it were reasonable to expect a shoulder like that to carry what she had been asked to carry.

The car that took her away had a cough like a laugh. The driver had the practiced gaze of someone who transports other people's histories as if they were boxes labeled fruit. The street watched in the humble way streets do, not sure whether it was being cruel or merely being itself. The hawk—a professional—completed another circle and filed its report with the sky.

It would be pretty to say that the child looked back, but her gaze was forward, as if some rumor of light was already instructing her to collect herself. She seemed to recognize that leaving one house is practice for entering another, and that the person who carries you may not be the person who keeps you, and that keeping and loving are cousins who only speak on holidays. On her lap she held the wooden lamb and the lamb, who knew how to be useful, kept the silence.

They crossed a part of the city where the street names knew famous vowels, and the buildings pretended to be taller than they were. People had invented different ways of walking and all of them were auditioning for gravity. The child felt her heart choose a tempo and then adjust it for the scenery. She liked the sign where a woman in a hat promised to be beautiful if she were purchased. She liked the way the sun became a rumor when it fell behind glass. She liked most of all the moment when the car paused at a corner and a girl with hair the color of an argument looked down at her and smiled, and the smile had no moral. It simply said: I see you. In a life that would later be cataloged by men with tidy pencils, this would be the first reliable artifact of joy.

She did not belong to anyone, not in the way that stays fixed in the mouth. She belonged to the idea of belonging, which is harder and also more interesting. She belonged to the afternoons that taught her how a room changes when you enter it and decide to be lenient. She belonged to the mirror that would one day learn to applaud her. She belonged to the kind of sadness that travels with its own trumpet and knows when to play quietly so as not to embarrass the host. She belonged to the hawk and to the prayer and to the duffel bag that did and did not happen. She belonged to a grandmother who believed sugar bowls gossip and to a mother whose mind rented out rooms to saints who were late for work. She belonged to a family that had lost its license to keep certain kinds of promises.

When the car arrived at the next address, the world did what it always does in the presence of a new story—it cleared its throat and pretended it had been expecting this. The woman at the door wore a dress that believed in the future. Her smile was practical and did not waste adjectives. The man behind her had a posture that could keep a roof in place. There was a bowl of apples on a table, and the apples looked like a picture of obedience.

The child stepped in and the house took her measure. Somewhere far off, a boulevard rehearsed its neon. Somewhere closer, a woman who had given birth forgot the name of a spoon and then, in a rush of courage, remembered it again.

Evenings came back, as they do, and brought their strange mercy. The child slept and dreamed the ocean was a hallway and each wave was a door, and behind each door was a room where someone said her name with the authority of love. In one of the rooms a mirror stood like a patient conspirator and showed her a girl with a mouth built for difficult promises. The mirror did not accuse. It was an accomplice. "We will do this together," it said, in the exact whisper a mother might have used in a better story. "We will pretend until it becomes true, and then we will continue pretending, because truth is a shy animal and needs company."

When she woke she was ready to practice surviving with elegance. She learned to say please and mean it and thank you and keep some of the thanks in reserve for later. She learned to enter a room as if the room were the nervous one. She learned that the smallest motion—tilting the head, pausing at the threshold, smiling in a way that allowed others to yoke their hopes to her—could convert suspicion to affection. She learned a hundred uses for her hands. The hands remembered the duffel bag and also remembered the ribbon. They knew which to hold and which to bless and which to let go as if letting go were a form of art.

Years later, when the name had changed and the light obeyed her, she would talk about childhood as if it had happened to a beloved stranger whose mail she still received. She would say, "I was a baby nobody kept," and then she would laugh into the silence the way a good actress rescues a scene. She would say, "But I learned, darling, that if no one keeps you, the world becomes a very large closet and all the dresses are yours."

People would think she was joking. People always think beauty is joking. But she would mean it. The joke would be the prayer. The prayer would be the rope. And the rope would be the ribbon tied around the secret that even she never fully untied: that once upon a time a little girl learned to be luminous in a house where love was counted like coins and spent like light.

The hawk still wrote its circles over Hawthorne when she no longer lived there. The prayers still chained themselves politely to supper. The duffel bag, in some version of the story, still waited on a chair, learning the patience of unchosen futures. The ocean rehearsed its forever.

And a grown woman with a borrowed name stood in rooms that could not believe their luck and gave them reason to. If you looked closely you could see the baby, serious as a ledger, decide again and again to survive with style. Not because it was easy or inevitable, but because something in her had been consecrated by refusal. She would not be kept. She would be kept, instead, by the very act of being unkeepable, which is a kind of custody the world cannot revoke.

When the lights later rose and fell on cue and the cameras made their industrial devotions and the men with pencils agreed to adore her and then forgot how, she would sometimes put a hand to her belly and count a safety into herself, the old Bolender habit, the modest arithmetic of breath. And if anyone had asked what she was counting she might have said, with the reckless accuracy of a saint, "The exits." She knew them all, and she knew also that the exit is sometimes the entrance if you are clever and if the dress fits. Which, for her, it always did, because she had learned to make it fit by learning to be the dress and the woman both, the garment and the glow, the baby appearing again in a series of rooms that did not deserve her and therefore needed her urgently.

If the world sometimes wondered how a girl like that could walk a rope and make it look like a boulevard, the answer was not complicated. She had been practicing since the cradle. In one hand she held the memory of order, of Ida's kiss like an oath, of a crib that made a lattice of lace across the wall. In the other she held the rumor of escape, of Gladys's duffel-bag devotion, of dangerous love with the charm of a broken promise. Between those two weights she carried herself—perfect posture, knees together, smile like a deadline—over every chasm the story offered. And whenever the wind rose—and it always rose—she would lower her eyelashes and let the wind believe it had been the one to make her move.

3

The Ghost Mother

The Bolender house smelled of oatmeal in the morning and furniture polish in the afternoon, a rhythm of starch and discipline that wrapped the days like tight gauze. Wayne Bolender worked with radios, tinkering late into the night with coils of copper and the mysterious hum of unseen voices, while Ida kept the household with the precision of a metronome. They were foster parents, not guardians. Caretakers, not family. But they were safe. And for a girl who had already learned, before she could speak, that safety was fleeting, that was no small thing.

Safety, however, had rules. Eat what's on your plate. Speak only when spoken to. Kneel for evening prayers. Say thank you. Say I'm sorry. Say nothing at all when you want to scream. Ida's voice, clipped and firm, carried the weight of those commandments. "Now, Norma Jeane," she would say, smoothing the collar of a plain dress, "a good girl listens. A good girl obeys." To neighbors she was "Aunt Ida," though the title carried no warmth of kinship—it was a role, as rigid as her posture. Wayne, quieter, offered little beyond the occasional nod of approval or the distant crackle of a radio catching stations from nowhere, as if he preferred the voices drifting through the ether to those under his own roof.

Norma Jeane tried to become the kind of girl who would be kept. She folded herself into silence, her hands folded in her lap, her eyes lowered during prayers until she learned to recite the words by heart, though they never felt like her own. She ate what was put before her, even when it churned in her small stomach, because Ida's rule was law. She said "thank you" when prompted, and "I'm sorry" when she hadn't the faintest idea what for. She learned the art of being invisible, a shadow with braids pulled so tightly her scalp ached.

And yet, something shimmered inside her—a flicker she couldn't suppress. She would stare at the wallpaper until it became a ballroom, dancers twirling across the faded floral print. She would press her face to the cracked window at dusk and watch the light flicker on in distant houses, each square of yellow like a movie screen playing a story she could almost imagine herself inside. Imagination was forbidden in the Bolender house, where salvation came through structure, not dreams. So she hid it—in scribbles, in half-whispered stories to herself, in the secret corners of her mind.

Years later, she would laugh softly when telling Susan Strasberg about those days. Susan, who grew up in the Strasberg household where the dinner table was a theater of argument, passion, and affection, could hardly fathom such quiet. "Your house was alive," Marilyn told her once. "Mine . . . mine was so neat it squeaked. If I dropped a fork, it was like dropping a bomb. If I said what I felt, it was like cursing God." She had envied Susan's noisy family, envied the mess of love on full display. In Hawthorne, love was folded, pressed, and put away in drawers, brought out only under strict conditions.

To Jim Bacon, years later, her recollections came tumbling out in torrents, long and rambling, sometimes circling back on themselves until he barely knew where to interrupt. "You know, Jimmy," she once began, her voice half-amused, half-broken, "they used to line us up for prayers, like little soldiers in dresses, and Ida would close her eyes so tight you thought she might pop. And I'd try to pray too, but all I could think about was the wallpaper—I was waltzing in my head while she was asking God to forgive us. Maybe He forgave me, maybe He didn't, but I couldn't stop dancing in my head. It was the only way to survive." Bacon said she could go on like that for two hours, words spilling like beads from a broken rosary, each one glinting with some unexpected light.

Ida wasn't cruel, exactly. Cruelty requires a spark of malice, and hers was a more numbing form of righteousness. She believed in salvation through structure, in the straight back, the folded hands, the silence of obedience. If she punished, it was not with the whip of anger but with the cold gaze of disappointment. "Aunt Ida's eyes," Marilyn told Bacon once, "were sharper than any switch. She could make you feel like your soul was crooked just by looking at you." Wayne, for his part, was present without ever being truly there. His world was made of wires and static, the voices of strangers leaking from radios that filled the house with a kind of ghostly chorus. To Norma Jeane, those disembodied voices seemed more real than his own.

And always, there was the ghost mother. Gladys hovered at the edges of that ordered world, her absence pressing in more heavily than her presence ever had. Sometimes she visited, sometimes she vanished for weeks, leaving behind only a trace of perfume or a rumor among neighbors. In the Bolender house, her name was spoken rarely, as though she were both forbidden and inevitable. Yet Norma Jeane felt her—in dreams, in shadows on the wall, in the restless sense that the house, however safe, was only temporary. "She was like a shadow I could never escape," Marilyn told Susan. "Even when I was good, even when I was quiet, I could feel her waiting just beyond the door."

The rules were Ida's gospel. But they were also chains. Norma Jeane would repeat them like liturgy: Eat what's on your plate. Speak only when spoken to. Say thank you. Say I'm sorry. Each phrase carved into her, shaping the contours of a girl who would one day become a woman who knew exactly how to perform gratitude, apology, silence—and also how to break free from them. To Bacon, she once mused, "I think Hollywood liked me because I already knew my lines. I'd been practicing them since I was a kid. Smile here, apologize there, pretend you're happy. By the time the cameras came, it felt natural. Too natural."

The Bolender house was neat, proper, Protestant—but it was never truly home. Home is where imagination is allowed to bloom, and in Hawthorne, imagination was smothered under layers of starch and polish. And yet, in secret, Norma Jeane's imagination grew like weeds through cracks in the pavement, impossible to suppress. She learned to dream silently, to hide her stories the way she hid her drawings under the mattress, the way she hid her longing behind bowed heads and whispered amens. She became good, she became invisible—but even then, something inside her shimmered. A flicker. A foreshadowing of the girl who would one day refuse to be unseen.

Evenings in the Bolender house followed the same script, as though Ida herself had written the play. Supper was modest—potatoes, a slice of meat, bread thick with butter if the week had been good. Norma Jeane ate quietly, watching the way Wayne bowed his head before taking the first bite, the way Ida's hands folded over her napkin like wings pressed in prayer. Then came cleanup, Ida humming half a hymn as she wiped down the counters until they gleamed with her sense of righteousness. Finally, as the dusk settled over Hawthorne, there were prayers. Kneeling at the bedside, small hands clasped, eyes tightly shut against any stray thought.

"I used to cheat," Marilyn confessed years later to Bacon, half-laughing, half-ashamed. "When Ida's eyes were closed, I would open mine. Just a peek. I wanted to see what God looked like when she was talking to Him. But all I ever saw was the wallpaper. I think God must have lived in that wallpaper—that's where I put Him, anyway. I didn't understand heaven, but I understood those flowers on the wall."

Wayne would finish the day fiddling with radios, the soft buzz of static filling the corners of the house. Norma Jeane lay in bed, listening to his machines pull invisible voices from the air. She thought of them as ghosts, drifting in and out, speaking languages she didn't yet know. Sometimes she imagined one of the voices belonged to her mother—far away, calling out to her in code, a sound only she could recognize. The voices seemed to promise that the world was larger than this house, that safety was only one version of life, and that somewhere out there, the story might change.

The Bolenders, for their part, believed they were giving her the greatest gift of all: order. To them, disorder was the devil's opening. Ida often told the girl, "God loves the obedient child best." Marilyn, remembering this with a sigh, once told Susan Strasberg, "Can you imagine? Love, as something you had to earn by being quiet. At your house, Susan, if someone raised their voice it meant they cared. At mine, if I raised my voice, it meant I was wicked."

Gladys haunted the ordered house like a phantom. She would arrive unannounced, with perfume that clashed against the polish and soap of Ida's world. She would scoop up her daughter and whisper stories into her ear—stories about movie stars she'd glimpsed at the studio, about parties that blurred into dreams. Sometimes she was tender, sometimes desperate, sometimes trembling with a sadness no child could understand. Her visits were unpredictable, her departures abrupt. Once, she promised Norma Jeane they would live together soon, just the two of them, and the little girl clung to that promise like it was scripture.

"She was always a ghost to me," Marilyn told Bacon. "Even when she was right there, I couldn't hold her. She was half here, half in another world. Sometimes I think she saw things I couldn't see—angels or devils, maybe. Sometimes I think she just saw her own pain."

The neighbors whispered about Gladys—about her fragile mind, about her erratic ways. Ida shook her head and muttered prayers when the visits ended, but she never forbade them outright. She must have known the girl needed her mother, even if her mother was little more than a shadow. Still, Ida reasserted her rules after every visit, as though to cleanse the air of whatever chaos Gladys had brought. Norma Jeane would kneel a little longer, speak a little softer, fold herself even tighter, trying to be the good girl Ida demanded. But the ghost mother lingered, whispering from some dark corner: you are mine, even if I cannot keep you.

As the years passed, Norma Jeane grew skilled at inhabiting two worlds. In Ida's world, she was obedient, silent, modest. In her secret world, she was a dreamer. She would draw faces in the margins of old notebooks, whisper stories to herself while scrubbing dishes, spin in circles in the yard until she collapsed dizzy, imagining she was dancing under a spotlight. That split—between what was seen and what was hidden—would define her life. To Bacon, she once mused, "I think I was always two people. The good girl they wanted, and the girl who was making up her own story. Maybe that's why I became an actress—I'd already been playing the role since I was a child."

Jim Bacon recalled evenings when Marilyn, years later, would drift into these recollections like she was falling backward into time. "It was like she was still there," he said. "I'd ask one question and she'd talk for two hours. Her words were like water breaking through a dam—they just kept coming." She told him how Ida braided her hair so tightly she thought her scalp might tear, how she learned to smile when she was scolded because it softened the punishment, how the smell of oatmeal could make her stomach churn even decades later. She told him about lying awake at night, whispering to herself, "Be good, be good, be good," as if the words might build a wall high enough to keep out the shadows.

To Susan Strasberg, Marilyn painted a different contrast. "At your house," she said, "everyone was allowed to feel. You could yell, cry, laugh—all of it. At mine, feelings were dangerous. They had to be hidden away. I used to think, if I could just sit at your table, I'd know what love was." Susan, moved, once told her that her longing showed through in every role she played—that the world fell in love with Marilyn Monroe because she carried that hunger for love into every frame of film. Marilyn only smiled, as if to say Susan had guessed a truth she never dared put into words.

In the Bolender home, though, love was not a word spoken lightly. It was implied through discipline, through order, through rules that were meant to protect even as they suffocated. Ida believed she was saving the child's soul, warding off the chaos that had consumed Gladys. And perhaps she did, in her way. But in saving the girl from chaos, she also taught her that survival meant silence, that being loved meant disappearing into obedience.

Years later, Marilyn would look back on those lessons with a mixture of gratitude and grief. "I suppose they saved me," she admitted to Bacon. "But they also made me . . . hollow. Like I was just a vessel waiting to be filled. And Hollywood, well, Hollywood was happy to fill me up with whatever it wanted."

The ghost mother never left. Even as Norma Jeane learned to bow her head and recite prayers, even as she tucked her imagination into hidden corners, Gladys lingered. She was there in the silence after supper, in the shadows that stretched across the wallpaper ballroom, in the static voices spilling from Wayne's radios. She was the absence that shaped the girl more profoundly than presence ever could.

And so the child grew—obedient on the outside, luminous in secret. A girl shaped by rules and haunted by absence. A girl who had already learned to perform, to split herself in two, to live with one foot in the visible world and one in the invisible. The ghost mother watched, unseen, as her daughter became a vessel of contradictions—good and rebellious, silent and dreaming, kept and unkeepable.

By the time Norma Jeane reached school age, the Bolenders' rules were etched so deeply into her that she moved through the classroom like a girl trained for chapel. She raised her hand only when called upon, sat straight in her desk, and finished every bite of her sandwich as though God Himself had ordered it. Teachers praised her as a "good girl," the kind of child who never caused trouble. She smiled at their praise, but inside she kept her secret theater alive. While the lesson droned on about arithmetic, she imagined the chalkboard turning into a movie screen, the dust from the eraser swirling into scenes only she could see.

When she shared any of this with Jim Bacon decades later, she delivered it as a stream of revelations, each one tumbling over the next. "Jimmy, I was so good, so quiet, but in my head I was talking all the time. You know what I used to do? I'd imagine the chalk squeaks were voices, whole conversations. The chalk was telling me secrets. And I'd laugh to myself—just a little giggle—and then the teacher would look at me like I'd broken the Ten Commandments. But I couldn't stop. My mind was . . . alive. Like a circus nobody else could see."

Bacon remembered sitting transfixed, chain-smoking while she spun her childhood back to life in rambling, fevered detail. He hardly needed to ask questions; she poured it out as if the words had been waiting decades for an open ear. "You don't know what it's like," she told him once, "to be invisible in one house and then to grow up to be the most visible woman in the world. It's like . . . like I was making up for all the times I couldn't speak. I was speaking for all the times little Norma Jeane had to stay quiet."

In those years, Gladys slipped further into the shadows. Her visits became rarer, more unpredictable. When she appeared, it was as if she'd emerged from another world entirely—hair disheveled, eyes clouded, a strange urgency in her voice. She would press kisses on her daughter's cheeks, then retreat, muttering about people who wanted to hurt them, voices only she seemed to hear. Ida stood stiffly by, equal parts watchful and resigned. After Gladys left, she would polish the furniture until her reflection stared back at her, as though order could erase the disorder that had just passed through the door.

To Norma Jeane, her mother's absences felt heavier than her presences. She dreamed of her at night, imagined her standing at the foot of the bed, watching silently, unable to touch. "She was like a ghost, Jimmy," Marilyn told Bacon. "Even when she was there, she wasn't really there. I'd reach out and feel nothing. And then I thought—maybe that's all mothers are, anyway. Just ghosts we chase forever."

Susan Strasberg heard the softer version of this truth. Marilyn confided to her, "When I was a girl, I wanted a family like yours. A noisy table, arguments, hugs—all of it. My house was . . . silent. And when my mother came, she was already half gone. I think that's why I loved being around the Strasbergs. You reminded me of what I never had."

The contrast between those two confidences—the raw confession to Bacon, the wistful longing shared with Susan—revealed the duality Marilyn had carried since childhood. She was both the child haunted by a ghost mother and the woman who yearned for the warmth of a family she could never quite claim.

As the 1930s deepened, the Great Depression shadowed Hawthorne. Neighbors lost jobs, families doubled up in cramped houses, radios carried grim news. But inside the Bolender home, order never faltered. Ida made do with less, stretching meals, patching dresses, braiding the girl's hair so tight it shone. Wayne repaired radios for cash, bringing home odd scraps of wire and solder that smelled of burned metal. The little girl watched, wide-eyed, as voices sprang to life from boxes, invisible people speaking out of the air. To her, it was proof that the unseen could be made real—that hidden worlds could burst into sound if you only knew how to listen.

When she told Bacon about those nights, her words spilled out in breathless wonder. "I thought maybe my mother was in those radios. That if I listened hard enough, I'd hear her voice. Sometimes I pretended the static was her singing to me. Isn't that crazy? But I needed to believe she was somewhere I could reach."

By 1933, Gladys's instability could no longer be ignored. Whispers grew louder. She had been seen wandering the streets, muttering to herself, eyes wild. She had accused neighbors of plotting against her, claimed strangers were following her. Finally, she was committed—locked away in a state hospital where her mind unraveled in a world of delusions. For little Norma Jeane, the ghost mother became fully ghost.

The Bolenders did not tell her much. Children were not owed explanations in their house. One day her mother was there, fragile and unpredictable; the next she was gone, absorbed into the walls of an institution. "They told me she was sick," Marilyn remembered later, her voice trembling. "Sick in her head. But how do you explain that to a child? I thought maybe I'd made her sick. Maybe I was too much trouble, too noisy inside, even if I was quiet outside. Children always think it's their fault. And I did. I thought I'd broken her somehow."

The sense of guilt lingered, a scar she carried into adulthood. Even in her brightest moments, she felt the pull of that ghost, the whisper that she was too much or not enough, that love could vanish without warning. Bacon heard it in her endless stories, the way she circled back to her mother again and again, as though speaking the ghost aloud might finally lay it to rest.

And yet, the child survived. She obeyed Ida, followed the rules, played the part of the good girl. But inside, the shimmer never dimmed. She still saw ballrooms in wallpaper, movie screens in cracked windows, angels hiding in radio static. She had learned to be invisible—but she had also learned to imagine herself visible. And that imagination, hidden though it was, became her secret weapon.

The day would come when she had to leave the Bolenders, when she would be passed again into another uncertain future. But even then, the lessons of the ghost mother and the gospel of rules would remain. She had learned silence, but also performance. She had learned absence, but also longing. She had learned to obey, but also to dream.

Years later, she would tell Bacon in one of her rambling, late-night confessions, "Jimmy, I think I was born twice. Once when my mother gave me away, and once when I realized I could invent myself. That second birth—that was the one that saved me."

And so the girl who grew up in the Bolender house—neat, proper, obedient—carried with her the ghost of a mother who could not keep her and the secret shimmer of a child who could not be erased. The ghost mother lingered, whispering from the shadows. The obedient girl bowed her head, folded her hands, and waited. And deep inside, the shimmer grew, biding its time, ready to burst into light.

4

Back with Mom

The end of childhood, if it can be said to have an end, came for Norma Jeane not with birthdays or schoolbooks but with the death of a small dog named Tippy. He had been her companion, her shadow, the single creature in her young life that offered love without condition or rules. His bark filled the stillness of the Bolender house, a bright interruption against Ida's rigid silences. Some neighbors hated it, muttering about the noise, the endless yapping that disturbed the order of their street.

Years later, in her memoir dictated with weary candor, she told it differently, more brutally—that a neighbor, driven past reason by Tippy's barking, had taken a garden hoe and severed him in two. A shocking image, gothic in its cruelty, and one that Marilyn carried as though the world had confirmed her worst suspicion: that anything loved could be destroyed without mercy. Family members later claimed the truth was less grotesque, that the dog had simply been struck by a car and Ida, ever practical, had used a hoe to move the body out of the road. But the detail hardly mattered. What mattered was what the child saw when she came running up the drive—Tippy's body mangled, a hoe nearby, death handled like yardwork.

She never believed Ida's explanation. In her mind, the neighbors had killed her dog, had taken from her the only friend who loved without judgment. "They killed him," she insisted. She said it again and again until Ida wondered if the girl was slipping into delusion, repeating the madness of her mother. But it was no delusion; it was defiance. Norma Jeane refused to accept a version of the world in which cruelty was mere accident. She knew, instinctively, that the world could be vicious. And so, Tippy became the first ghost of her life, haunting her with the memory of unconditional love stolen too soon.

Not long after, Gladys appeared again, as if conjured by the child's grief. Ida, weary and perhaps unnerved by her ward's fixation on the dog's death, phoned her. "It would be best now if you came and took Norma Jeane," Ida told her. "She's very upset. I think she needs her mother." So Gladys arrived, not with open arms but with the impersonal blare of a car horn. She sat in the driver's seat while her daughter dragged her small suitcase down the gravel drive, the house receding behind her like the end of a long, stern sermon.

Back in her mother's care, the world was different. Gone were the tidy acres of the Bolenders, the strict prayers, the polish that made every surface shine like a reflection of Ida's own self-control. In their place was a cramped Hollywood apartment, shared with another woman: Grace McKee. Grace was Gladys's friend, a coworker at Consolidated Studios, where they spliced film negatives together in the endless churn of studio production. Grace was lively where Gladys was withdrawn, glamorous where Gladys was frayed. She painted her lips, curled her hair, and laughed loud enough to turn heads. To a little girl starved of sparkle, Grace seemed like a fairy godmother.

Grace saw in Norma Jeane what no one else had yet dared to name: the potential for beauty. "Show them how pretty you are, Norma," she would say, coaxing the child to pout, to smile, to bat her lashes in imitation of Jean Harlow. She curled the girl's hair, dabbed her lips with rouge, spoke lightly of a nose job someday, as though beauty was a destiny to be prepared for like school lessons. Marilyn, years later, recalled these moments with both tenderness and unease. She had been only eight. She had not yet grown into her own face, and already Grace was casting her in a role—a child rehearsing for a womanhood that would not wait.

Yet the apartment was no haven. Gladys was unraveling, sinking further into the shadowed corridors of her mind. Depression thickened around her like fog, muffling her daughter's small voice. Within months, her breakdown came. The world she shared with Grace collapsed into chaos. Unable to care for the child, they placed her temporarily with George and Maud Atkinson, a British couple who lived nearby.

Norma Jeane learned, once again, what it meant to be passed along. "I thought I was going to a prison," she would later remember. Each move was an erasure. Each suitcase packed was a reminder that she belonged to no one. Yet in August 1933, Gladys purchased a house—three bedrooms in Hollywood, a fragile attempt at stability. She moved her daughter back in, along with the Atkinsons. The house was full of smoke, laughter, the clink of glasses. They played cards, sang songs, danced in the evenings. "They liked to drink a little, smoke, dance, and sing and play cards, all the things that I had been taught were sinful," Marilyn would recall. "And they still seemed like very nice people to me."

It might have been happiness, if only it had lasted. But Gladys's mind could not bear the weight of ordinary life. By 1934, she suffered another breakdown and was institutionalized, this time for good. The ghost mother receded permanently into the shadows of the state hospital, her absences now sanctioned by law and medicine. Grace stepped forward, assuming legal guardianship of the child.

Grace McKee was no ordinary guardian. She believed in movies the way others believed in scripture. To her, Hollywood was not a place but a destiny, a stage where beauty became immortality. She dressed Norma Jeane in little outfits, curled her hair, painted her lips. "Just like Jean Harlow," she would say, presenting the child like a prize at the studio where she worked. Colleagues looked on with amusement or disapproval, but Grace was undeterred. She told the girl she would be famous one day, that she had the face of a star.

But dreams were fragile things in the Depression. Grace's own life was a series of marriages and disappointments. By 1935 she was on her fourth husband, Ervin "Doc" Goddard, a towering man of six-foot-five, with a resemblance to Randolph Scott and a hunger for success he would never quite satisfy. He had three children from a previous marriage—Eleanor, Nona, and Josephine (later known as actress Jody Lawrance)—and times were hard. Another mouth to feed was more than he wanted. Within months, Grace packed Norma Jeane's bags and delivered her to the Los Angeles Orphans' Home Society.

"I thought I was going to prison," she said again, words etched into her memory like scars. "What had I done that they were getting rid of me? I was afraid of everything and afraid to show how scared I was. All I could do was cry."

The orphanage was a place of gray walls and strict schedules, where children learned quickly that they were not special. But Grace, perhaps guilty, did not abandon her ward entirely. Every week she visited, bringing small gifts—dresses, lipstick, little trinkets that smelled faintly of Hollywood. She spoke of movies, of stardom, of Shirley Temple and Jean Harlow. "One day," she told her, "you'll be just like them. Just wait and see."

To other children, Grace's visits must have seemed like a cruel tease, a glimpse of a world none of them could touch. But to Norma Jeane, they were lifelines. She clung to the idea that she was destined for more than these gray walls, that someone believed she was meant for light and not for shadows. Yet the weekly reminders of what she lacked were also wounds. She went to sleep dreaming of cameras, of applause, of escape—only to wake in the same narrow bed, still just another orphan.

Marilyn, looking back, remembered how Grace's words both saved and cursed her. "She made me believe I could be somebody," she told a friend. "But she also made me believe I had to be somebody. There was no choice. If I wasn't beautiful, if I wasn't a star, then what was I? Nobody."

At the orphanage she learned to hide her pain behind smiles, to perform gratitude for every small kindness. She smiled for the staff, smiled for Grace, smiled even when her heart ached with loneliness. Each smile was a mask, practice for the role she would later play for the entire world.

In June 1937, after nearly two years behind the orphanage gates, Norma Jeane was allowed to leave. She was just eleven, still more child than girl, but already carrying the exhaustion of someone who had lived a dozen lives. Grace signed the papers and swept her back into the world, determined, at least outwardly, to give her ward another chance at home.

But the home she returned to was no sanctuary. Grace was now married to Doc Goddard, and the atmosphere in the house had shifted. Doc, tall and broad-shouldered, seemed to fill every room with his presence. He had once nursed dreams of the movies—a few stand-in roles, an extra in *Babes in Toyland* as a toy soldier—but those dreams had died quickly, leaving behind only bitterness and whiskey. To Norma Jeane, he was a looming figure, both fascinating and frightening, the kind of man whose mood could dictate the air you breathed.

She remembered him drinking in the evenings, his voice growing louder as the glass emptied, his laugh edged with something dark. "Aren't you going to give me a kiss?" he asked her once, the words slurred, his hand reaching too close. She froze, every lesson of obedience from the Bolenders returning at once. But obedience here was dangerous. She slipped away silently, avoiding him in corners and corridors.

Years later, she told James Dougherty, her first husband, about that night, about the kiss that was not a kiss but a violation in disguise. "He scared me," she admitted. Others corroborated the story—fragments from different witnesses, biographers piecing together the evidence. Whether once or more than once, whether clumsy drunkenness or something darker, the memory settled like a stone in her. It was another confirmation of what she already half-knew: that men could be dangerous, that safety was an illusion.

After that, her time under the same roof as Doc and Grace was brief. Poverty may have played a role, as some biographers suggest, but the incident with Doc became part of the lore, the whispered explanation for why she spent much of her adolescence in other homes. She was sent to live with Grace's aunt, Ana Lower, on Nebraska Avenue—a kind woman who gave her a quieter, gentler home than most she had known.

Yet the pattern was unbroken: each new roof was temporary, each guardian a stopgap, each suitcase packed and unpacked until she no longer knew what permanence looked like. She once described it simply: "I was more alone and separated from anything than I had ever been." Loneliness became her constant companion, shaping her like Ida's rules once had, embedding itself into her bones.

With Ana she found some respite, a steadier rhythm. But soon she was sent again, this time to Aunt Olive Monroe's house in North Hollywood. Olive, abandoned by her husband Marion, struggled to raise three children of her own. To drop another child into that mix was less salvation than survival. "I was feeling the predicament of my life," Marilyn would later recall, "and that frightened and depressed me so much, I would get sick and couldn't eat. When I did, I would often throw up." Her body spoke the language of distress even when her lips said nothing.

From house to house she went, never certain where she would sleep next month, never certain whom she might have to call "Aunt." Each goodbye confirmed the truth that had stalked her since infancy: she was not a girl to be kept.

Still, Grace remained a presence. She visited, she wrote, she whispered her gospel of movies. She continued to believe, or at least to tell the girl she believed, that destiny awaited her in Hollywood. When she brought her back again, to live under her roof, it was with that same strange mixture of care and betrayal. Grace could not keep her, yet she kept feeding her dreams.

By her mid-teens, Norma Jeane began to emerge from the cocoon of invisibility that had defined her childhood. At Van Nuys High School, she became noticeable. Her hair, naturally brown but already kissed by the California sun, caught the light. Her smile, practiced in front of mirrors, charmed classmates. She was shy, but not unseen. She drew the gaze of boys, the whispers of girls, the kind of attention that both thrilled and embarrassed her.

Among her companions was BeBe Goddard, Doc's daughter from his previous marriage. BeBe was a bridge into the ordinary rituals of adolescence: walking home from school together, gossiping about teachers, lingering near lockers. And then there was Jim Dougherty, five years older, a former football player with shoulders as wide as the horizon. He drove her and BeBe home sometimes, his presence reassuring, his grin easy. To Grace, ever the matchmaker of fate, he seemed perfect. To Norma Jeane, he was just a boy, kind but unremarkable, not yet the stuff of dreams.

Grace had other concerns. Doc was offered a promotion, a position as Head of Sales for Adel Precision Products' East Coast branch. It meant a move to Huntington, West Virginia—a new start for them, but not for the girl. Norma Jeane, still legally their ward, was not going with them. The orphanage loomed again, its gates waiting like a prison door.

Desperation sparked in Grace. She turned to her friend Ethel Dougherty, Jim's mother, with a plan. "What if your son married Norma Jeane?" she proposed. "That would keep her out of the orphanage, and it's not as if they don't already like each other."

It was pragmatic, almost businesslike, the way she had once groomed the girl for stardom—as though lives could be arranged like wardrobes, like roles in a studio casting book. Norma Jeane, when told, was torn between fear and resignation. She asked Grace if perhaps the marriage could be only in name, a friendship, a protection without intimacy. Grace gave her a smile meant to soothe but heavy with dismissal: "Don't worry. You'll learn."

And so the decision was made. At sixteen, barely past childhood, she was to become a wife. It was not romance but logistics, not passion but protection. "The Goddards couldn't support me," Marilyn would later say. "And they had to work out something. And so I got married."

To Bacon, years later, she recounted the moment with a kind of bitter humor. "Imagine that, Jimmy. They said I was too young for Hollywood, but old enough to get married. Sixteen years old and already playing house like a grown woman. I didn't even know who I was yet."

The wedding was modest but memorable. On June 19, 1942, a few weeks after her birthday, Norma Jeane walked down a staircase in a borrowed gown. Foster parents Ida and Wayne Bolender were there—the only real family she had known—watching with quiet pride. Grace was absent, already preparing for her move east. Gladys was absent too, locked away in her hospital. The girl who had been passed from hand to hand was now handed to a husband, the arrangement sealed with vows spoken more out of necessity than love.

To the world, it looked like a beginning. To Norma Jeane, it felt like another transaction. Childhood had ended with Tippy's death; adolescence ended with the signing of a marriage certificate.

The morning of June 19, 1942, broke clear and bright, though to Norma Jeane it felt heavy, as if the sky itself had been pressed down by the weight of what was expected of her. Sixteen years old, fresh from classrooms and hand-me-down dresses, she was stepping into the role of a bride, not out of love but because it was the only way to keep from returning to the orphanage. The plan had been made for her, agreed upon by adults who spoke of her future as though it were furniture to be moved into the right room.

The borrowed gown was white, the veil thin as gauze. She remembered climbing the staircase in the Goddards' home, the way everyone turned their heads upward to see her. Her foster sister Nancy Jeffrey would later recall how beautiful she looked at the top of the stairs, a vision almost glowing in the light. But in Marilyn's own memory, the day carried a bitter edge. "The Goddards couldn't support me," she told an interviewer years later. "And they had to work out something. And so I got married."

The ceremony was simple, a minister, a few witnesses, no grand celebration. Grace was already gone east with Doc, her absence more telling than any words could have been. Gladys, her real mother, was locked away in the sanitarium, a ghost presence that hovered over every milestone of the girl's life. But Ida and Wayne Bolender were there—the guardians of her earliest years, the ones who had drilled her in rules and prayers. Their presence was both comfort and reminder: even in marriage, she remained the child who had been passed from hand to hand.

Jim Dougherty stood tall, dutiful, his smile steady. Five years her senior, he had been a student body president, a football player, a young man whose path seemed assured. To him, this marriage was not a romance either; it was an arrangement, one he accepted with the pragmatism of his mother's persuasion. They had dated a few times, awkwardly, without sparks. Now they were husband and wife.

To Bacon, decades later, Marilyn described the moment with wry humor. "Jimmy, I didn't even know what it meant to be married. I thought maybe we could be like roommates. I asked Grace if that was possible. She just laughed and said, 'Don't worry, you'll learn.' But what was I supposed to learn? Nobody had ever told me how to love somebody. All I knew was how to survive."

The wedding night was quiet, restrained. Jim was kind, not forceful, but Norma Jeane's body carried the weight of fear. Every touch was a question she wasn't ready to answer. She had grown up wary of men, wary of the dangers hidden in their smiles and voices. Doc Goddard's looming presence still haunted her, the echo of his drunken grasp a warning etched into memory. She wanted safety, not intimacy. She wanted a bed where she could sleep without fear of being moved again.

In the small apartment they shared afterward, she tried to play the role of wife. She cooked simple meals, washed dishes, smiled when visitors came. Jim went to work, steady and predictable, the kind of man who believed in routines. To him, this was ordinary life. To her, it was another performance. She was practicing again, as she had under Ida's roof, playing the part expected of her, reciting the lines of gratitude, apology, silence.

Yet there was a flicker, even then, of the woman she would become. She looked in the mirror and practiced her smile, not just for Jim but for herself, for the reflection of a girl who still believed Grace's promises that she might one day be someone more. She curled her hair, dabbed on rouge when she could, not because she wanted to seduce Jim, but because she was rehearsing for a future stage.

"Marriage didn't make me feel like a woman," she told Susan Strasberg years later, speaking in that confessional tone that always left Susan shaken. "It just made me feel safe from the orphanage. That's all it was. Safety papers."

The safety, however, was thin. She was still lonely. Jim was kind but distant, older, living in a rhythm she couldn't match. She found herself daydreaming, just as she had in the Bolender house, staring at wallpaper and imagining it as a ballroom. Now she stared at the small apartment walls and saw movie screens, herself projected larger than life, adored instead of overlooked.

To Bacon she confessed, "I used to lie in bed and imagine cameras flashing, people calling my name. Jimmy was asleep, and I was pretending I was someone else. That's how I got through it. Pretending. I'd been pretending my whole life."

Her marriage was, in truth, another foster placement, another arrangement decided by others. She belonged to Jim now, legally and socially, but the girl inside her was still the orphan, still the dreamer, still the child who had learned that survival meant playing the part others wanted. The difference was that now, her part was wife.

Outside, the world was at war. By 1942, America was fully engaged in the Second World War. Factories buzzed, young men marched off to training camps, ration books determined what could be cooked in kitchens. Jim would soon enlist, joining the flood of boys-turned-soldiers. For Norma Jeane, the war years would open a door she could not yet see—the chance to work in a defense plant, to pose for photographs that would catch the eye of a photographer, and to begin the transformation into Marilyn Monroe. But for now, in 1942, she was just a sixteen-year-old bride trying to keep her place in the world.

When she looked back on it years later, the bitterness was never far from her words. "They said it was to protect me," she told Bacon, "but it felt like another way of losing myself. First to Ida, then to Grace, then to Doc, and finally to Jim. I kept thinking, when do I belong to me?"

The wedding photograph captured her with wide eyes, a soft smile, innocence draped in lace. To the world, it was the image of a girl stepping into womanhood. But behind the smile was the same refrain she had carried from the orphanage: What had I done that they were getting rid of me? Only this time, marriage wasn't the end of rejection but the mask of belonging.

Ida and Wayne Bolender, standing in the pews, must have seen her differently. To them, she was still the foster child they had raised in prayers and obedience, now stepping into her next chapter. Perhaps they believed she had been saved from the fate of her mother, from the chaos that haunted Gladys. They could not have imagined that the girl in lace would one day belong to the world, her face stamped on billboards and magazines, her name whispered in every language.

The marriage gave her shelter, but it did not give her a home. Home was something she had never truly known—a place where she was kept, not passed along. She smiled for the photographs, said her vows, cooked the dinners. But deep inside, the shimmer remained, the secret self who had once seen ballrooms in wallpaper and heard angels in radio static. That girl was still there, waiting.

The end of this chapter in her life was not an end at all, but another beginning in disguise. A girl who had been an orphan, foster child, ward, orphan again, was now a wife. She was no longer in danger of being sent back behind the gates. She had escaped one prison only to enter another. And in that confinement, the dream began to grow.

5

The Unofficial Orphan

On the 30th of September 1935, a promise broke. Grace McKee, who had sworn to Gladys Baker that she would always look after her daughter, walked eight-year-old Norma Jeane up the drive of the Los Angeles Orphans' Home Society, handed her over to the matron, and left her behind. Grace wept that morning, or so the story goes—tears streaking the rouge she loved to wear, her sobs echoing down the corridors. But the tears did not change the fact that she was leaving the girl there, registering her as the home's 3,463rd ward. A number in a ledger. A mouth off her hands.

Norma Jeane understood promises in the way children do: literally, eternally. If Grace had promised her mother, it meant safety, forever. To see her guardian walk away was to see the world split open. She felt it not as paperwork or guardianship but as abandonment, hot and raw, like the sting of a burn. Later she would say, "When a little girl feels lonely and that nobody cares or wants her, it's just something she can never forget as long as she lives." That morning was the seed of her lifelong certainty that love could vanish in a blink.

The orphanage stood at 815 El Centro Avenue in Hollywood, a city already shimmering with movie magic. Its walls were high, its gates stern, its buildings lined with neat brick and windows that did not open wide enough to let the dreams fly out. Founded in the late nineteenth century, it was meant to be a refuge for children like her, but to Norma Jeane it was another house of rules, another stop in the long procession of roofs she was shuffled under.

As Grace disappeared, the child was led into the dormitory, where rows of iron beds stretched like pews in a church. Twenty-six other girls shared the room, their laughter and tears blending into the air like incense. She set her small suitcase down and stared at the bed assigned to her. Everything here had been used before, by other children whose names she did not know. She was not special, not beloved. She was simply next.

That night, lying in the narrow bed, she listened to the sounds of breathing all around her—some soft, some jagged, some muffled by the effort not to cry. She wanted to call out for her mother, for Grace, for anyone, but silence pressed harder than her voice. So she whispered to herself, the way she had in the Bolenders' house, a litany of survival: *Be good. Be quiet. Be invisible.* If she followed the rules, maybe she would be safe.

Outside the dormitory window, she could see the silhouette of the RKO Studio water tower, looming like a sentinel over Hollywood. At eight years old she didn't yet know what it meant, but the sight branded itself into her imagination. That tower belonged to another world, one of cameras and stars, a world she was forbidden but already beginning to covet.

Days at Hollygrove were ordered by the clock. Wake at dawn, line up for prayers, file into the dining hall where oatmeal waited in tin bowls. Eat quickly, don't waste, don't complain. Chores followed: scrubbing floors, washing laundry, tending the grounds. Then school at Vine Street Elementary a few blocks away, where the children from the orphanage were easy to spot—their clothes a little plainer, their hair not quite as neat, their eyes carrying the unmistakable weight of wards.

To her classmates she was simply another poor child, another girl without parents. To herself, she was already becoming something stranger—an unofficial orphan. Her mother still lived, locked away in a sanitarium. Grace still existed, visiting now and then, bringing small gifts, rouge and ribbons, promises of stardom whispered like fairy tales. But none of them kept her. She was in between: not quite abandoned, not quite claimed.

This limbo became her identity. She learned to live in the margins, to act the part of the dutiful child while secretly inventing herself anew. Every smile was practice, every curtsy rehearsal. At Hollygrove, survival was performance, and Norma Jeane played her role with heartbreaking diligence.

The matrons noticed how obedient she was. She didn't fight, didn't scream, didn't make trouble. She cleaned her plate, folded her blankets, said her prayers. They praised her, just as teachers once had, for being "a good girl." But inside, she was rehearsing something else—the art of pretending to be good while longing to be seen for who she really was, though she had no words yet for that person.

She looked around at the other girls and saw her reflection in them: children who had been promised something and then forgotten, children who cried in the night but still lined up in the morning. Some would vanish, fostered out to families, only to return weeks later with stories they could not tell. Others grew tough, mean, their laughter sharp as knives. Norma Jeane stayed quiet, watchful. She filed every expression, every posture, into her memory—like an actress studying for future roles.

She had already lived in more homes than most adults, and yet each time she carried her small suitcase into a new room, she hoped this would be the last stop, that someone would finally keep her. Hollygrove was no different. The adults told her she was there "for her good," "for her safety." The words were meant to comfort but landed like condemnation. They meant: *You are too much trouble to be kept.*

It was at Hollygrove that she began to grasp the depth of her wound. She was not merely alone; she was unclaimed. That difference etched itself into her bones. She did not belong to anyone, and so she would have to belong to herself.

The days at Hollygrove learned her name before the people did. Bells called her more faithfully than adults ever had—first bell for waking, second for prayers, third for the march to breakfast where the oatmeal steamed in rows like fog rising from a field. She learned the hallway shine of waxed floors, the laundry's ghost-breath of lye, the papery rustle of donated dresses that never quite fit. There was always a rule attached to a kindness: the dress if you kept your knees together, the extra orange if you finished your chores, the pat on the head if you swallowed whatever hurt you wanted to tell.

She discovered how to be excellent at small things. Hospital corners on the sheets so tight you could bounce a penny. Towels folded by thirds, stacked like quiet hymns. Shoes aligned beneath the iron bedframe so that the aisle look of the dormitory pleased the matron's eye. Little obediences kept the world from tilting; little obediences earned invisibility, which sometimes felt like safety.

At Vine Street Elementary she sat toward the middle, not too far forward to draw questions, not so far back the teacher's disappointment could find her. She brought home perfect penmanship from a place that was not home, the loops and stems of her letters obeying lines as if the page were a picket fence she dared not climb. The girls who belonged to mothers wore ribbons that matched their socks. She wore whatever the donation barrel decided she would be that week: a blue cardigan pill-balled at the wrists, a skirt with a hem that had learned too many bodies. Still, she made it neat. Ida's gospel had not left her; neatness felt like a spell strong enough to keep chaos outside.

Sometimes at lunch she would count—how many steps from the school gate to the corner where the view opened and the city began to shine. How many breaths between the teacher's last word and the bell that shook her loose. How many afternoons until visiting day, when Grace might come.

Grace came, and when she came, she glowed with that particular studio radiance that seems to cling to anyone who touches film for a living. A scarf draped just so. Lipstick with a name like "Crush" or "Siren." She smelled faintly of cold cream and cigarettes, a scent Norma Jeane would forever associate with the idea of possibility. Grace never arrived empty-handed. A ribbon. A little compact mirror from a set someone had discarded at Columbia. Once, a tiny bottle of rouge so bright it looked like it might burn through the tin. "Just a dot at the apple of your cheek," Grace said, tapping her own face with a painted pinky, "and you'll look like Jean Harlow's sunbeam." She made glamour sound like a language only the faithful could speak.

The girls in the dormitory watched from their cots. Some envied, some mocked, but most simply stared, as if they, too, smelled on Grace the door that led out of here. After the visit, the matron would be gentler for the rest of the day, as if a little of the glamour had rubbed off on her as well.

Grace spoke in future tense. "A camera will love you." "One day you'll be on a set instead of outside the fence." "Don't slouch; starlight is posture, too." She made the world beyond El Centro Avenue sound like the kingdom where forgotten girls were renamed and crowned. If there was guilt in her for leaving the child here, confection covered it—praise frosted over regret. She told the story she needed to believe: that the orphanage was a vestibule to the church of pictures, that she was preparing her little parishioner for the altar.

At night, in the dormitory thrum—the coughs, the muffled crying, the small negotiations over blankets—Norma Jeane practiced. Not with rouge (the matron would have taken it), but with the parts of her face nobody could confiscate. She learned the difference between a polite smile and a bright one, between a mouth that meant "thank you" and a mouth that meant "please keep looking." In the warped shine of her tiny compact, she studied expressions like they were vocabulary: surprise, delight, shyness, listening. She could feel how each one rearranged her inside life as well, tugging at breath, at pulse, at the way a thought stands up or sits down in the body. Acting, though she would not have named it yet, was not pretending to feel but summoning the feeling until it obeyed.

Sometimes, when the matron switched off the overheads and the city rose into its night—neon flickers, distant laughter—the girls would begin the quiet daisy chain of talk. Who had mothers who might return, who had fathers who had vanished into states even the maps did not bother to name, who had been "placed out" to families that sent them back like dresses that didn't fit. Stories passed like contraband. The older girls could make whole houses out of their words; the little ones moved in gratefully and slept there. Norma Jeane did not have the best stories, but she had the most careful ones. She told them like she folded her towels: smooth, no loose threads. The other girls listened because something in her voice promised that the telling itself could tidy you.

Yet beneath the tidy would not stop humming. It was loneliness, yes, but also a sharper hunger: to be singled out not as the next bed or the next mouth, but as the next miracle. "I used to think as I looked at the Hollywood night," she would say years later, "There must be thousands of girls sitting alone like me, dreaming of becoming a movie star. But I'm not going to worry about them. I'm dreaming the hardest." At 8, at 9, she did not yet own the sentence, but the sentence was already owning her. The tower at RKO grew into a punctuation mark for desire—each time she saw it, the wish inside her ended with an exclamation point.

Hollygrove's routines were not heartless; they were simply designed for many, and she was learning to be a singular. The milk was measured, the prayers were measured, the minutes under hot water were measured, and she learned how to convert scarcity into ritual so the lack did not swallow her. She washed her hair with the exact movements older girls taught her, rinsed with the pail's last mercy, wrapped the towel like a turban because a star would have done so. The small mirror on the wall gave back a foggy child. She squinted until the fog cleared and a future face floated there, the one Grace kept predicting. If she held very still, she could almost hear camera shutters like crickets in summer grass.

On Sundays, visiting hours dressed the campus like a holiday. Men who might be uncles, women who might be cousins, couples who might be auditioning for parenthood, all with their good intentions ironed. Norma Jeane learned to greet the hopeful strangers without promising herself away. The matrons watched body language carefully, like casting directors. A girl whose answers were crisp, whose hair shone from clean discipline, whose shoes were polished—such a girl might find herself placed. Norma Jeane could do all that. But sometimes, as she stood before these kindly adults, something in her tightened. It was not defiance. It was the early, animal sense that belonging offered too easily could become another exit. She had been placed and replaced; she knew the seam where "welcome" could split.

On the afternoons when Grace did not come, she invented her. She'd sit on the low cement lip near the yard and draw with her finger in the dust: a lipstick tube, a hand mirror, a tiny comb like a fishbone. She imagined dialogue, Grace's Coaching Voice: "Hold your chin a bit higher." "Don't let them see your fear; let them see your light." Sometimes she imagined the opposite scene, one that had never happened: a woman staying, a hand that did not let go at the intake desk. She rehearsed that fantasy, too, until it loosened its grip. Better to court the future than be haunted by the past.

There were girls who could snatch laughter from the smallest thing and make it into candy for everyone. There were girls who had learned how to disappear even while standing between you and the doorway. Norma Jeane was somewhere between: she did not vanish, but she did not blaze either. She shone the way a coin shines when you tilt it to see if it's real. Teachers liked her: polite, attentive, the small nods at the right moments. The janitor liked her because she always dragged the mop bucket back to the closet without spilling a stripe across the polished hall. The cook liked her because she thanked him even when the oatmeal congealed. Gratitude was another language she mastered—smooth, quick, unaccented—because gratitude made adults breathe easier, and adults who breathed easier were less likely to send you away.

One winter evening, rain stitched the city into a single wet cloth and the dormitory smelled faintly of wool and sleep. A volunteer came to read aloud—some book about brave children in an old country. He pronounced the hero's name with reverence, as if the syllables themselves had done something noble. Norma Jeane lay very still and thought: names can be capes. If you choose the right one, it can blow behind you like wind and make you look faster, freer, almost airborne. It was not yet the thought of "Marilyn," but it was its seed. The orphanage's ledger had recorded her as Ward No. 3,463—a number that hid her like tall grass. One day, she would step out of the grass and pick a name that glinted.

Grace's talk of Harlow wasn't only glamour; it was strategy. Harlow was proof that a girl from nowhere could be renamed into everywhere. "Platinum," Grace would murmur, twisting a lock of the child's brown hair between two fingers as if she could rub the metal up through the strands. "You have the face for it." The matron once told Grace she was filling the child with foolishness. Grace smiled and replied that foolishness was the raft you built when the ground kept giving way.

The raft worked. On the hardest nights—when a girl cried so long she hiccupped herself to sleep, when a rumor passed that someone's father had come and turned away at the gate—the raft bobbed in Norma Jeane's mind. She lay on it and looked up through the dormitory darkness and imagined the stars repositioning themselves into studio lights. It soothed her that the same night covering Hollygrove also covered the backlots where people were paid to pretend. Pretending, here, was survival. There, it was work. She considered the possibility that survival might one day be her work.

Once, as the girls filed toward supper, she made a small mistake: she hummed. Not loud. Barely a thread of tune. But the matron snapped without turning, "Quiet, Miss Baker." Shame flamed her cheeks. And then, a second later, something inside her answered back with a coolness she hadn't known she possessed: *I will be anything you require in your building. But I will not forget the music.* It startled her—the clarity of it, the adultness. It didn't make her rebel. It made her careful about where she put the song. That is how stars are built: not out of noise, but out of the cunning storage of noise until the door opens and you can let it out like weather.

By the spring after she arrived, the staff knew what they had in her: a tidy child with a talent for being good. They leaned on that. She was made a helper to smaller girls, the one who tied shoes, buttoned a dress that always seemed to have one button missing, found a ribbon's wandering end and coaxed it into a bow. It taught her another lesson she would carry into studios and marriages: caretaking grants temporary belonging. If you are necessary, you may be kept a little longer. She learned to pour necessity out of herself like warm water. People softened under it. Keeping her felt like keeping calm.

Grace's visits flickered between generosity and urgency. She'd talk fast, as if she were running out of the right to dream on the girl's behalf. "They've got an opening at the lab," she'd say, or, "I saw a test—nothing came of it, but the look was all wrong; you wouldn't make that mistake." She kept the Hollywood door propped with her foot and a smile. And yet the foot would tire, the smile would wilt, and she would hurry away, leaving behind, on the girl's pillow, the trace of something cosmetic and a sentence that pulsed like an artery: *One day, you'll be just like Shirley Temple. Just wait and see.* The sentence was absurd—Temple was a comet, and the orphanage had no sky for comets—but absurdity is the exact size of hope.

When birthdays came, they came quietly. The home had a way of making individual days belong to the group—cake cut in even squares so no one could argue luck. Still, she made a private ceremony of it. In the bathroom mirror she studied herself the way a director studies rushes. Where had the year switched her? Cheekbones a little higher. Mouth a little surer of its corners. A look in the eyes she couldn't yet name—watchfulness touched with dare.

She was 8 turning 9, 9 turning 10. The ledger did not change its mind; it did not cross out the number and write "beloved." But each year she smuggled more of herself through the days—tiny stowaway parcels of will, beauty, and nerve. She did not tell the other girls. Some of them could not help mocking any girl who declared a dream out loud. Dreams, in a place like this, were like jewelry: if you wore them where everyone could see, someone might take them.

Late one night—a summer heat clogging the dormitory with sweetness from the pepper trees—she woke to find most of the room asleep and the far window glowing with city haze. She slipped from the bed and padded across the floorboards. At the glass she pressed her forehead and felt the whole of Hollywood tremble through the pane: the distant studios like beehives, the boulevards flowing with their separate insomnia, the RKO water tower a dark punctuation against a lighter sky. She thought, suddenly, not of being rescued but of rescuing herself. The thought frightened her so completely she almost said sorry to the window. Then she stood up straighter, the way Grace told her, and looked out again until the fear bent its knee.

By then she knew: Hollygrove was not the end of her belonging but the proof that belonging might be invented. She would not wait for a family to keep her. She would build a face the world would not return. She would make a name that turned heads when it was spoken, a name that meant you could never again be misfiled as Ward No. 3,463.

By 1937, Hollygrove had pressed its order into her like a watermark. The bells no longer startled her; she moved in rhythm with their demands. Yet inside, something untamable kept pushing. Every time she smoothed her sheets, every time she stacked the towels, every time she forced herself to chew the same pale oatmeal, she was storing up the disobedience of wanting more.

She had learned how to live in two registers: the outward girl who followed rules with quiet obedience, and the inward girl who whispered stories to herself. She told herself she was not merely Norma Jeane, orphan ward number three-thousand-something. She told herself she was someone who could not be erased. And once she told herself a story, she could believe it.

It was in the evenings, after supper, when she felt the crack between the two lives most clearly. The matrons would herd them back to the dormitory, twenty-seven girls marching like little soldiers of sorrow. Some dragged their feet, some darted into line hoping to vanish, and some, like Norma Jeane, walked steadily, eyes down, already drifting into an invented world.

The window became her confessional. She pressed her forehead to the glass and saw the RKO Studio's water tower. At first it had frightened her, a strange black figure rising into the night. But as the months passed, the tower transformed. It was a lighthouse for the shipwrecked, and she was its audience of one. If she stared long enough, the tower seemed to lean toward her, whispering that there was another world across the fences.

From that tower came her first great prayer, one she whispered so many times it became a rhythm in her pulse: *There must be thousands of girls sitting alone like me, dreaming of becoming a movie star. But I'm not going to worry about them. I'm dreaming the hardest.*

Dreaming the hardest: it became her vow. In a place that flattened individuality, where every bed and every bowl was the same, she dared to compete not for affection, not for family, but for the future. She would out-dream them. She would conjure a destiny out of thin air, and no one would dare return it like an unwanted foster child.

Grace still visited, though less often than the child longed for. She would appear with her bright smile, her studio gossip, her careless glamor, and leave behind little gifts that felt like contraband. A ribbon here, a dab of rouge there, sometimes just a sentence that lit her like fire: *Don't forget, Norma, you're meant for pictures.*

Norma Jeane absorbed the contradictions without complaint. Grace had promised to keep her, then left her at the orphanage. Grace made her into an orphan, yet also made her believe she was destined to be a star. The two truths were never reconciled. They simply lived side by side, like mismatched roommates in the dormitory of her heart. One whispered betrayal, the other whispered destiny. She grew up learning to live with both.

She watched the other girls carefully. Some hardened, faces turning sharp as they prepared to survive a lifetime of rejection. Some grew resigned, their eyes dull before they reached 12. And some simply vanished, placed out to families or disappearing into the system's cracks. Norma Jeane studied all of them like lessons. What she learned most was this: if you could not be loved, you could still be remembered.

At Vine Street Elementary, she learned to keep her head down, but even there she caught glimpses of another self. Teachers praised her neat work, her perfect handwriting, her quiet attentiveness. Yet in group recitations, she noticed how her voice carried differently, a little rounder, a little sweeter. The other girls teased her once for singing to herself under her breath, and she stopped—outwardly. Inwardly, she never stopped. She was stockpiling sound, like a bird waiting for the right spring.

On visiting days, she felt the ache most keenly. Families came and looked the children over, searching for the one who might fit into their lives. She stood politely, answered their questions, even managed her small, rehearsed smile. But when the adults walked away, choosing another child, she felt not relief but confirmation: she was not chosen. She was no one's daughter, no one's little girl. And if she was no one's, then perhaps she could be everyone's.

That is what she would later become: not private property, not kept by a single family, but a dream projected to millions. The unofficial orphan who reinvented herself into a public fantasy.

But at nine years old, in the shadow of Hollygrove, she could not see that far. She could only see the tower, the night sky, the dreams she was daring to dream harder than anyone else.

By June 1937, her time at Hollygrove ended. She packed her suitcase again—the same ritual she had performed so many times it felt like second nature. The matrons signed the papers, Grace returned to claim her, and the gate opened. But leaving did not feel like freedom. It felt like another transfer, another chapter in the book of being passed along. She walked out carrying her little suitcase, but also carrying the invisible luggage of her orphan years: the loneliness, the fear, the sharpened watchfulness, the need to perform goodness, the vow to be remembered.

Years later, she would speak of Hollygrove with contradictions. Sometimes she made it sound harsher than it was, playing up her suffering as part of her legend. Other times she softened it, remembering small kindnesses, little joys among the children. The truth was that it had been both: cruelty and tenderness, despair and dreaming. It had been her crucible.

What Hollygrove left in her was not just scars but strategy. She had learned to create a self that adults wanted to keep. She had learned to mask her fear with a smile. She had learned to dream harder than the girls around her, to believe that if she kept believing long enough, belief itself could become a future.

When she looked back, she saw the orphanage not just as a place she had survived, but as the place where she began to invent herself. The orphan was not chosen, not named, not kept. So she would choose herself. She would name herself. She would keep herself.

And in time, the world would know that name: Marilyn Monroe.

6

The Wrong Father in Every Frame

Before she knew the weight of her own name, before the world renamed her with a golden surname, Norma Jeane learned to whisper another man's name into the silence of her rooms: Clark Gable.

It began with a photograph her mother Gladys pressed into her hands like a relic. Gable's grin shone out of the still from *It Happened One Night*, half roguish, half reassuring, his eyes glinting as if they held secrets just for her. Gladys, already drifting into her own storms, told the child in a matter-of-fact voice, "He's your father."

Not literally. Even Gladys, who could braid delusion into daily life like ribbon in a child's hair, did not mean that the King of Hollywood had crept into their apartment one night. She meant it spiritually, mythically, in the way a church gives you a savior when flesh-and-blood fathers have vanished. In Gladys's church of make-believe, Clark Gable was the deity assigned to her daughter.

For the girl who had no father to steady her hand or lift her chin, the declaration was a gift. Fathers, she had been told, were supposed to claim you. She had never been claimed. But if Gladys's word could be believed, then a photograph could claim her. A man's face could become a lineage. She could belong to a smile in a studio portrait.

She stared for hours at that photograph, her child's eyes tracing the corners of his grin, the strong line of his jaw. She let herself believe that somewhere in the world, this man was thinking of her, perhaps wondering what had become of his daughter. She imagined letters he never wrote, embraces he never gave, lullabies he might have sung if only MGM had not kept him so busy. In her mind, he became the father stolen by lights, cameras, and premieres.

This was not a childish game. It was survival. In the vacancy where a father should have stood, she placed the figure who filled every movie screen, who was hailed in every fan magazine as "The King of Hollywood."

The magazines themselves seemed to conspire in the illusion. *Photoplay* called him the man every woman wanted and every man wanted to be. Louella Parsons declared him America's favorite leading man. His smile, printed a million times on glossy pages, made him everyone's property and thus, in a peculiar way, hers. To read those words was to be told, over and over, that he was chosen. And if he was chosen, then perhaps she was chosen too, by extension.

At night she whispered to his picture, telling him the things she could tell no one else. She told him about the loneliness of the dormitory, the rows of iron beds that clanged like prison doors, the smell of lye and starch that clung to her clothes. She told him how she missed her mother even when her mother was near, how she felt invisible in rooms where she tried so hard to be good. She asked him questions she did not know how to phrase aloud: *What is a father supposed to do? Do they tuck you in? Do they laugh at your jokes? Do they love you without needing a reason?*

And sometimes she imagined the answers. In the half-dark, while other girls whispered or cried into their pillows, she heard his voice low and steady: *Yes, I see you. Yes, you are mine. Yes, I will never leave you.* She repeated the words until they became lullabies stronger than the clanging beds, stronger than the sting of bleach, stronger than the ache of being unwanted.

The orphanage itself was another kind of parent—stern, metallic, impersonal. The iron bedframes lined in rows like soldiers. The food: oatmeal that congealed, bread gone stiff by afternoon, milk with the faint aftertaste of tin. The daily devotions Ida Bolender insisted upon, hymns rising into rafters where the plaster was cracked. On Sundays the children were herded into pews, told to call God their father, though none of them quite believed it. Fathers were the men who never came back, the ones whose names were smudges in court ledgers.

In that world, Norma Jeane's secret conversation with Gable was rebellion. While others clutched dolls or prayed to the ceiling, she pressed her secrets into a photograph. A celluloid father might not tuck you in, but he also never turned drunk or mean. He never vanished. He never said no.

Gladys encouraged the fantasy, feeding it with scraps of magazines and her own cracked certainty. Once she held up a publicity still of Gable in riding boots, cigarette dangling, and said, "See? The same mouth. The same nose. You have his smile." It was nonsense, but to a child aching for kinship, it was gospel. She practiced that smile in the mirror, stretching her lips until she thought she could see him staring back at her.

And she didn't stop at Gable. Hollywood was her gallery of fathers and uncles, men who paraded across the screen as though they had been conjured for her. Gary Cooper with his tall grace—she imagined him as the uncle who might sneak her ice cream cones. Spencer Tracy, dependable and solid, became the grandfather who would have walked her to school. Cary Grant, mischievous and elegant, was the older brother who might have taught her how to dance. Even actors who flickered briefly across the screen—Charles Boyer with his Continental sigh, Tyrone Power with his swashbuckling grin—found their way into her scrapbook of surrogate kin.

She clipped their pictures from magazines, pasted them alongside Gable's face, and studied them like scripture. Each man represented a possibility. Cooper's honesty. Tracy's steadiness. Grant's wit. But Gable was always the sun. He was the one her mother had chosen, the one whose name made her heart skip when she saw it on a marquee.

Sometimes, in her dreams, the borders between picture and reality dissolved. She imagined him at the beach with her, hoisting her onto his shoulders so she could see farther than the tide. She pictured him at the kitchen table, sipping coffee, looking up from the newspaper to smile at her. The child rehearsed these visions so often they became memories, as vivid as the real ones of bleach and bread and iron beds.

And she rehearsed with her body as well as her mind. In front of the mirror, she tried out voices: the little-girl whisper, the teenage lilt, the womanly coo. She wanted to know which one would please him, which one might keep him from leaving. She studied his smile and practiced it until it became her own. She bent her posture into poses she thought matched his stride. She built herself as his daughter, his reflection, his creation.

The orphanage faded around her when she played these games. The other girls might gossip, giggle, weep into their pillows, or whisper about real fathers who might one day return. But Norma Jeane had her own secret lineage. She belonged not to ledger entries or state custody, but to the King of Hollywood.

Her fantasy expanded with each film she managed to see. When Gable strode across the deck in *Mutiny on the Bounty*, she whispered to the screen, *That's my father.* When he clutched Jean Harlow in *Red Dust*, she saw her parents reunited in a jungle romance. When he smirked his way through *San*

Francisco, she imagined him pulling her out of the rubble, saving her from the quake of loneliness.

By the time she was a teenager, the line between survival fantasy and preparation for stardom had blurred completely. She didn't just want to be Gable's daughter. She wanted to step through the screen and live in his world, where fathers saved their children, where smiles meant permanence, where the wrong father in every frame was still better than no father at all.

As the years unspooled, the rituals she had once practiced in secret began to spill into every corner of her life. By 14, she no longer just whispered to the photograph of Gable hidden in her scrapbook—she spoke to him through the mirror. She tilted her chin and let her lips tremble with the innocence she imagined he wanted to see. She widened her eyes until they seemed to shine with childlike trust. She even practiced laughing alone in the dormitory bathroom, listening to the echo bounce back, as if the walls themselves could tell her whether the sound carried sweetness or seduction.

Each gesture was an offering, and each offering a rehearsal. The father she had conjured in celluloid became her first audience, and she learned how to make him stay with her through a smile, a pose, a whisper. Later, when photographers marveled at her instinct for the camera, they had no idea they were inheriting the work begun years earlier with a movie still and a lonely child's imagination.

Other girls talked about the fathers who visited them, who worked shifts at factories or drove trucks or came back from the war with medals pinned to their chests. Norma Jeane said little. She let them boast about real men of flesh and paycheck while she carried a secret father whose face was known in every theater from Kansas to Cairo. When she stayed quiet, it wasn't shame—it was reverence. Her father was too important to belong to anyone else's chatter.

By the time she left Hollygrove, the practice of invention had become second nature. She didn't simply make up stories; she lived inside them. When she posed for her first modeling shots, she leaned toward the lens as though it were Gable's eyes, wide and steady. Every camera was a father now, every flashbulb a promise that someone, somewhere, finally saw her.

Her early marriages bore the same fingerprints. Jim Dougherty was not a husband so much as a placeholder, a stand-in from the casting department of life. He was steady, older, protective—qualities she had once sought in Gable's on-screen fathers. But he wasn't permanent. None of them were. When the studio came calling, when her beauty began to draw lenses like moths to light, she stepped out of the marriage without hesitation. She had already learned: men left. Pictures stayed.

Joe DiMaggio was closer to the myth. Brooding, heroic, his jaw as chiseled as any matinee idol's—he could almost have stepped from her scrapbook. For a time, she believed he might be the protector she had been rehearsing all her life. But Joe wanted a wife, not a daughter. He wanted silence where she craved applause. His protection turned into a cage, and cages were nothing new. She broke free, though part of her still ached for the steadiness he had promised.

Arthur Miller was another kind of surrogate father: intellectual, stern, disappointed. He reminded her of the men in pulpits at Hollygrove, frowning down at wayward children. She tried to win his approval as she had once tried to please the photographer—adjusting her smile, softening her voice, offering herself as both child and muse. But the applause he gave was rare, and her rehearsals with him ended in the same silence that had filled her childhood.

Even her affairs carried the trace of the pantheon she built as a girl. Sinatra with his swagger, Montand with his Continental charm, Kennedy with his dangerous aura—each of them played roles she recognized from her private theater. But none of them stayed, none of them ever truly claimed her. She was still the girl whispering to the wrong father in every frame.

And then prophecy turned flesh. In 1960 she stood across from Clark Gable on the set of *The Misfits*. The child who had whispered to a photograph in a dormitory lined with iron beds now faced the man himself under the Nevada sun. The circle was complete.

By then she was 34, luminous but worn, her body sustained by pills, her spirit heavy with fame's cruel weight. He was 59, his once-golden face marked by time and disappointment. Yet when she looked at him, she saw not the weary cowboy costume nor the lines around his eyes, but the man who had raised her in silence. Every gesture he made—the way he tugged at his hat, the rumble of his laughter—was familiar to her. She had been studying them since childhood.

To Arthur Miller, to Eli Wallach, to anyone who would listen, she confessed: "He's the only man I ever really loved." The world assumed it was another Monroe exaggeration, another scandalous headline. But she meant it as truth. Not romantic love. Not desire. But the love of a daughter for the father she had created out of celluloid.

On set she drifted toward him like a moth to the projector's beam. She watched him with eyes that blurred the lines between memory and reality. The man before her was both stranger and kin. She had carried him for decades in whispers and scrapbook clippings, and now here he was, breathing, speaking, standing within reach.

And then, in one last act of cruelty, the script turned against her. Gable collapsed of a heart attack soon after filming ended. Marilyn wept as if the ground had opened beneath her. She had lost her father all over again. Perhaps she had lost him for the first time in flesh.

It was almost biblical, the way her life bent back into myth. The girl who had prayed to his photograph ended her career standing beside him in his final role. The orphan who whispered to his stills became the woman who whispered her love for him as he slipped away.

This was her tragedy: that even as the world crowned her Marilyn Monroe, she remained the unofficial orphan, still begging for a father who never came. Every marriage, every affair, every flashbulb was a rehearsal for belonging. Yet behind it all was still the little girl in the dormitory, whispering to a picture, asking questions that no man ever answered.

But it was also her triumph. Out of silence, she built story. Out of absence, she conjured presence. From the wrong father in every frame, she learned how to become the right woman in every one of hers.

Hollywood had given her nothing, but she took everything. She took the water tower outside Hollygrove and made it a beacon. She took her mother's half-mad declaration and turned it into prophecy, fulfilled on a desert set in Nevada. She took the photograph of Clark Gable and made it scripture.

The wrong father in every frame had raised her more faithfully than any man who ever lived in her house.

7

Sundays with Mother

Sundays were sacred. Not for God, not for rest, but because they carried the shimmering possibility of her mother.

On Saturdays, Norma Jeane polished her shoes until they gleamed like little moons. She laid out her best dress across the chair by her bed, smoothing its creases with palms that trembled with anticipation. She brushed her hair over and over until it shone, as though light itself might persuade her mother to stay. She whispered bargains to the clock, prayers not from scripture but from the small catechism of a foster child's hope: let her come tomorrow, let her smile at me, let her stay.

The other children in the Bolenders' house looked forward to Sundays as a day of church, hymns, and the gentle indulgence of Ida's home-baked rolls. But for Norma Jeane, the day was charged with a different electricity. Her God might have been absent, distant, unreachable—but her mother could still appear on the doorstep, arms full of dreams or madness, and claim her for an afternoon.

The knock was always the true beginning of Sunday. She could hear it before anyone else, or so she believed, her ears trained to pick out the difference between a stranger's rap and her mother's hurried fists. And when it came, she flew to the door like a sparrow loosed from a cage.

Perfume arrived first, a ghost slipping through the crack before the woman herself. Then came the sight: red lipstick a little crooked, hair either perfectly styled or falling out of pins, hands forever rummaging in a purse. Gladys's face was a kaleidoscope, never the same woman twice.

Sometimes she was the glamorous mother, the one who brought gifts. A doll with glass eyes that blinked when tipped backward. A tin of sugar cookies that grew damp and soft in the foster home's heavy air. A ribbon, a scrap of fabric from the film lab where she worked—objects that to any other child might seem trivial but to Norma Jeane were treasures, each one proof that her mother remembered she existed.

Other times she was the storyteller. She spoke of movie stars whose gowns she'd brushed against at the lab, whose tired faces she'd seen without makeup. Her words painted moving pictures in the child's mind: Jean Harlow's laughter echoing in a corridor, Joan Crawford's gloves lying forgotten on a table. The stories were half-true, half-sad, and wholly intoxicating to a little girl who lived among hand-me-down dresses and borrowed beds.

And then there were the darker Sundays. Gladys would arrive late, her lipstick smudged, her voice distracted, as if she were speaking through fog. She might sit at the table for hours, staring at some invisible figure across the room, or burst suddenly into tears, whispering, "You don't look like me at all." In those moments, the child's heart twisted between shame and pity, longing and fear.

But whether her mother came with gifts or silence, laughter or ghosts, Norma Jeane clung to every visit. She counted Sundays the way other children counted birthdays. For those few hours she was no longer a ward of the state, no longer one name among thousands on an orphanage ledger. She was a daughter—claimed, seen, loved, if only in fragments.

The brightest Sundays happened at the beach.

Gladys in a cardigan, squinting at the horizon, her arm looped loosely around her daughter's shoulders. The Pacific was a raucous playground, waves folding in on themselves like white linen sheets being shaken out. The sand burned the soles of Norma Jeane's feet, but she didn't care. She chased gulls, collected seashells, and returned to her mother breathless, holding each treasure as if it were proof: *Look, I found this for you. Don't leave me.*

Sometimes Gladys laughed, and the sound was sharp and sudden as breaking glass, startling in its brightness. For an hour or two, mother and daughter were stitched together by sunlight and saltwater, as if the ocean itself had decided to make them whole. Gladys would tilt her head back, eyes closed, lips parted, letting the wind undo her careful hair. And Norma Jeane would study her with the reverence of a disciple: this was what beauty looked like, fragile and dazzling, a lighthouse against the blur of foster homes.

They ate sandwiches wrapped in wax paper, drank sodas from sweating glass bottles, and for a fleeting span the world felt normal. Other children built castles, other mothers spread towels, and the Bolenders' foster child pretended she belonged among them. The moments were fleeting, but in her memory they replayed endlessly, each retelling a small resurrection.

Not every visit had sunlight. There were Sundays at Echo Park, where Gladys pushed her on the swings with a distracted rhythm, her gaze fixed on something no one else could see. Sundays at Griffith Park, where she sat stiffly on a bench while Norma Jeane clambered on jungle gyms, too wary of her mother's mood to call out for attention.

Yet even those shadows were brighter than silence. A distracted mother was still a mother. A weeping mother was still hers.

Back in Hawthorne, life with the Bolenders was austere but steady. Ida was devout, her faith stitched into every seam of the household. She believed discipline was salvation: children rose early, folded their blankets, bowed their heads before meals. Hymns floated through the house like a second wallpaper. Albert was quieter, content to let Ida steer the ship, but his presence was a steady anchor, a reminder that not all men vanished.

The Bolenders' home always smelled of starch and hymnals, a fragrance that mingled sanctity with soap. For all its strictness, it was the most stable life Norma Jeane ever knew. She learned to fold laundry until the corners met perfectly, to recite prayers in a voice that trembled with eagerness to please, to move in rhythm with the Bolender children like another note in the family hymn.

And yet even in that steadiness, she kept her Sundays holy. She believed in them the way Ida believed in scripture. She believed in the next knock, the next whiff of perfume, the next chance to be held.

Once, Gladys showed up at the Bolenders' front door unannounced, eyes wild, clutching for her child. She locked Ida out the back door and tried to spirit Norma Jeane away in a duffel bag, as if motherhood could be smuggled past the neighbors. Ida fought her back, pried the bag open, restored the child to safety. It was a frightening scene, whispered about long after, a scandal tucked between psalms and laundry lines.

To Norma Jeane, though, even that madness was proof of love: her mother wanted her enough to try to steal her back.

The line between safety and danger blurred early. Gladys could be the glamorous mother with gossip and cookies, or the frantic stranger with trembling hands. Sundays became lessons in unpredictability. A child learns fast: love can arrive dressed as perfume or as panic, and you never know which until the door opens.

And so she grew, small and hopeful, keeping vigil for a mother who flickered in and out of reach. The Bolenders gave her a bed and boundaries, but Gladys gave her something else—longing. It would follow her like a shadow into every frame of her life.

The duffel bag incident became a legend in the Bolender household, though no one spoke of it openly in front of the child. It lived in whispers, in Ida's tight lips when neighbors asked too many questions, in Albert's quiet sighs at the dinner table. But for Norma Jeane it was not gossip—it was a memory she could not forget.

That Sunday had begun like any other. She had polished her shoes the night before, tied her hair with a ribbon, and sat waiting for the knock. When it came, her heart leapt. Gladys stood in the doorway, eyes bright with a kind of fevered urgency, her smile too wide. She swept into the house with the energy of a storm, and before Ida could object she had scooped her daughter up, pressing kisses on her cheeks that smelled of powder and cigarettes.

"I'm taking her home," Gladys announced. It wasn't a request; it was a decree. She clutched Norma Jeane by the wrist, dragged her down the hall, and in a moment of desperation stuffed her small body into a duffel bag, zipping it up as if she could pack motherhood away and carry it off like luggage.

Inside, Norma Jeane felt the canvas close around her, smelled the oil of the fabric, heard the frantic rasp of her mother's breathing. It was dark and airless, terrifying and exhilarating all at once. Terrifying, because she could barely breathe. Exhilarating, because it meant her mother wanted her—wanted her enough to steal her back.

Ida returned through the back door, her voice sharp with alarm. A struggle followed: Ida prying, Gladys clutching, neighbors peeking in through lace curtains. Finally, the zipper slid open, and Norma Jeane tumbled out into Ida's arms, gasping for air. Gladys collapsed into tears, shouting about conspiracies, about people who wanted to take her child away.

For Ida, it was proof of madness. For the neighbors, a scandal to be retold. For the little girl, it was something else entirely: proof of love. Love so desperate it broke rules, love so fierce it bent into madness. She didn't forget the terror, but she remembered most of all the urgency of those arms, the feeling of being wanted enough to be fought over.

Not long after came the brief reunion. At 7, she was allowed to live with her mother again, in a small Los Angeles bungalow where the furniture sagged and the walls seemed to lean inward. For a few fragile weeks, she felt the thrill of being claimed. Gladys tucked her in at night, cooked her meals, walked her to school. The world felt stitched together again.

But the seams did not hold. Gladys's moods swung violently, her paranoia tightening like a noose. She muttered about people watching through the windows, about voices whispering in the walls. One morning she stood frozen in the kitchen, clutching a knife not at her daughter but at invisible enemies. The child stood still, heart racing, not knowing whether to run or to soothe.

Then came the inevitable: men in uniforms, the sound of a stretcher creaking down the hall, her mother's wild eyes flashing as she was taken away. Gladys was institutionalized, and Norma Jeane returned once more to foster care, carrying the bewilderment of a child whose Sundays had vanished.

The years that followed were marked by absence. Foster homes blurred together: one with a strict aunt, another with strangers, each temporary, none permanent. But memory filled the void. Norma Jeane replayed the beach outings, the perfume in the doorway, the laughter like broken glass. She polished them until they gleamed, until they felt like whole years instead of fragments. Memory, for her, was not a record but a resurrection.

Even as Marilyn Monroe, the Sundays continued to echo. She never erased Gladys from her life, no matter how much the studios urged her to. Publicists insisted she was an orphan, a myth cleaner and more marketable. She repeated the lie, sometimes with a practiced smile, sometimes with an inward wince. To the world, she was rootless, parentless, sprung from nowhere like Aphrodite from the sea. But in private, she kept her mother tethered to her story.

She paid for Gladys's care, covering hospital bills, arranging housing, making sure the woman who could not raise her was never abandoned. It was loyalty born not of logic but of longing. Love, even broken love, bound tighter than absence.

In 1952, when a journalist revealed that Marilyn's mother was still alive, the truth shattered Gladys once more. The woman who had once tried to steal her child in a duffel bag now wept in an institution, crushed by the exposure. Marilyn carried the guilt like a scar. Even her fame—perhaps especially her fame—was dangerous to the fragile woman she still called mother.

And yet she kept reaching back. She visited Gladys, sent letters, pressed money into the hands of nurses. She kept her mother in her orbit even when that orbit grew as wide as Hollywood, even when lovers and husbands told her to let go.

Her last meeting with Gladys came in the summer of 1962, just weeks before her own death. Marilyn was luminous and fragile, still juggling pills and insomnia, still chased by paparazzi. She sat with her mother in the quiet of a hospital room, two women bound by blood and brokenness. They spoke little. Gladys drifted between lucidity and delusion, sometimes smiling at her daughter, sometimes staring past her at ghosts. Marilyn held her hand, whispering promises she could no longer keep.

Afterward, she left in tears, driving away with the weight of Sundays pressing against her chest. Within weeks, she too would be gone.

The arc of their bond was a crooked line: visits and absences, laughter and paranoia, tenderness and terror. But through it all, Norma Jeane kept the ritual alive. Sundays were holy, even when they did not come. She carried the belief like Ida carried her Bible—a faith in the next knock, the next chance, the next fleeting moment of being claimed.

The truth is, her mother gave her two gifts. One was longing—the ache of absence, the wound of inconsistency. The other was imagination—the ability to take fragments and build from them entire worlds. From cookies and perfume, she built memories of belonging. From a cardigan and a day at the beach, she built the dream of family. From silence and sorrow, she built resilience.

And perhaps this was the greatest inheritance. Gladys could not give her stability, but she gave her the tools of invention. Marilyn would use them to conjure herself into existence, to turn Norma Jeane the foster child into the most famous woman in the world. The ritual of Sundays—the waiting, the preparing, the believing—became the ritual of her life. She was always waiting for love, always preparing for the knock, always believing in what might come through the door.

That belief was her tragedy, and her triumph.

Sundays with Mother became the template for all the relationships that followed. She dressed and waited for Joe DiMaggio, hoping he would appear steady at the door. She polished herself for Arthur Miller, praying his approval would come. She whispered bargains with fame itself, trusting that if she were beautiful enough, radiant enough, someone would finally stay.

But no one stayed. No one ever stayed the way she dreamed her mother might.

And yet she never abandoned the ritual. Until the end, she counted Sundays.

8

The Pillow

The day began in the ordinary way, which is why it never warned her of what was coming.

Morning at the Bolenders' was a liturgy of starch and hymn. Ida tied on her apron like armor and warmed the kitchen with the clatter of pans; the house smelled of oatmeal, scorched coffee, and soap sharp enough to sting the nose. Albert moved through rooms with the steady hush of a metronome, oiling a hinge, smoothing a splinter, straightening a picture frame that had never tilted. The other children slid into their chairs and folded hands for grace. They prayed with the sleepy obedience of those raised to the rhythm of bells. For most of them, Sunday felt like any other day stitched with a little more church. For the girl in the corner, it felt like waiting.

Norma Jeane watched the way the Bolender children bowed their heads, copied the angle of their chins, and whispered the amens a beat late, as if she were translating a language she had not quite learned. She buttered her toast as carefully as if the bread might break under too much attention. She was good at careful. Careful was a house where trouble did not notice you.

She thought about her mother. She always did on Sundays, even when she told herself she wouldn't. Gladys had not come last week. She might come this time. Or not. With her, the rules were made of fog. Some Sundays she arrived with a tin of cookies that went soft in the damp air of the little house. Some Sundays she brought a doll whose glass eyes blinked when you tilted its body, as if the toy were pretending to sleep like a polite girl. Some Sundays she brought stories from the film lab: how she had spliced together the dreams of strangers, how she had seen a star's face without makeup and decided it was human after all. And some Sundays she did not come at all, and the hours moved like a procession in a church where the God you were promised had stepped out and left a note you could not read.

The child carried all those versions of her mother inside her. She was the glamorous mother with the painted lips. She was the jittery mother who looked through you as if you were glass. She was the absent mother whose silence could be louder than hymns. A girl learns to live with fragments when she has no whole.

After breakfast came chores. The Bolender children swept and dusted with the briskness of those used to Ida's stern eye. The house gleamed with polish and soap. Even play had rules here: toys put away quickly, voices kept at a respectable pitch, nothing left out of place. It was the opposite of Gladys's world, which was all clutter and sudden laughter, the kind that ended with tears. At the Bolenders', the rhythm was predictable, and predictability was its own kind of comfort.

Norma Jeane scrubbed the floor until her knees ached. She thought of her mother as she worked—how Gladys's laugh sometimes burst out like a firecracker, how her hands shook when she lit a cigarette, how she once whispered that Hollywood stars were like gods, only lonelier. To hold such a sentence in your head at eight is to feel a storm forming beyond the hills.

By midmorning a thin coastal light spread across the street, the kind that makes even small lawns look practiced. A streetcar chimed, the sound skating along power lines. In the yard, Albert checked the fence slats, tamped a loose nail, nodded at his own sufficiency. He was a man who spoke in completions rather than words.

When the chores were finished, the house settled into its Sunday hush. Ida mended a collar at the table, each stitch an argument against chaos. Children whispered rules to games invented on the fly, bargaining with boredom as if it were a shopkeeper. The radio in the neighbor's kitchen leaked a sentimental waltz. Everything ordinary. So ordinary the air seemed to believe itself.

Inside the girl, a separate weather gathered. She watched the door the way sailors watch a sky that might turn. If Gladys came, it would be like wind entering a closed room—perfume before voice, urgency before meaning. If she did not, the day would collapse into an ache that had no name. She wanted both things at once: the arrival and the relief of being spared it.

At supper they bowed their heads again. The potatoes steamed like fresh laundry. Albert said a quiet blessing, more exhale than prayer. After, Ida washed plates and stacked them with an exactness that seemed like faith. The children read Bible verses at the table, halting in their diction, saintly by assignment. When the sun slid behind the roofs and the house put on its night face, the girl's breath grew shallow without her telling it to. The body keeps its own ledger.

In bed she turned her pillow to the cool side. The sheet felt starchy against her calves, not unpleasant, just decisive. She positioned the blanket precisely, as if right angles could keep out the dark. From a room away came Albert's single cough, the lighthouse signal she had learned to count on. A bus went by—one long growl, then quiet. The quiet had thickness to it, the way fog sometimes feels like something you could lift with both hands.

She closed her eyes and tried a new prayer, because the old ones had never once altered the night: Let it be safe. Let love be light. Let the door stay only a door.

Presence arrived before sound. It was a pressure on the room, a change in temperature along the skin. When she opened her eyes she saw a shape in the doorway. The moon had threaded a needle through the curtains and pulled a narrow line of light across the floorboards. In that slice stood her mother.

Gladys's face was unlit, unreadable, a mask a child might try to solve like a riddle. In her hands, a pillow. She held it the way a woman holds laundry she means to carry to the line—ordinary, thoughtless. But her knuckles were pale and squared, the way knuckles are when the hands forget they are hands and remember only gripping.

The girl did not speak. Stillness had always been her quickest language. Somewhere in her, older than words, something said: don't move.

The first contact was almost tender—an adjustment a mother might make when she thinks a child has kicked off the blanket. Then the cloth sealed. Warmth became pressure. Pressure became absence. The faint taste of soap rose along her tongue. The air narrowed to a pin.

Her body tried to become logic. Inhale, exhale, solve for x. But there was no x. Inhale was a locked door; exhale ran down the hallway and disappeared. She turned her head, and the pillow turned with her like a second skin. The bed felt too small to hold all that panic; her legs kicked once, twice, a fish rehearsing the idea of land.

Above the pillow, her mother's breath. Ragged, torn, threaded with words that had no grammar: the men the men they're listening God keep you safe hush now be quiet or they'll . . . The voice was not cruel. It was desperate, as if the act were a shelter built wrong.

Time turned fluid. The room tilted slightly and the moonline broke across the floorboards into pieces. Her hands found the edge of the pillow and pushed, then weakened, then pushed again, small waves that knew the shore would not move. A sound escaped her—not a cry, just the syllable the body makes when it argues with night.

Then the weight lifted.

Air rushed back, uninvited and generous. She gulped it the way thirsty people drink from faucets. The bed steadied. Her mother stepped backward as if woken from inside her own body. The pillow sagged. Gladys said something that splintered into air, a sentence without subject or object, and turned away. Each board in the hall spoke under her feet. Then the hallway ended, and the sound with it.

The girl did not scream. That would have invited witnesses, explanation, and the peril of being told she had dreamed. She lay very still and counted her heartbeat until numbers grew meaningless. When the dark thinned at the edges to the color before morning, she rose, washed her face, and walked into her day.

No one said a word at breakfast. Ida buttered toast with liturgical precision. Albert unfolded his paper and became a man-shaped wall against the world's weather. The other children argued in the register of the righteous, more pastime than battle. Gladys did not appear. Silence sat with them, politely, like a cousin who had come from out of town and didn't know where to put their hands.

What is not spoken grows roots. By midafternoon the girl had made herself a private set of rules: do not sleep on your back; hug the pillow longways, to keep it from remembering tricks; keep one hand close to your mouth, just in case. No one taught her any of that. Children invent the tools their lives require. Somebody else's doll becomes your guardian. A line of ants on a windowsill becomes a parade you control. A pillow becomes a thing you watch.

That night she tried not to sleep at all. She tracked the hairline cracks in the plaster with her fingertip and named them rivers. She gave the ceiling a map and then explored it until fatigue erased the borders. When she did slide under, she woke moments later with her heart sprinting, the room unfamiliar, the window a square of pale accusation. The dream had been the beach—the wave lifting and then not lifting, a sheet of water spread over her face. She lay on her side and counted to one hundred and then again. Numbers are a kind of raft if you repeat them enough.

The days pretended to be normal. She performed normal back at them. At school, she copied letters with a fierce neatness, as if tidy penmanship could keep the night out of the margins. She was polite to the point of invisibility. When teachers praised her, she smiled with an angle she had already perfected—gratitude, but small, like a bow done at a distance. Ida was pleased with order; the girl offered order as proof that she belonged. Albert tightened a loose bolt on the gate and she leaned against the post, liking the way solidity felt on her spine.

Night remained a country without visas.

Sometimes she moved the bed so the headboard met the wall and she could feel the house itself behind her, a witness big enough to matter. Sometimes she left the lamp on until Ida's steps came down the hall and the click of the switch corrected her. "Electricity costs money," Ida would say, and the girl would nod and turn her face into the dark and pretend the dark was fabric she had chosen.

Children are archivists. They keep and they label. She filed the pillow under: things that can turn. Later, she would add other entries—faces, rooms, promises—but the first was a square of ticking and cloth. The lesson held.

Years would carry her into other beds in other houses under other names. The Los Angeles Orphans Home, where bells told children when to wake and when to fold and when to be done. A rented room behind a yard that smelled of laundry steam and orange peels. Later, dressing rooms and studio bungalows where the light was always being engineered into kindness. The pillow traveled with her in the small of her mind, a folded square of caution.

Insomnia taught her skills. She learned to narrate her way through the dark: telling herself a story slow enough that sleep might slip in and finish it. She learned to build rooms in her head—one with curtains she could open, one with a radio she could switch to a station that played only rain. She learned to breathe in counts, to outlast the hour the body believes is worst. When none of it worked, she lay still and met the night without blinking, as if respect might earn her a passage.

Later the world would call her Marilyn and build pillows around her like thrones. Photographers would ask her to drape herself across satin as if safety and softness were the same noun. They would call to her from behind their machines—Chin up, baby, eyes here—and she would give them what they wanted with such generosity that no one thought to ask what the prop meant to the woman holding it. The public would make a religion out of the image: a bed as invitation, a pillow as promise. It is an old trick of myth, to confuse the altar with the god.

Doctors came with tidy desks and pens that made prescriptions look official enough to quiet doubt. They offered her little boats for night crossings—downers to drop the curtain, then, when morning refused her, small suns to raise it again. Balance, they said. Regimen. She learned the choreography:

take one, then the other, then pretend you are not balancing a tray through a crowded room.

Lovers learned only the symptoms. Joe found her walking rooms at 2 a.m. and said come back to bed, and she said I'm coming and stood still for another hour. Arthur looked up from his pages and said you have to sleep, as if sleep were a country you could enter with a passport and a good coat. Others were kinder or worse; none could build her a night that did not remember. She loved them the best she could. She kept count of her breaths as if love might ask for a tally later.

There were mercies, too; it would be unfair not to say so. Days when the house felt aired out and ordinary, when toast was a sacrament, when the neighbor's radio played a song that seemed to have been written to walk her through a morning. Afternoons when she could nap with the window open and wake to the sound of sparrows arguing like relatives. Nights when the beach returned, but this time the wave lifted her and set her down like a mother who had learned gentleness late.

She forgave Gladys because hate is a mortgage, and she had rent enough to pay. She told herself versions of the truth that were survivable: protection gone wrong; love mistranslating itself; a night that mistook smothering for shelter. She paid for her mother's care with money that never felt like money—pieces of herself exchanged for rooms with linoleum and nurses with patient shoes. She brought flowers. She let administrators call her Miss Monroe, and nurses call her sweetie, and practiced being both women at once.

If there was a God in Ida's church, He never explained Himself. If there was a god in Hollywood, He explained too much. Between them she built a third practice: continuance. You get up. You put on your shoes. You butter toast. You go to work. You lie down at night and you go on lying down until either sleep or morning finds you. You keep one hand near your face and the other near the lamp, and you count if counting helps.

What do you do with a night that taught you softness can kill? You turn softness outward and learn it as a craft. You make it visible, so you can't be ambushed by it; you design the light, you choose the angle, you place the pillow yourself. You let the world believe the picture, because pictures are easier to survive than explanations. And you keep the truth small and folded, a square you carry without showing.

Once, much later, she visited Gladys in a room where the windows didn't open. Her mother's eyes were sometimes still, sometimes stormy. They spoke of carnations and tea and the nurse who might be new or might be the same and it hardly mattered. On her way out she pressed her palm to the doorframe as if to steady the building and laughed softly at herself, a woman who still negotiated with wood.

That night she turned her pillow and found the cool side and told herself the oldest story she knew: a girl in a small bed, counting to one hundred and then again, learning the shape of breath. She closed her eyes and waited, not for safety—that was a child's contract—but for enough morning to make another day.

9

The Orphanage Clock

The Los Angeles Orphans Home was meant to inspire trust from the outside. Its walls were whitewashed, its hedges clipped as neatly as a soldier's haircut, its front steps scrubbed clean of dust each morning by the older children. Neighbors passing on Pleasant Avenue might have thought it a modest school or a convent, a respectable place where order reigned and children were kept safe. But order was not love, and safety was not belonging. Inside, the air was heavy with soap, starch, and silence—a silence that pressed itself into the children's bones until they learned not to speak unless spoken to.

The bell was her first memory here. It hung above the courtyard, iron darkened by years of fog and sun, and when it rang, it did not suggest. It commanded. It pulled children from sleep, pushed them into line, marched them to meals, sent them to lessons, and finally drove them back to the dormitories at night. Its clang was absolute, stripping away individuality, replacing each child's heartbeat with its iron pulse. Even when it was quiet, Norma Jeane felt it reverberating in her chest, a reminder that time here belonged to the institution, not to her.

The dormitory stretched long and narrow, a barracks for the small and forgotten. Cots stood in rows, iron frames painted white but chipped at the corners, their mattresses thin and scratchy. Sheets smelled perpetually of lye, blankets heavy and rough against bare legs. The air carried the sour tang of disinfectant, mingled with the human smells of too many bodies confined together. At night the room was a chorus: coughs erupting suddenly, a child whimpering for a mother, the squeak of bedsprings as others tossed in restless sleep. Norma Jeane learned quickly to lie still, her eyes open to the ceiling, her breathing controlled, so that the matron making her rounds would pass without noticing her wakefulness.

The mornings began with a ritual as precise as any liturgy. Shoes polished until the leather shone like mirrors, hair combed into neat parts, hands washed and inspected for dirt. The older children supervised the younger, tugging braids too tight, scrubbing cheeks until they were raw. Breakfast was ladled into bowls in a cavernous hall that echoed with clattering spoons and murmured grace. The food filled the stomach but never satisfied—thin oatmeal, toast that crumbled into dust on the tongue, coffee for the matrons but hot water for the children. Ten minutes, no more. The bell tolled again, and the trays were gathered up, hunger lingering like an echo.

Other children learned to beg for seconds, flashing wide eyes or feigning stomach aches, but Norma Jeane discovered that prettiness could be its own currency. A smile carefully timed, a "thank you" sweetened like syrup, might earn her a slightly larger ladle of stew or a softer tone from a matron. She did not yet understand performance as an art; she understood it as survival.

The classrooms smelled of chalk and mildew. Lessons were drilled by rote: multiplication tables, Bible verses, handwriting exercises that cramped small fingers. Children recited in unison, their voices drained of individuality until they sounded like a single weary organ. Norma Jeane mouthed the words, copying the rise and fall of others, careful never to stumble. She discovered early that invisibility was the safest posture. To be invisible meant no punishment, no scolding, no extra chores. Trouble fell on those who drew attention, and she had already learned in her short life that attention could wound.

Yet invisibility carried its own kind of ache. Some children wanted to be noticed so badly that they fought for it—tugging at a matron's skirt, raising their hands in class, volunteering for every task. They believed attention might be the bridge to adoption, that if they performed well enough, smiled brightly enough, someone might finally choose them. Visitors sometimes came through the halls, wealthy couples dressed in hats and gloves, their eyes scanning rows of children as if browsing wares in a shop. The children straightened their spines, widened their smiles, displayed themselves like hopeful merchandise.

Norma Jeane tried, too. She brushed her curls smooth, stood with hands clasped, offered her best smile when eyes fell on her. She was always noticed. The matrons whispered about her prettiness; the visitors paused longer at her face. Yet when the day ended, it was always someone else who left holding a stranger's hand. Each rejection pressed another stone into her chest. She learned to retreat behind her smile, to hold herself steady even as hope drained away.

At night the clock took over from the bell. A large wall clock in the dormitory ticked with merciless rhythm, its pendulum swinging like a judge's gavel. Tick. Tick. Tick. The sound counted her invisibility, each second another reminder of how long she had been waiting for a mother who never came, for a father she had never known, for someone—anyone—to claim her.

She whispered to herself in the dark. If the matrons heard, they thought she was praying, and perhaps she was. But not to the God in the hymns. She prayed to faces she had cut out from magazines, to fathers she invented whole cloth, to Clark Gable, whose photograph she believed could hear her. She told herself stories: that her father would arrive with flowers, that her mother would walk in radiant and healed, that a hand would reach for hers without hesitation. These were not idle daydreams. They were rehearsals for the life she was teaching herself to survive.

Other children clung to dolls with missing eyes or blankets worn thin. Norma Jeane clung to her imagination. She built entire worlds inside her mind: houses with porches, mothers who cooked suppers, fathers who laughed at her jokes. She imagined birthdays with cakes tall as towers, Christmas mornings where wrapping paper exploded like confetti, family dinners where no one ever left the table. Each vision was stitched from scraps of movies she had seen or stories she had overheard, but in her heart they felt as real as the iron cot beneath her.

One night she whispered so vividly about a family picnic—the checkered blanket, the fried chicken, the lemonade sweating in glasses—that the girl in the next bed began to cry, begging her to stop because it hurt too much to imagine what could never be. Norma Jeane learned then that her imagination was not just a shield for herself; it was a weapon, too sharp for some to bear. She began to keep her visions private, cradling them like fragile pets that only she could feed.

But she never stopped rehearsing. She practiced smiles in the cracked mirror of the lavatory, tilting her head just so, parting her lips in a way that seemed both innocent and knowing. She copied the mannerisms of matrons, the inflections of girls who had been adopted, the gestures of stars she glimpsed in magazines. She did not yet call it acting. She called it surviving.

The matrons varied. Some were briskly kind, offering a rare pat on the head or an extra spoon of porridge. Others were cold, their faces carved with fatigue, their voices sharp as wire. None tucked the children in at night, none kissed scraped knees, none lingered with affection. Love was rationed like sugar in Depression-era Los Angeles—a scarce luxury, dispensed sparingly if at all.

On Sundays the children were marched to chapel, shoes scuffed but polished, hair combed to glossy obedience. They sang hymns in a chorus that rose into rafters too high for their small voices. Norma Jeane mouthed the words but drifted into the colors of stained glass, the reds and blues painting the floor like a secret cinema. To her the shifting light was more real than the God in the hymns. She felt safer in the story told by glass than the silence she met in prayer.

She learned from the children around her, too. There was Lillian, the girl in the next cot, who wept each night for a mother whose letters never came. There was Ruthie, sharp-tongued and quick to fight, who once clawed Norma Jeane's arm for daring to sit too close to the radiator. There was Annie, small and birdlike, who became her friend for a season, whispering secrets until the day she was suddenly gone—chosen by a family in Pasadena. The absence of Annie was worse than the fights with Ruthie. It was proof that people disappeared, that bonds could dissolve overnight, that love, when it arrived, was always borrowed.

Norma Jeane folded these lessons into herself. Do not cling too tightly. Do not expect permanence. Do not trust love to stay. Smile, even when the smile is armor. Pretend, even when the pretending hurts. These were the catechisms of the orphanage, more enduring than any sermon.

And so she waited. She waited through the clang of the bell, through the scrape of spoons, through the hiss of starch on laundry, through the tick of the dormitory clock. She waited with her smile, with her whispered stories, with her body lying still as stone while her mind built worlds where she was wanted.

The orphanage had meant to discipline her. What it gave her instead was Marilyn Monroe.

The city outside the gates had no interest in children like these. Los Angeles sold itself as a paradise of oranges and sunshine, a city of movie palaces and palm-lined boulevards, but tucked behind those promises were institutions like this, where the children of the forgotten were hidden away. The Depression had flooded the orphanages with wards of the state, their faces thin, their futures uncertain. Newspapers printed photographs of them sometimes, lined in rows for charity appeals, but the captions reduced them to numbers. No one wrote their names.

The matrons reminded the children of this often: you are lucky to have a roof, lucky to have meals, lucky to have beds. Luck, in the orphanage, meant you were not starving on the street. But luck never stretched to love. No one said you were lucky to be cherished, lucky to be chosen, lucky to be held. Those luxuries belonged elsewhere.

Norma Jeane carried the weight of that distinction every day. The orphanage did not bruise her body, but it bruised her spirit in subtler ways. Indifference was a wound that did not bleed but ached endlessly. To be one among many, never singled out for love, was its own cruelty.

Yet within that cruelty she found an odd kind of power. Invisibility allowed her to observe. She studied the matrons, the way their faces softened when confronted with charm, the way a smile could disarm a scolding. She studied the other children, noting who was rewarded for sweetness, who was punished for defiance. She filed these lessons away as if preparing for a role she had not yet been cast in. Later, on film sets, she would know exactly how to angle her chin, how to let her voice catch at just the right moment, because she had been rehearsing since she was nine years old.

The orphanage gave her something else: a stage. Not a literal one, but the space of her imagination, where she performed for herself each night. She invented families who applauded her jokes, fathers who carried her on their shoulders, mothers who braided her hair with gentle hands. She whispered dialogues into her pillow, sometimes mouthing both parts, until the fantasy felt like memory. These rehearsals became muscle memory, etched so deeply that when the cameras finally found her, she did not need to invent from scratch. She only needed to recall.

She learned, too, from the departures. Every time another child was chosen, a silence fell across the dormitory. Bedsprings stood empty, lockers gaped hollow, and the child's name ceased to be spoken. At first she felt jealousy, then grief, then a harder emotion she could not name—the knowledge that she had not been chosen again. Each absence reminded her of her own invisibility. But each absence also carved into her a determination: if the world would not choose her, she would find a way to make it impossible to look away.

Adoption was the fantasy most children clung to, but Norma Jeane began to cling to something else. She wanted not just a family but an audience. She wanted the eyes that passed her over to stop, to linger, to see her fully. If she could not be loved by one, perhaps she could be adored by all.

The Depression years marked her like chalk on a blackboard. She saw men lined at soup kitchens, women scrubbing stairs for pennies, families packing everything into battered cars and heading west for work that rarely materialized. Los Angeles was both haven and illusion, a city where riches were promised in studio lights even as poverty spread in its shadows. The orphanage was a microcosm of that contradiction: whitewashed walls masking the hunger inside.

Sometimes the matrons spoke of Hollywood as if it were another planet. Some of the children whispered about being discovered, about movie stars adopting them, about luck that could catapult them from cots to silver screens. Norma Jeane listened, but she did not laugh. She believed, perhaps more deeply than anyone, because she needed to. She believed in the movies the way others believed in scripture. She believed the screen could deliver her into visibility, into belonging.

She was already collecting faces. Clark Gable, of course, remained her mythic father. But she began to notice others: Jean Harlow's platinum hair, Carole Lombard's mischievous grin, Greta Garbo's melancholy gaze. She cut their photographs from magazines when she could, tucking them into her small drawer like talismans. Each image was both an escape and an instruction manual. This is how you are noticed, the faces seemed to say. This is how you are remembered.

The clock in the dormitory ticked on, indifferent. Tick, tick, tick—like a heart that belonged to no one. For many children, the sound lulled them into sleep. For Norma Jeane, it was a metronome of anxiety. She could not surrender to slumber easily. Sleep had been a danger since the night of the pillow, since her mother's trembling hands pressed down. At the orphanage, the danger came in other forms: nightmares of abandonment, the fear that she might vanish like the children who disappeared into adoption. So she lay awake, watching shadows stretch across the ceiling, telling herself stories until exhaustion finally claimed her.

That insomnia never left her. Years later, when she reached for pills to force sleep, she was still the child in the orphanage bed, listening to the clock, afraid of what dreams might bring.

Yet the orphanage did not erase her spirit. If anything, it sharpened it. The hunger for love became a furnace. The absence of family became a challenge. The loneliness became a stage on which she learned her lines. Each smile practiced in the mirror, each whispered fantasy, each silent rehearsal prepared her for the role of a lifetime.

The matrons believed they were instilling discipline, but what they gave her was something unintended: ambition born of deprivation. They taught her invisibility, and she turned it into visibility. They gave her silence, and she filled it with performance. They denied her love, and she transformed that absence into a hunger so fierce it made her unforgettable.

When she finally left the orphanage, carrying little more than the scars of invisibility, she also carried the tools that would one day build Marilyn Monroe. The world thought the studios created her, that makeup and publicity and gossip columns invented her allure. But long before the lights and cameras, the Los Angeles Orphans Home had forged the essential parts: the smile as shield, the insomnia as ghost, the hunger as engine.

The orphanage thought it had reduced her to one among many. What it had done was create a girl who would never again be content to be invisible.

And so the clock ticked on, indifferent, unaware that one of the children lying awake beneath its gaze was already plotting her escape. She would not be a ward forever. She would not be forgotten. One day, the world would know her name, and the ticking of the orphanage clock would be drowned out by applause that did not stop.

10

Ana and the Nebraska House

The Nebraska Avenue house was the opposite of spectacle. A single-story bungalow with a porch that sighed in summer and a roof that ticked in winter, it kept its head down the way modest people do. Paint flaked softly from the eaves. The screen door rasped a quiet warning before it opened. Honeysuckle made a shy attempt at claiming the fence, and someone—always, unfailingly—swept the front steps each morning so the day would have a clean place to begin.

To anyone passing on foot it was simply another house on another Los Angeles block. To a twelve-year-old who had slept in rows of iron beds and woke to bells that owned her pulse, it was a miracle disguised as wood and stucco. It was a door that opened and kept opening to the same room, the same bed, the same table set for breakfast the next morning. Continuity, the most ordinary magic in the world, finally within reach.

Edith Ana Lower—Aunt Ana, though no blood tied them—carried that same ordinary magic in the way she moved through rooms. She had a librarian's patience and a nurse's practical hands. She wore her hair coiled and pinned; her dresses, modest and clean, made a quiet argument for order. She believed in Christian Science with the calm certainty of a sunrise: spirit over matter, thought over pain, prayer over panic.

To a child whose life had been drafted by chaos, Ana's voice was a metronome set to mercy. It didn't make the world less complicated, but it made the day decipherable. She didn't ask what you felt so much as what you were going to do next—wash, read, sweep, set the table, fold the towels while they were still warm so their edges would meet. Responsibility, she said, was how love stayed tidy.

Norma Jeane would confide to Jim Bacon that inside, the house smelled of furniture polish and wood cleaner. Floors shone, not in a proud way, but in the way a face shines after being washed and dried and kissed on the forehead. The kitchen was a little orchestra of useful noise: kettle purring on the back burner, spoon tapping against a mixing bowl, the soft thud of a drawer closing on neatly stacked dish towels. In a glass jar on the counter, sugar made a small mountain; nearby, a tin of tea waited like a quiet promise. Every object had a place, and—more importantly—kept it. The stability gathered around the girl like an Afghan pulled up to the chin.

The backyard felt larger than it was. A sliver of lawn pushed up against a narrow border of roses; hollyhocks kept watch along the fence line like tall, kindly aunts. In spring, bees stitched the air into a hum that made thoughts feel less jagged. On warm afternoons, laundry flapped itself dry on the line and the clothespins clicked like punctuation. The sky above West Los Angeles was big and indifferent and somehow soothing. She learned the look of it at different hours—bruised lilac at dawn, milky at noon, dramatized gold in the last gasp of day—and the sky learned the shape of her longing.

Life there ran on small rituals that added up to something large. Breakfast at the round kitchen table: toast, a smear of jam when the budget could stand it, porridge eaten plain when it couldn't. A short prayer that asked for nothing and thanked for everything. Shoes on, books hugged to the chest, a glance back at the doorway for reasons she could not name. School, then home, then chores: sweep the front room, dust the mantle, polish the picture frames until the faces inside them looked like they were breathing. After supper, Ana read aloud from the Bible or from Mary Baker Eddy, and for once words about unseen things did not feel like a trick or a test. They felt like scaffolding for the heart.

School was Nora Sterry first, Emerson Junior High later. Norma Jeane walked there with other children, and the sidewalks grew familiar under the soles of her shoes. She learned the houses by their front gardens: a little grove of geraniums that always looked like a small parade; a lemon tree that made its own light; a patch of dirt where a neighbor swore wildflowers would come back "any day now" the way some mothers swore they'd come back, too. In class she was attentive, careful with her answers. Teachers liked her because she made liking her easy: yes ma'am, no sir, eyes bright and steady, the homework folded neatly in half. She was not a star pupil so much as a star listener, and adults are softer toward children who listen as if listening might save a life.

Children can be kind in the morning and cruel by lunch. She learned to navigate both weather systems. A boy with a cowlick brought her a stick of gum and turned scarlet when she thanked him; a girl with a precise braid announced at recess that Norma Jeane's dress was "church-ish," like a slight you could press between two pages and keep forever. After school, a pair of sisters asked if she wanted to walk home with them; the next day they forgot she existed. The currents of belonging were shallow and shifting, but they were currents. In the orphanage, there had only been undertow.

The mirror in her little room took on the authority of an oracle. Oval, a little clouded at the edges, it returned a face that kept surprising her: the softening roundness of childhood giving way to angles and shadows that made people look twice. She practiced smiles the way other girls practiced scales. A hint of teeth, then not. Chin down, eyes up. Shoulders back, a secret she didn't know she knew moving behind her collarbones. She learned what light could do to a cheekbone even when that light came from a stubborn window that never opened all the way. The mirror did not flatter; it told a story. Someday, it seemed to say, you will be looked at like a language people suddenly remember how to speak.

Sometimes she imagined the mirror was a camera and that a photograph could catch the version of herself she did not yet know how to keep. She would tilt and turn and try to feel what she thought beauty must feel like: not superiority, but permission. Not "I'm better," but "I'm allowed." The mirror taught her that being looked at and being seen were cousins who did not always speak, and she filed that knowledge for the years ahead.

Letters began to arrive like thin wings. Kentucky stamps, looping script, paper that held the faint scent of a house she'd never been inside. Berniece. Just the name steadied something inside her, like finding a handhold chipped into a cliff. She learned the fraternal rhythm of sisterhood one envelope at a time. Berniece wrote about her own mother, about a city whose winters bit and whose summers swelled, about work and dresses and little wishes she tucked into prayer.

In return, Norma Jeane wrote everything and almost nothing: the brand of soap Ana liked, the way the honeysuckle reached for the fence, the thrill of finding her own name in someone else's mouth on paper. She reread each letter until the creases went white and the ink grew faint at the folds. At night, she held those letters against her chest and pretended the paper was skin.

Christian Science threaded the days without strangling them. When she complained of a headache, Ana's hand was cool on her forehead and her voice was steady in her ear: We are not at the mercy of what seems to hurt. The words didn't deny pain so much as refuse to hand it a crown. For a child who had been ruled by other people's storms, it mattered to be told that the inside could sometimes be louder than the outside. It mattered to be told there was a way to talk back to fear without becoming noise.

Los Angeles in those years was a study in contradictions. The Depression hadn't quite let go; the war in Europe was tightening a fist across the ocean. Men waited at day-labor corners hoping for trucks that didn't always come. At night, radios poured out news that made adults' faces pinch and children's spines straighten. And yet—Hollywood. Marquees flared like sunrise at the wrong hour, and lobby cards promised lives so glossy they squeaked.

On Saturdays, if chores were done and coins were found in a sugar jar Ana swore had no bottom, the two of them took the streetcar and let the city carry them toward a picture palace. They sat in the velvet dark and watched other people's problems be solved in ninety minutes with a kiss, a laugh, a last-minute revelation.

On the way home, the streets looked different, as if the movie had peeled a film from the day and left everything a little raw and glittering. Norma Jeane collected faces the way some children collect pressed flowers. Garbo's solitude, Harlow's champagne sparkle, Lombard's mischievous ease. Dietrich like a secret you only tell yourself in the dark. She did not want to be them exactly. She wanted to speak the language they were speaking: the dialect of notice. She wanted to be fluent in being looked at and not lost.

At Emerson, a teacher handed back a composition with a small star penciled at the top and said, "There's music in the way you say things." It was a throwaway kindness, but it held. She walked home lighter, as if the day had agreed to carry half her satchel.

On the sidewalk a neighbor snapped a photo with a Brownie—"Stand just there, honey, the light is nice"—and later handed her a print where her face looked like it had decided something. She stared at the photograph until the edges curled. The camera had been plain; the picture was not. It made her wonder whether seeing herself was the same thing as recognizing herself, and she decided it wasn't. Recognition takes time. Sometimes it takes years and applause and the right dress and a name you weren't born with.

Stability did not erase the tremor underneath. It softened it, the way sand muffles the sound of a wave. But the wave was there. Once, after school, she let herself into the quiet house and set her books on the table, and for a second she could not hear anything but her own breath and the clock. Panic brightened everything. She called out. No answer. Panic sharpened everything. She called again, smaller. Then Ana's footsteps, unhurried as always, and her voice: "I'm here, child." The relief was so sharp it hurt. She laughed it off and never told anyone that some days she lived on the knife-edge between belonging and bolt.

On warm Sundays, if chores were done and the day had behaved itself, Ana packed a small tin of sandwiches and a glass bottle of lemonade and they rode the bus toward the coast. The Pacific did not care who you were; it touched everyone. She stood barefoot where the water folded over itself like clean sheets and let the sand make promises around her toes. The horizon was a straight line that refused to bend, and that stubbornness comforted her. When the sun slipped its shoulder into the sea, she felt a clarity she couldn't name: the sense that even if nothing lasted, some things returned, and sometimes that was enough.

She learned the neighborhood as a kind of scripture. The elderly man who shuffled each morning to collect his newspaper always saluted the sun as if it were a captain. The laundress who beat sheets with a willow switch and sang hymns so softly the air blushed to hear them. The little boy who practiced marbles in the gutter with the seriousness of a surgeon. If you know a place well enough, it starts to know you back. She began to feel known—not by fate, not by fame, but by the block. The block is a small thing to belong to, but it's a start.

With adolescence came the awkward tenderness of a body catching up to itself. Dresses were let out, hems negotiated. She learned where to put her hands when she didn't know what to do with them. Boys looked longer; girls looked aside and then, when she turned, looked back. The attention was hot and confusing and sometimes kind. She learned to say "thank you" as if it belonged to her and to say "no" as if it belonged to them. In the mirror she tried on versions of herself like costumes: the girl who knows, the girl who doesn't, the girl who will someday walk into a room and the room will forget its name.

Sometimes at night, after the house had folded itself into quiet, she'd take Berniece's latest letter from its place between the dictionary and her vanity and read by the narrow light of the lamp. She read slowly, the way you eat when there isn't enough. The words brought another life into the room and made the air feel full. Once a photograph slipped from an envelope—Berniece in a day dress, one hand at her waist, the corner of her mouth caught mid-thought. The resemblance wasn't an echo so much as a chord. She pressed the picture to the mirror and stood beside her sister's face. Family is a story we tell our blood until it answers back.

Ana's faith allowed no indulgence in self-pity. When the war grew nearer, when ration books appeared beside the sugar jar, when the radio crackled with dates that would later be circled in history, the house stayed faithful to its rituals: prayer, supper, folded towels, the garden watered before dusk so the roses would not scald. Fear was acknowledged like a visitor who could not be allowed to stay the night. In that discipline, there was a tenderness that never announced itself as such. You knew it by the way a blanket was tucked, the way a shirt was mended so the seam lay smooth against the skin.

At school she joined a library club because the stacks smelled like possibility and dust. She found a book on Greek myths and fell in love with the idea that gods could enter a room disguised as strangers and wreck your life with beauty. She read novels where girls were rescued and others where girls rescued themselves, and she tried to decide which was more dangerous. She wrote little scenes in a notebook—dialogues that had the shape of the conversations she longed to have. The notebook, unlike people, was never too busy to listen.

She began to notice that the camera loved stillness more than movement. On a dare at the five-and-dime photo booth, she held herself as calm as a held breath and watched the strip spool out: four small squares where her face looked like it was telling the truth for the first time. She slipped the strip into her book of myths as if secrecy could charge it with power. The myths and the photos slept back-to-back and taught her that immortality is often just repetition that refuses to die.

Sometimes Gladys drifted through these years like weather: a note in a shaky hand, a visit that arrived and left her moving like someone walking across a floor that could give way. Love was not absent, exactly. It was volatile. Between those gusts, Aunt Ana's steadiness became ballast. It did not solve the ache; it kept the ache from knocking the walls down. In the space Ana made, the girl learned to breathe without bracing.

The city kept instructing her. Hollywood Boulevard was a catechism in lights: neon creeping up the night like ivy, ladies in fox collars pretending not to be cold, men whose laughter sounded like pocket change. On a streetcar she caught her reflection in the window—superimposed over a billboard of a woman whose mouth was a red rule. The reflection startled her: she was not the woman on the billboard, but she had learned the grammar. How to be sentence and silence at once. How to be question mark and answer.

In the Nebraska Avenue house she learned the choreography of domestic mercy. The way you set a table so a guest feels expected. The way you open a window when a room has forgotten how to breathe. The way you say a person's name like they are the only person who has ever had it. Those lessons didn't look like training for a future that would fling her image across the world, but they were. She would carry them onto sound stages and into hotel rooms and into marriages: an instinct for where comfort could be placed, how to build a place to stand with nothing but hands and voice.

Not everything gentle can last. That truth haunts even the steadiest house. But gentleness can leave a residue on the soul, a shine that holds when the furniture is carried out. In these years she gathered small, durable things: the habit of making a bed smooth enough to lie to sadness; the practice of keeping letters where you can reach them in the dark; the certainty that even if you cannot keep a mother, you can keep a promise to the child you were. She promised that child a future in which the clock would not order her life, in which the bell would ring because she wanted it to.

The girl who had learned invisibility in the orphanage learned here how to be present without apology. Not yet the woman on the screen, not yet the name that made strangers dream, but a person in a room who could bear being seen. She carried water to the roses and noted how flowers behave when you look after them: they lean toward light even when they've been through wind. She did not yet have the words for what she was becoming, but she felt the direction in her bones. Toward, always toward.

One evening, the radio announced a headline that would become a door into a different decade, and Ana reached for the knob and turned the volume down until the words lost their edges. They ate bean soup with torn bread. After the dishes were washed and set upside down to dry, after the last passage had been read, after the porch had given up its heat to the dark, Ana said, "We will do what we can. That is enough." And for once the girl believed her. Enough is not abundance; it is permission to go on.

In bed, she lay on her side and watched the moon throw a little silver on the wall. She thought of Berniece, somewhere under the same coin of light. She thought of a father who was an outline she could not shade in. She thought of her mother floating somewhere between love and a hospital ward. And then she thought of herself—not the self the mirror returned, not the self the camera might prefer, but the self who could get up in the morning and make the day decent. That self felt like a thread she could hold. She promised to hold it.

Years later, when people wrote about her as if she were sudden, as if she had sprung fully formed from a studio's forehead, they would miss this: a small house on Nebraska Avenue where a girl practiced belonging until the muscle remembered. A woman with a calm voice who taught her that habit could be a kind of hope. Letters from a sister that stitched blood to paper and paper to heart. A mirror that told the truth and then forgave it. A city that glittered and groaned and offered her a stage she was not yet brave enough to step onto, but would be. The Nebraska house didn't make her famous. It made her ready.

When she finally drifted toward sleep, it came without the old fight. The clock on the mantel ticked like a patient animal. Somewhere outside, a cat negotiated with the night. In the yard, the roses held their breath. In the room, the girl loosened hers and let it go. Morning was coming, predictable as mercy. The same steps to sweep, the same prayers to fold into the day, the same mirror to stand before and study the face that was learning the miracle of being its own.

She would not always live there. The world had plans for her. The world had plans for the part of her that had learned to look like light. But the part that learned how to make a bed, how to write a letter, how to drink lemonade slow on a hot afternoon so sweetness didn't hurt—that part would come along, too. It would insist upon kindness in rooms that had forgotten the word. It would know where the window latch was and how to lift it when the air went stale. It would remember that being noticed and being loved are not synonyms and would try, in the secret hours, to choose the latter even when the former was easier to find.

The Nebraska Avenue house taught her how to keep house with her own spirit. Go slowly. Put things back. Say thank you out loud so the air hears it. Water the thing that leans toward light. Answer the door when it knocks, but keep a small latch on your heart in case the visitor is weather. Read to yourself in a voice that forgives. And if you must leave—and you will, the world will insist—leave the room a little better than you found it. Leave a folded towel, a washed cup, a letter on the table that begins, Dear Berniece, I am all right.

11

The Lost Girl

They were not sisters not quite friends, not family in any way the law could name. They were the ones who appeared like half-remembered songs, bright for a verse, gone by the chorus. Girls who passed through the foster homes and orphanages of Los Angeles the way sparrows dart through alleys—here and gone, sometimes leaving only the echo of wings. To Norma Jeane, they became a constellation. She traced their faces like stars and told herself that if she could just connect them, she would not be alone.

The first and brightest was Doris, who lived down the block on Nebraska Avenue. Doris had a braid so tight it looked like rope, eyes wide with permanent surprise, and a voice that could cut through the shriek of trolley brakes. She was daring in ways that thrilled and terrified: daring Norma Jeane to slide down banisters until her stockings ripped, daring her to lick frost off the metal railing in winter, daring her to pocket sugar cubes from Ana's pantry and call them medicine for sadness.

One Saturday they tried pancakes. Doris insisted she could cook, though her mother never let her near the stove. They mixed batter that slopped like wet cement, poured it too thick, burned it black on one side and raw on the other. The kitchen filled with smoke, and Norma Jeane's eyes streamed until she thought she might cry for real. They buried the evidence under the rosebush in the yard, laughing so hard their knees gave way. "We'll blame the dog if anyone asks," Doris declared. But the dog was long gone, a casualty of too many missed feedings.

At night, lying side by side in Doris's room during sleepovers, they whispered as if the plaster walls had ears. Doris's father was a heavy presence: boots on the porch like hammers, snores rattling the windows, a voice that made everything sound like an argument. "I'll run away," Doris swore. "Hollywood, maybe. Or New York. Somewhere I can sleep without him shaking the house."

Her eyes burned with the kind of certainty only the desperate carry. Norma Jeane whispered back, clutching her pillow as if it could keep her safe: "I'll marry Clark Gable." The vow sounded foolish even to her, but Doris nodded like a priest accepting confession.

They made maps of escape—arrows drawn on notebook paper, dotted lines pointing toward bus stations, ship docks, train yards. They folded the maps into tiny squares and tucked them inside shoes. "Just in case," Doris said.

The brightest of their adventures took them to the beach. The air smelled of tar and salt, the sand so hot it scorched their feet until they ran shrieking into the Pacific. They built castles too fragile to last, chased gulls that scattered like paper blown from a fire, screamed when waves knocked them off their feet. For those hours they were not foster children or daughters of drunks. They were queens of the shoreline, saltwater baptizing them into a secret faith. Later, when Doris's family packed up and moved, the memory of that afternoon stayed with Norma Jeane like a seashell she could press to her ear.

If Doris was flame, Ruthie was fruit. She always smelled of oranges, her family living above a grocery store. Her dresses carried that perfume of citrus and figs, and she bragged about sneaking down at midnight to eat straight from the crates. "You don't know heaven till you've had figs in the dark," she said, licking juice from her wrist. "Someday I'll be a movie star, and I'll order them by the pound."

Ruthie dazzled with her certainty. She spoke of skyscrapers in New York as if she had already booked her room. "I'll marry Tyrone Power," she declared. "Not Gable, he's too old. Tyrone." Norma Jeane didn't argue; she was content to watch Ruthie claim a destiny as easily as someone calling shotgun.

The apartment above the store sagged with age, wallpaper peeling like scabs, the ceiling stained from leaks. But to Norma Jeane it was a palace because Ruthie was there. They sat cross-legged on the floor, eating figs until their fingers were sticky. Ruthie's mother hummed in the kitchen, pots clanging like bells, the air so thick with sugar it made Norma Jeane dizzy. For a girl used to starch and hymnals at the Bolenders', this was another world—noisy, fragrant, alive.

Saturdays meant the trolley downtown. The girls clung to the metal poles, hair whipped by the open windows. They pressed their noses against department store windows, marveling at satin gowns with wasp waists and rhinestone shoes. "Someday," Ruthie whispered, "those will be ours." Norma Jeane nodded, even though she could hardly imagine a future where dresses belonged to her.

They pooled coins for the matinee at the Million Dollar Theater. In the balcony, they watched Deanna Durbin sing until the air itself seemed to shimmer. Norma Jeane leaned forward, drinking in the applause as if it could spill over to her. "That'll be you someday," Ruthie whispered. The words burrowed deep, a seed wrapped in the sweetness of figs.

In the orphanage she found Millie, who had eyes too old for her face and fingers that moved with needle precision. Millie stitched torn hems before anyone noticed, patched socks with speed that bordered on magic. She treated the orphanage like a station. "Don't get attached," she warned. "Girls don't stay long." Her words were heavy with truth, but in the laundry room, where steam hung thick and machines thundered like timpani, she softened.

They sang Bing Crosby tunes, their voices nearly drowned by the clamor. They laughed so hard at their own off-key harmonies that they forgot for a moment where they were. Millie showed her how to thread a needle, guiding her hands with patience. "It's not about the thread," she said. "It's about holding things together long enough to get by." Norma Jeane stitched her first crooked hem that night and felt as though she had stitched herself into survival.

Betty was older, sharper, with a knack for glamour. She had a way of walking down the orphanage corridor like it was a runway. She taught Norma Jeane how to paint nails with stolen polish, crimson slick and glinting under dim light. "Mystery," Betty whispered. "That's the trick. Tilt your head, half-close your eyes. Make them wonder."

They draped scarves into gowns, clomped in shoes far too big, paraded before the younger girls who clapped as if they had been transported to Paris. Norma Jeane went last, chin tilted, lips pursed in a look she had practiced in mirrors. For the first time she felt the hush of attention wrap around her like a cloak. She was not invisible. She was someone worth watching.

The girls created a secret club, solemn as any church. They met under blankets with flashlights, pricking thumbs to swear blood sisterhood. Their commandments were simple: share candy, share secrets, believe each other. They whispered about crushes, about parents who drank, about dreams of movie screens and husbands who would rescue them. Norma Jeane listened like someone kneeling in prayer.

But the commandments cracked. Once, Millie told Betty's secret—that she had kissed a boy behind the orphanage gate—and Betty refused to speak to her for a week. The silence was punishment, heavier than slaps. Norma Jeane tried to broker peace, but the fissure taught her that even sacred vows could fracture. Love, even in the form of friendship, was fragile glass.

Still, they laughed. Norma Jeane stuffed grapes in her cheeks until she looked like a chipmunk, crossed her eyes until Ruthie nearly choked with laughter, mimicked teachers so mercilessly that even Millie's serious face cracked. She sketched the matron in chapel with snakes for hair, passed it to Doris, and was caught. Punishment was swift, but the memory of laughter endured longer than the sting of reprimand.

Lila was the quietest. Freckles dotted her nose; her voice was barely louder than a whisper. One night, in the secrecy of their blanket fort, she confessed that a boarder in her foster home had "looked at her too long." She didn't explain more. She didn't need to. The words hung heavy, the air gone sour. No one had the language to answer. Norma Jeane reached across and held her hand. It was the only prayer they knew.

The world beyond them was changing. Soldiers in uniform filled the streets, their boots echoing on sidewalks. Adults whispered about war, about Hitler, about sons drafted. The girls treated air-raid drills at school like games, ducking under desks, giggling until shushed. But fear seeped in anyway, like smog thickening the horizon.

Billboards on Sunset gleamed with Judy Garland's smile, Shirley Temple's curls. The lost girls read them like scripture, promises painted 10 feet tall. They walked home in threadbare shoes, their pockets empty, but their imaginations blazing with futures where their names would one day shine.

Betty was the first to whisper the idea of slipping away. They were huddled on the orphanage steps one dusky Saturday, the air heavy with starch and cabbage from the supper hall, when she leaned in with a sly smile. "We could take the trolley downtown. Just once. No one would notice." The suggestion was reckless and radiant, like striking a match in a dark room. Norma Jeane's pulse quickened. Even Millie, who prided herself on caution, bit her lip as though weighing the punishment against the thrill.

When the moment came, they slid through the fence where the wire sagged, hearts pounding. The trolley screeched to a halt, doors opening like a promise. Inside, the seats rattled and the driver didn't ask questions. Neon signs flickered even in the afternoon, perfume counters spilled sweetness into the streets, and the smell of roasted peanuts drifted from vendors' carts. They clutched their nickels and stared wide-eyed at a city that felt bigger than the sky.

At the Million Dollar Theater, they pooled coins for balcony tickets. The lobby gleamed with gilt and marble, chandeliers hanging like frozen fireworks. Inside, the air was cool, thick with popcorn and cologne. Deanna Durbin's voice filled the dark, luminous and impossible, as if it came from heaven itself. Norma Jeane leaned forward until her elbows dug into her knees. She wanted to swallow that light whole, to believe it might someday fall on her. "That'll be you one day," Ruthie whispered, sticky from the orange she had smuggled in. Norma Jeane couldn't answer. She only stared, her throat aching with the wish.

When they slipped back through the fence later, faces flushed with triumph, it was as if they had carried the city home with them. They piled under blankets with a flashlight and swore never to forget what it felt like to sit in the dark, together, believing in futures larger than their bodies.

Nights in the orphanage were their true cathedral. Two chairs draped with quilts became a temple, the flashlight their flickering candle. They declared themselves a secret order, sisters sworn by thumb-pricked blood and whispered vows. Candy was shared like communion, secrets exchanged like currency, promises bound in the kind of solemnity only children could summon. In that glow, they became each other's salvation. Millie confessed that she feared turning 15, when the state might push her into the world without anchor. Ruthie admitted she sometimes hated her sisters for stealing their mother's attention. Betty revealed that she had kissed a boy behind the fence, her voice trembling as though she had named a crime.

When Norma Jeane's turn came, her voice caught. "I just want a home," she whispered. The flashlight illuminated her wide eyes, the sudden silence that followed. Then Lila, freckles scattered across her nose like ash, reached for her hand. It was enough.

But even holy covenants cracked. One afternoon, Millie, stung by Betty's sharp tongue, spat out her secret. Betty's cheeks flamed. "You broke the rule," she hissed, withdrawing into silence. For a week she walked with her chin high, her eyes averted, punishing them all. Norma Jeane tried to patch the wound, clowning with crossed eyes, drawing caricatures of the matron with horns, anything to stir laughter. When Betty finally relented, the Sisterhood resumed, but something delicate had broken. Love, Norma Jeane realized, was not invincible.

Summer brought heat that pressed on their backs like iron. When a church group herded them onto buses for a trip to the beach, they shrieked with delight. The Pacific unrolled before them, vast and glittering, the air sharp with salt. They plunged into the surf until the waves toppled them, came up coughing, hair plastered to their cheeks. On the sand, Ruthie sculpted herself a throne, Betty paraded like a queen of beauty, Millie fortified moats with engineer's seriousness. Norma Jeane built fragile spires, towers so delicate they collapsed at the first touch of the tide. She rebuilt them, again and again, her small hands shaking with determination.

As the day waned, they huddled in borrowed blankets, watching the horizon burn gold. Lila whispered that she had never seen the ocean before. "It feels alive," she said, her voice barely louder than the gulls. Norma Jeane nodded, hugging her knees. She wanted to tell them she could feel her mother in the waves, that she imagined Gladys laughing beside her, skirts soaked, hair wild in the wind. But she held the vision close, afraid that speaking it aloud would dissolve it.

The ride back was quieter, the bus humming like a lullaby. The girls leaned against one another, lulled into drowsy silence, and Norma Jeane pressed her forehead to the window, promising herself she would return one day, not as a foster child chaperoned by charity, but as someone who belonged.

The betrayals that mattered most came in whispers. One evening, Lila bent close in the dormitory, words trembling. A boarder in her foster home had touched her, eyes lingering too long, hands worse. She did not have to explain. The room went still. Doris clenched her fists, Betty cursed under her breath, Millie looked down at her shoes. Norma Jeane, not knowing what else to do, took Lila's hand. It was the only prayer they could muster.

But secrets leaked like water. Within a week, the story was repeated in cruel mouths. A girl outside their circle jeered, called Lila spoiled, ruined. Lila fled, sobbing. The Sisterhood fractured again, but this time there was no easy mending. Norma Jeane felt the breach in her chest like a fissure. She lay awake that night, the ceiling pressing down, whispering a vow into the dark: someday, someone would believe her.

The world beyond the orphanage was changing with a thunder none of them could ignore. Uniforms filled the streets, soldiers marching with shoulders squared, eyes hungry. Newsreels at the matinees blared images of war in Europe. At school, they practiced air-raid drills, ducking under desks as if wood could save them from bombs. They giggled nervously, but the fear lingered afterward, as stubborn as smog.

On street corners, radios crackled with Roosevelt's voice. The girls lingered at shop windows where mannequins wore satin gowns and rhinestone shoes. Betty pressed her palms against the glass. "One day," she swore. Ruthie nodded fiercely. Doris scoffed but stared as long as the rest. Norma Jeane hung back, studying her own reflection superimposed over the glamour: a girl in hand-me-downs, eyes wide with hunger for a future she could not yet name.

They teased each other about marrying soldiers, about singing for troops, about the famous lives they were destined for. Norma Jeane laughed along, but inside she kept her true prayer quiet. She wanted not marriage, not even fame—but safety. A place no one could send her away from.

The city spread its arms wider each time they ventured into it, and each time it reminded her how small she was. Still, the girls clung to each other as if their laughter, their whispered vows, could hold back the tides of war, hunger, men, abandonment. For a little while, they succeeded. For a little while, they believed.

The days lengthened, and with them the feeling that childhood was a temporary lodging, a hotel room from which they might be evicted at any hour. Norma Jeane sensed it in the way the matrons glanced at the older girls, measuring hips and hemlines, already deciding their futures. "Too pretty for her own good," she overheard one of them say once, and the words clung to her like a burr. She was learning that beauty was not a blessing but a sentence.

Still, the girls made their own sanctuaries. On hot nights, when the air inside the dormitory pressed heavy on their chests, they dragged mattresses near the windows and whispered stories until dawn. Doris described a house she had once known, its kitchen full of pie crusts and singing. Ruthie invented elaborate futures in New York, with skyscrapers and doormen and furs. Millie pretended she wanted nothing, though her voice trembled when she said it. Betty told them she was destined for the screen, her name in lights.

And Norma Jeane? She told them pieces, never the whole. That she wanted to be wanted. That she dreamed of a door that would open for her and never close again. She never admitted the darker wish—that she could be someone else entirely, someone whose name was already written in stars.

One evening, the girls dared each other to sneak into the attic. The stairs groaned like tattletales, the air thick with dust and mothballs. Trunks lined the walls, filled with forgotten clothes, cracked photo albums, broken toys. Ruthie draped herself in a moth-eaten fur and paraded like a movie star, Betty powdered her nose with century-old rouge, and Doris found a record player that whined out a ghostly waltz. They twirled until they collapsed in laughter, dizzy with dust and possibility.

Norma Jeane found a cracked mirror leaning against the rafters. She lifted it carefully, studying the reflection that wavered in the fractured glass. For a moment she didn't see the girl in hand-me-downs, the foster child with uncertain eyes. She saw a figure haloed by light, a face worth watching. She smiled into the shards, practicing. Later she would call it acting, modeling, performing. In truth, it was survival—learning how to become visible before the world decided to erase her.

The war shadowed everything. Posters demanded sacrifice, ration books clipped their meals, blackouts dimmed the city. Soldiers crowded the trolley cars, flirting with girls too young to understand the danger of the attention. Betty leaned into it, tossing her curls; Doris recoiled, sharp-tongued with refusal. Norma Jeane stood somewhere between—half flattered, half afraid, feeling the eyes on her like heat she could not escape.

One soldier offered her a stick of gum and asked her name. "Norma," she whispered, then quickly added, "Jeane." He repeated it, testing it on his tongue as though it might belong to someone else entirely. She never saw him again, but she carried the sound of it for weeks, savoring how her own name could feel foreign, new, as if it belonged to another girl who might yet be born.

The Sisterhood frayed as the months wore on. Doris was sent to relatives in Bakersfield, Millie to another foster home across town. Ruthie's family moved east for war work, and Betty was adopted by an aunt who dressed her like a doll and paraded her in patent leather shoes. Each departure was a wound. They promised letters, they swore they'd meet again, but absence stretched like an ocean. One by one, the circle dissolved.

On the last night before Doris left, the girls gathered in their blanket fort one final time. The flashlight flickered weakly, their blood-pact papers scattered around them like fallen leaves. No one wanted to speak of endings, so they told jokes instead, silly and desperate. When the light sputtered out, they sat in the dark, listening to each other's breathing, memorizing it. Norma Jeane felt their presence press into her skin, as if their shapes would remain imprinted long after they were gone.

She did not cry when they left. She had learned too well that tears changed nothing. Instead, she carried them with her—Betty's bravado, Doris's laugh, Millie's steadiness, Ruthie's dreams, Lila's trembling hand. They became ghosts who whispered to her in quiet moments, reminding her that she had once belonged, if only briefly.

Years later, on studio lots and dressing-room couches, she would find echoes of them in other women. The way Susan Strasberg clung to her arm, the fierce protection Natasha Lytess offered, the laughter of co-stars who drifted in and out of her life. She recognized the same hunger for connection, the same fragility disguised as strength. The lost girls of her childhood had prepared her for those bonds, teaching her both the sweetness of intimacy and the inevitability of its loss.

Walking the city streets alone, Norma Jeane often imagined she saw them again—on trolleys, in shop windows, slipping through the crowd at Grauman's. She would blink and they were gone, as if they had been inventions all along, conjured by a lonely child desperate to believe in sisterhood.

But in her heart, they were real. Real as the sand between her toes at the beach, as the taste of stolen fruit, as the shiver of blood-oaths under a quilted canopy. They were her first family, chosen not by birth or law but by need. And though they scattered, though the world swallowed them one by one, they left behind an unspoken legacy.

They taught her to survive by linking arms, to trust laughter even when it cracked, to believe that love—no matter how brief—was worth the risk. And when she finally stood before cameras and crowds, offering herself to a world that wanted to devour and adore her in equal measure, it was those lessons that held her steady.

She would always be, in some part of her soul, one of the lost girls. And that girl would always be waiting for the others to come back, believing they might step through the door again with stories, secrets, and promises of forever.

12

Uncle Marion's Big Camera

The story of Uncle Marion always began the same way in the Monroe family, whispered like a prayer too painful to say aloud but too heavy to ever forget. His name was Marion Otis Elmer Monroe, born in 1904 under the red-dirt skies of Oklahoma, the third of Della Monroe's brood and the most restless of them all. He was Gladys's brother, the handsome one, the sailor, the boy who looked best in uniform. And he was the one who never came back.

In the autumn of 1929, as the country collapsed under the Great Depression, Marion vanished into the streets of Los Angeles like a character written out of his own story. One morning he went to the US Submarine Base at San Pedro, where he worked as a seaman, and by nightfall he was gone. No note. No body. No explanation. The newspapers never carried his name. The police shrugged. The Navy recorded him as absent. His wife Olive put the children to bed and waited until waiting became unbearable, until she understood that nothing was returning but silence.

For Gladys, already fragile, it was a wound without sutures. She carried Marion's absence like a shard of glass in her chest, cutting deeper with every heartbeat. For Della, her mother, it was another chapter in a family saga that seemed cursed with instability. First, the broken marriages. Then the endless moves westward, chasing the fantasy of California sunshine that never quite warmed them. Now, a son who had disappeared in a city that swallowed people whole.

They told the children he was probably dead, though even that was only half-believed. "Presumed lost" became the official phrase. It carried the weight of tragedy but left the door ajar, as if one day he might stroll back through it in his sailor's cap, smiling sheepishly, explaining that he'd been away at sea. But the sea did not give him back.

In family photographs, he lived on: a young man with dark hair slicked back, eyes squinting against the glare of the California sun. In one cherished photo, Marion stood beside Della and little Jack, a cousin. Gladys kept that image like contraband, pulling it out in moments of solitude, as if staring hard enough might will him back to life. The photo became an icon of both beauty and grief, a reminder that sometimes the people you love most become ghosts before you even have the chance to say goodbye.

Norma Jeane would be born years later, in 1926, three years before Marion's vanishing. She never met her uncle, but she grew up in the echo of his absence. The adults spoke his name in hushed tones, their faces closing like shutters whenever questions were asked. For a child, silence is louder than truth. She felt the hole he had left, even if she could not yet name it.

Marion's disappearance was more than a family tragedy; it was a pattern, another seam ripped open in the Monroe fabric. Men left. They died, they drank, they strayed, they vanished. Gladys's own father had deserted the family long before, leaving Della to scrape by with what dignity she could salvage. Now her brother had simply walked out of the frame of their lives. For Norma Jeane, absorbing these stories as she grew, it planted a terror that would haunt her forever: the fear of abandonment, the fear of being left behind with no explanation.

The family tried to remember Marion as the bright one, the daring one. They spoke of his sailor's adventures, his laughter, the way he could charm a room. But shadows always hovered at the edge of those recollections. There were rumors, never spoken aloud in front of children, about gambling, debts, perhaps other women. The Great Depression made men desperate; Los Angeles swallowed them whole with promises it couldn't keep. Did Marion run from his responsibilities? Was he pulled into darker waters by forces unseen? Or did he fall victim to something more brutal, the kind of crime that left no trace but absence?

Gladys carried these questions with her like stones. She had already endured so much: the loss of custody of her first two children, the grind of working at the film lab, the gnawing instability in her own mind. Marion's disappearance became another fracture in her sense of safety. If her brother could vanish without explanation, so could anyone. So could love itself.

When Norma Jeane was old enough to understand, she was shown the photograph of Uncle Marion. It was offered with the reverence of a relic. "That's your uncle," someone whispered—whether Gladys or Della or another relative, she could not remember later. What she did remember was the face: strong, handsome, a stranger whose blood ran in her veins. To a little girl desperate for family, for belonging, the photo became proof that she came from somewhere, that there were people tethered to her name.

But it was also a warning. Here was a man whose absence had defined an entire family, a reminder that even the ones who loved you could disappear without a trace. For the rest of her life, Norma Jeane would treasure photographs—snapshots, headshots, publicity stills—as if they could pin people in place, prevent them from vanishing. In photographs, everyone stayed. No one left. No one disappeared into the Los Angeles night, never to be heard from again.

Marion's story ended in mystery, but its shadow stretched long. It fell across Gladys, across Della, and finally across the little girl who would one day become Marilyn Monroe. She would carry that shadow into every role, every marriage, every desperate attempt to hold onto the people she loved. The missing uncle became more than a family ghost. He became a metaphor for the fragility of love itself—the way it could dissolve without warning, leaving only a picture and a story no one wanted to finish.

As the years passed, Marion's disappearance began to shift shape in the Monroe household. It was less an event than a legend, less a loss than a parable whispered over kitchen tables. Children weren't told the full story, but they caught fragments, like torn pieces of film reel spliced together: "the Navy," "San Pedro," "never came home." For Norma Jeane, those fragments became a private fairy tale, except this one ended not with happily-ever-after but with a door swinging shut in the dark.

She would overhear the grown-ups when they thought she wasn't listening. Della insisting, "He was a good boy, my Marion, he wouldn't have left us like that." Gladys muttering, "People don't just vanish. Somebody knows." Others shrugging, "That's Los Angeles. Swallows men whole." The not-knowing was the cruelest part, a wound that never scabbed over.

Children are sponges, and Norma Jeane soaked it all up. She knew she came from a family where men drifted away. Her grandfather, her father, her uncle—all gone, each in their own fashion. And she understood, even before she had the words, that this pattern might repeat, that the world was full of doors men walked through, never to return.

That's why she clung so hard to photographs. A photo didn't disappear. A face, once caught, could not vanish. Gladys kept Marion's photograph close, and when Norma Jeane first saw it, she felt a jolt of recognition: a stranger, yes, but one whose eyes were familiar. She traced his jawline with her fingertip. She stared at the uniform, the proud set of his shoulders. She whispered questions to the picture when no one was around. Where did you go? Why didn't you come back? Would you have stayed for me?

Sometimes, she dreamed of him. In her dreams, he was not lost at sea or swallowed by Los Angeles, but alive, standing in the doorway like a returning hero. She imagined him scooping her up, spinning her around, telling her she looked just like her mother, just like family. She invented conversations with the man in the photograph, as if a picture could answer back.

Gladys, fragile and brittle, also wrapped herself in those fantasies. Marion's absence seemed to loosen her grip on reality even further. She would talk about him in the present tense, as if he had merely gone away for a while. "When Marion comes home . . ." she'd begin, and then trail off, her eyes glassy. Sometimes, she'd weep suddenly, clutching at Norma Jeane as though the child might vanish too.

That fear seeped into the little girl. It taught her that love was never guaranteed, that even family could be stolen by silence. At the orphanage, when bells dictated her hours and strangers dictated her meals, she remembered Uncle Marion's photograph and felt kinship with his absence. She was absent too, in a way—absent from her mother's home, absent from the security other children seemed to have.

The Monroe family spoke of Marion's disappearance with the same mixture of reverence and resentment that they spoke of other tragedies. It was folded into their larger story: a history of abandonment, instability, and dreams deferred. For Norma Jeane, it became a warning that men could be dangerous in more ways than one. They could hurt you by what they did. They could hurt you by what they failed to do. And worst of all, they could hurt you by simply not being there.

Later, when Norma Jeane was older and the world began photographing her in earnest, she thought often of that photograph of Marion. Did he know, when the camera caught his image, that it would outlive him? That it would become his legacy, his only proof of having been? Perhaps that was why the camera felt like a spell to her, why she trusted it to hold her in ways people never seemed to. A camera couldn't walk out. A camera couldn't disappear.

The irony was inescapable: the girl who grew up clinging to a single photograph of a vanished uncle would one day become the most photographed woman in the world. Her entire career would be built on the faith that if a camera caught you, you couldn't be erased. Each flashbulb was her defiance of absence, her declaration against disappearing.

In quiet moments, though, the shadow of Marion still lingered. Fame couldn't erase family ghosts. Love affairs couldn't undo inherited wounds. Even at the height of her stardom, when men crowded around her and the world seemed to belong to her image, she still feared that at any moment it could all vanish—like a sailor walking to work one November morning and never coming home.

In Hollywood, Norma Jeane became Marilyn Monroe, but she never stopped being the little girl who whispered to photographs. Behind every camera flash that gilded her face, there was the ghost of Uncle Marion, caught in a single picture and then gone. She often said that photographs felt more real than people, and perhaps that was why. People left. Film remained.

Her marriage to Jim Dougherty, the boy next door who became her husband at sixteen, was in some ways an attempt to anchor herself against that pattern of disappearances. He was steady, kind, the opposite of vanishing. Yet even as she folded his shirts and packed his lunches, she sensed how fragile permanence could be. When he went off to sea with the merchant marines, she kissed him goodbye as if she were kissing her uncle's ghost, bracing herself for another loss.

When the photographers at the munitions factory first turned their lenses on her, she felt the old thrill—not of being admired, not yet, but of being secured. Every snap of the shutter meant: you exist, you are here, you will not be forgotten. Unlike Uncle Marion, she would leave behind thousands of images. The camera was her insurance policy against disappearance.

But insurance is never the same as peace. Even at her most radiant, she carried within her that undertow of abandonment. Lovers spoke of it—how she could be intoxicating one moment and unreachable the next, as though her soul had one foot always halfway out the door. "Don't leave me," she whispered to more than one man, her plea echoing the prayer she had once made to a photograph.

She rarely spoke of Uncle Marion in public. He was part of the private Monroe tragedy, and the studios preferred their blonde bombshell to have a cleaner lineage. Yet in her private conversations, she would mention him—"my uncle who disappeared." She said it with a strange mixture of awe and fear, as if his absence were a family inheritance, a shadow passed down like eye color.

Even in her final years, when she posed for Bert Stern in that famous *Last Sitting*, her vulnerability was less about nudity than about presence. She was offering herself fully to the lens, insisting: I am here, I exist, remember me. The ghost of Uncle Marion hovered, as he always had.

The truth is, Norma Jeane never solved the riddle of his disappearance. No one did. But the not-knowing shaped her more profoundly than any answer could have. It taught her that absence can be louder than presence, that silence can be more enduring than speech. And it made her resolve, consciously or not, to fill the world with her image until there was no space left for forgetting.

When she died in 1962, the headlines announced it around the globe. Millions mourned. Her face was printed on the front pages of newspapers from Los Angeles to Tokyo. She had become unforgettable. And perhaps, in some corner of her restless soul, that was the victory she had been chasing all along—the triumph over the fate of Uncle Marion, the sailor who disappeared and left behind nothing but a picture.

For Norma Jeane, the photograph had always been more than paper and ink. It was the promise that a life, once seen, could not vanish without a trace.

Norma Jeane as a young child, playing on a beach in a striped bathing suit. Getty Premium Access / Hulton Archive / Stringer

Norma Jeane at age four, standing with a little boy outdoors. Getty Premium Access / Hulton Archive / Stringer

Norma Jeane playing with dogs in a rural garden, circa 1933. Getty Premium Access / Silver Screen Collection / Contributor

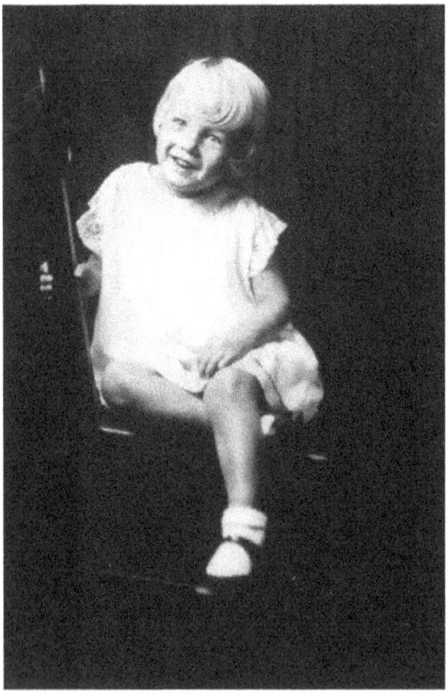

Norma Jeane at age five. Getty Premium Access / Hulton Archive / Stringer

Norma Jeane on the beach as a toddler with her mother, Gladys Baker, circa 1929. Getty Premium Access / Silver Screen Collection / Contributor

Norma Jeane Baker (bottom right) with her mother, Gladys Baker (top right), and friends, circa 1929. Getty Premium Access / Silver Screen Collection / Contributor

Norma Jeane Baker (right) with two small friends and a birthday cake, circa 1936. Getty Premium Access / Silver Screen Collection / Contributor

Norma Jeane Baker at a Chinese restaurant with members of her family, circa 1942. Getty Premium Access / Silver Screen Collection / Contributor

Norma Jeane Baker (right) on the beach as a small child, circa 1930. Getty Premium Access / Silver Screen Collection / Contributor

Newly signed 20th Century-Fox contract girl Marilyn Monroe poses for a portrait in 1947 in Los Angeles, California. Getty Premium Access / Earl Theisen Collection / Contributor

Marilyn Monroe with her first husband, police officer James Dougherty. Getty Premium Access / Sunset Boulevard / Contributor

Actress Marilyn Monroe, then known as Norma Jeane Mortenson, poses for a portrait in 1946 in Los Angeles, California. Getty Premium Access / Donaldson Collection / Contributor

A teenaged Norma Jeane Baker circa 1940. Getty Premium Access / Silver Screen Collection / Contributor

Norma Jeane Baker as a teenager, circa 1938. Just behind her is Ana Lower ("Aunt Ana"), a family friend with whom she lived for a while. Getty Premium Access / Silver Screen Collection / Contributor

Actress Marilyn Monroe poses for a portrait in 1947. Getty Premium Access / Michael Ochs Archives / Stringer

13

The First One Who Touched Her

It began with trust. The kind that only a child can give—unquestioning, wholehearted, naïve. He was a friend of the foster family, a man with an easy smile, the kind of visitor who carried candy in his pocket and seemed to know the names of children without ever being told. His laughter filled the kitchen like sunshine, his voice dipped with concern when he asked about school, about her health, about how she was settling in. To a girl who was passed from house to house like an afterthought, his attention felt like a gift.

Norma Jeane had learned early how to read adults. She could tell which ones were likely to scold and which ones would slip her an extra cookie after dinner. She had learned to weigh every glance and gesture, to anticipate moods the way sailors watch the weather. But this man confused her. He looked at her with a kind of focus that was neither fatherly nor careless. It was a gaze she didn't yet understand but felt somewhere deep in her bones, a vibration of unease she had no words for.

That afternoon the house was too quiet. The Bolenders were out. The walls seemed to hum with stillness. He told her she was pretty. Not in the way Ida did when she brushed out her curls before church, not in the way Albert did when he said she looked neat and respectable. No—this was different. His voice lingered on the word, soft and heavy at once, as if it were a secret just between them.

She smiled the way she had been taught to smile when grown-ups noticed her, but her stomach twisted. When he reached out, his hand landing on her shoulder as if to steady her, she froze. Children are not equipped for betrayal; they don't expect it from those who seem safe. She did not flinch, did not pull away. When his hand moved lower, she went still as glass.

He told her it was their secret. That she was special. That no one would believe her if she said otherwise. His words fell into her like stones into a well, sinking, sinking, until they touched the bottom of her silence. She did not scream. She did not run. She learned, in that single moment, the terrible trick of leaving her body behind, floating up into her mind while the skin below her stiffened and endured.

Afterward, she adjusted her dress, smoothed the fabric, and tried to pretend nothing had changed. But everything had.

The room looked the same—the same wallpaper, the same dull light filtering through the curtains—but its safety had evaporated. The chair by the window was no longer just a chair; it was the place where she had been made to feel like a thing instead of a girl. The floor beneath her feet had betrayed her by staying still when she wanted it to open and swallow her whole.

That night, lying in bed, she held her pillow close. Not for comfort but for protection, as though clutching it might keep it from turning against her the way her own trust had. She stared at the ceiling until her eyes burned, afraid to close them, afraid of what waited in the dark. Sleep, once a fragile refuge, had become a place of ambush.

And yet she told no one. Not Ida, whose stern faith left little room for the messy confessions of a frightened girl. Not Albert, who had always seemed kind but distant, too reserved to be burdened with what she didn't even know how to name. Certainly not Gladys, who floated in and out of her life like a ghost, incapable of tethering herself to her daughter's pain.

Silence became her armor. If she never spoke it aloud, perhaps it would fade. Perhaps it would not be real.

But silence, she would discover, does not erase. It burrows. It festers. It becomes part of the marrow.

The days that followed blurred together, but inside her, something sharp had taken root. She walked through the Bolender house with the same obedient steps, folded her hands for grace at the table, memorized her hymns and her lessons—but a thin film now separated her from the rest of the world. She was present but untouchable, like a ghost pretending to be a girl.

She avoided being alone with him again, though she never asked aloud to be spared. That would have meant speaking of what happened, and she had locked it away. Instead, she practiced invisibility. She became expert at disappearing into corners, at finding errands to run or chores to busy herself with when he came around. If she had to cross the same room, she smiled too brightly, laughed too quickly, cloaked herself in a performance so rehearsed that even the Bolenders believed in it.

She was still only a child, but she learned then the oldest trick of survival: make yourself agreeable, entertaining, untouchable by pretending you are exactly what they want. She smiled when it hurt, spoke when she wanted silence, laughed when she wanted to cry. She became two people—the one who endured and the one who performed.

At school, she tried harder to be liked. She memorized classmates' jokes, carried extra pencils to lend, helped the younger children with their sums. If she was indispensable, maybe she would also be safe. But the boys' glances lingered too long, and she felt that familiar unease rising again, like a shadow slipping under the door. Their eyes were not yet his eyes, but they carried the same seed of entitlement.

One afternoon, walking home, she caught her reflection in a shop window. For the first time, she did not see only a little girl. Her dress hung differently on her growing body, her curls framed her face in a way that felt older, her mouth seemed too knowing. She turned away quickly, unsettled. Beauty, she realized, was dangerous. Attention was a blade that could cut both ways.

But she also saw, in that same reflection, a kind of power. If people were going to look at her that way, perhaps she could decide what they saw. Perhaps she could control the gaze, shape it, play with it. She was too young to name this as performance, but instinctively she began to rehearse. In the mirror at home she practiced smiles—shy, coy, dazzling. She tilted her head just so, lowered her lashes, discovered which angles softened her features, which ones made her eyes burn brighter.

It wasn't vanity. It was self-defense disguised as charm.

The world thought she was harmless, a pretty child. But inside, she was already a strategist. Already learning that if she gave them what they wanted on the surface, she might protect what was breaking underneath.

When years later interviewers asked about her childhood, she often said she never really had one. This was the reason. The moment that man touched her, the carefree part of her girlhood collapsed. In its place grew the beginnings of Marilyn Monroe—the smile that could disarm a room, the laugh that covered wounds, the eyes that promised secrets no one was ever truly allowed to touch.

But at night, when the house was still, the mask slipped. Alone in her narrow bed, she curled around her pillow and let her mind drift far away. She imagined her father—whether Clark Gable, as her mother once teased, or some faceless man who might still come to claim her. She imagined a family who would keep her safe, who would not let strangers into the house, who would fight off the shadows on her behalf. She whispered these daydreams into the dark like prayers, though she did not know who, if anyone, was listening.

The world would never know this part of her. They would see the performance and call it seduction, call it charm, call it magic. They would not understand that it began as a shield. That before she learned how to conquer the camera, she first had to conquer the terror of being touched when she had no say.

It was the first fracture in a life that would be full of them. The first scar she carried in silence. The first rehearsal for the role that would one day consume her.

By the time she was fourteen, the memory had hardened into silence. It was not a story she could tell, not to the Bolenders, not to Grace, not to the girls at school with their easy chatter about dances and lipstick shades. It lived inside her like a knot of glass, invisible yet sharp enough to cut whenever she brushed against it. She learned to step carefully around it, even in her own thoughts.

But silence does not erase. It echoes. In the way she flinched at the sudden brush of a hand. In the way her body stiffened when a compliment lingered too long. In the way she laughed at jokes that made her stomach twist, because laughter was safer than protest.

Men noticed her earlier than most girls. Her figure, still soft with childhood but quickening into curves, drew glances that she had not asked for. She carried books against her chest like a shield, but the eyes still followed. Some were boys from school, awkward and overeager. Others were older—boarders in the houses where she stayed, men in hats passing on the street, shopkeepers whose smiles slid into something else. She told herself they were only looking. But she remembered how quickly looking could turn to touching, and how quickly touching could turn to shame.

So she practiced defense by disguise. She smiled. She tilted her head. She let her voice lift into playfulness when she wanted to scream. Better to control the attention than to be caught off guard by it. She learned to trade in gestures: a glance that suggested promise, a laugh that suggested permission, even when she meant neither. This was not flirtation. It was survival.

And yet, deep inside, she carried another truth. That touch, unwanted and unspoken of, had awakened something she despised and desired in equal measure: the knowledge that she could move people. That even as a child, she had held a kind of power that men recognized before she did. It was a dangerous power, but it was hers. And once she understood that, she began to experiment—not recklessly, but with a quiet, secret curiosity.

In front of the mirror she became her own audience. She practiced expressions, poses, half-smiles that hinted at more than they showed. She was still years away from the studio lights, but already she was rehearsing Marilyn. Already she understood that attention could be molded, shaped, turned like a spotlight. If she had to endure it, she would also learn how to command it.

Her friends sometimes teased her for being dreamy, for staring too long at her reflection in a shop window. They didn't know she was studying herself the way other children studied textbooks, trying to unlock the secrets of protection and belonging. They didn't know that every gesture was an experiment in control, that every smile was armor polished to brilliance.

The wound did not heal. It calcified into performance. When she was fifteen and a boy pressed her hand too tightly at a school dance, she smiled through it. When another whispered something crude in her ear, she laughed as though she'd heard a joke. None of them knew that behind the laughter was the echo of the man who told her no one would believe her.

But the silence was not empty. It was filled with longing—for someone to believe, for someone to see her not as a body to be claimed but as a girl still trying to understand herself. That longing bled into her friendships with other girls. With them, she could be playful, goofy, unguarded for a few moments. They became her refuge, her rehearsal space for a kind of intimacy that was safe. She clung to them, perhaps too tightly at times, hungry for the trust she could not give to men.

And yet, she could not escape the paradox. The same beauty that drew her friends close drew men closer still. She was already caught in the contradiction that would define her life: the need to be loved and the fear of what that love would cost.

Later, the world would look at Marilyn Monroe—the woman draped in silk, the woman whose lips parted like an invitation, the woman whose body shimmered on screen—and believe she had been born to seduce. They would not know that seduction was first a shield, forged in the terror of a child too young to name what had been done to her. They would not see the ghost of the little girl who clutched her pillow at night, whispering to a father who never came, promising herself that next time she would be ready, next time she would not be caught so defenseless.

The first one who touched her left no visible scar, but the invisible ones shaped everything. They shaped the way she walked into rooms, the way she leaned into cameras, the way she balanced innocence with allure as if her life depended on it—because once, it had.

And though she never told, though she locked the story away behind laughter and lipstick, it lived inside her. Every time she played the part of the woman who wanted, she remembered the girl who had no choice. Every time she smiled for the world, she remembered the silence she had swallowed. And every time she lay awake at night, staring at the ceiling, she remembered the weight of hands that had turned her childhood into something she could never get back.

That was the truth beneath the myth. Before the spotlight, before the icon, before the dream that became Marilyn Monroe, there was only Norma Jeane—a girl whose first lesson in love was betrayal, whose first lesson in desire was danger, and whose first performance was survival.

14

The Night the Clock Went Dark

The Los Angeles Orphans Home sat on its little rise above Pleasant Avenue like a reprimand. From the street it looked almost prim: pale walls, straight hedges, a front walk scrubbed so clean it seemed no one had ever tracked real dirt across it. But it was the fence that told the truth. The iron bars climbed higher than any child's reach, their spear-tips pointed at the sky as if to warn heaven itself to keep its distance.

And above the fence, above the roofline, rose the tower.

The clock lived there.

Its white face and black hands looked down on the children with the same blank attention the matrons used. It did not smile, did not soften. It simply marked their days in segments—wake, wash, eat, pray, work, sleep—like slices of bread cut from the same hard loaf. To everyone who worked in the Home it was the Orphanage Clock, dependable and dutiful. To the children, it was the warden.

When nine-year-old Norma Jeane first arrived, clutching a small satchel that held almost nothing, the social worker's hand rested on her shoulder like a temporary claim. "This will be good for you," the woman said, the way people did when they wanted to be finished with a hard thing. "You'll be safe here."

Safe. The word had teeth.

The matron signed the papers, asked the questions she always asked—name, age, religion, next of kin—and then, as if remembering an afterthought, glanced down and added, "Pretty child." The social worker nodded, as though prettiness could be listed on a form.

While they talked, the clock struck the hour. The sound rolled down over the roof and into the tiled corridors, into the dining hall, into the dormitories, into the nursery where a baby had begun to cry. The clang swallowed the baby's sobs. It swallowed the matron's words. It seemed to swallow even the small space where a frightened girl might have imagined an escape hatch.

In that sound, she heard forever.

Orphanage life taught her quickly that time did not belong to children. Time belonged to the institution.

Wake-up came with a bell and the matron's hard-soled steps on linoleum. Beds had to be made tight enough to bounce a coin. Faces and hands scrubbed in basins of water that was always either too cold or too hot, never simply kind. The girls lined up by height, then by age, then by whatever order pleased the matrons that morning. Breakfast was ladled, not served: oatmeal that could have caulked windows, toast that shattered into crumbs like it had been baked during the Hoover administration.

Ten minutes to eat. The clock watched.

Then school: rows of desks, chalk dust floating in stale light, lessons delivered in the sing-song rhythm of people who had said the same words so often they no longer heard them. Multiplication tables. Bible verses. Penmanship. The girls bent over their copybooks, the boys over theirs, all of them trying to fit their crooked childhoods into the straight lines of the letters.

After that came chores. Scrubbing floors, polishing railings, pulling weeds from a patch of dirt dignified as "the garden." They tended that stubborn little square of earth like it might reward them with something more than cabbages. Mostly it gave them blisters and something to bend over so they didn't have to meet anyone's eyes.

Even playtime had borders. The playground was fenced in like a smaller version of the institution itself: swings that complained loudly on rusted chains, a slide that burned bare legs in summer and numbed them in winter, a patch of grass that was always somehow both worn and off-limits. But here, for a few minutes each day, the clock's voice softened into the background, and the children tried to remember what it was to be simply young.

On the swing, Norma Jeane found her favorite rebellion. She pumped her skinny legs with all the force she had until the chains slackened for a heartbeat at the top of the arc. In that weightless moment she felt she might fly—not just over the fence, but away from every wall that had ever contained her. She could almost hear the clock protesting behind her, its hands still ticking, still insisting that she return to earth and schedule. But she kept chasing that slack moment, that breath where gravity forgot her name.

It was the closest thing to freedom the orphanage allowed.

Nights were ruled by the clock even more cruelly than days. The dormitory was a long room of iron cots and whitewashed walls, the ceiling light caged in wire as though the bulb might try to escape. The baby down the hall cried like an alarm the world refused to answer. Eventually, even the baby tired out, and the hush that followed was worse. Silence in the orphanage was not peaceful; it was a held breath.

In that hushed space, the clock's ticking expanded. Tick. Tick. Tick. It was not a gentle sound. It was precise, accusatory, like a pencil scoring lines through days on a calendar no one had promised would lead anywhere.

Sleep had never been simple for her, not since the night her mother's shaking hands had pressed a pillow too long over her face. Even here, in a place with rules and bedtimes and inspections, danger clung to the dark. She lay rigid on her narrow mattress, breathing carefully, one hand on her chest to reassure herself it still rose and fell. If she pressed the pillow against her own face now, she could choose when to pull it away. That choice belonged to her. It was a small kind of power, borrowed from the same place as the swing's slack chain.

Across the rows of cots, other girls wept in silence. They had been taught not to wail, not to demand, not to be noisy in their grief. The orphanage was full of unshed tears that ended up in dishwater and laundry basins instead of on anyone's shoulder.

Sometimes, in the soft, rule-breaking minutes after lights out, the girls traded stories—not candy, not toys, but stories. They dealt in futures the way gamblers dealt in cards.

"My daddy works on a ship."

"My mama's just sick. She's in a sanitarium. When she gets better, she'll come."

"My auntie promised she'd send for me."

Some of them believed their own stories. Some did not. Belief was not the point. The act of saying the words aloud made the waiting less deadly.

When it was her turn, Norma Jeane embroidered her tale like a seamstress who had only scraps but refused to admit it. Her mother was away, but only for now. Her father was important, busy, maybe a movie star. They would come for her when things were better. She spoke with such quiet conviction that sometimes, in the half-light, even she found herself fooled.

The one story she never shared was about the pillow.

The clock also presided over departures.

Sometimes a child was chosen. There was always a hush that settled over the dormitory when the news rippled through: So-and-so is leaving. Relatives had written, or strangers had applied, or a couple had walked through the halls and pointed. The chosen child's bed was stripped, their meager belongings folded into a suitcase or tied into a bundle. The others watched with a mixture of envy and dread. They smiled, they hugged, they wished good luck. Then they returned to their rows and lay awake that night staring at the empty bed, as if it might accuse them of being left behind.

Rescue was not always safe. Some of the chosen ones came back months later, quieter and smaller, their eyes older than their bodies. Others never returned at all, their names slipping out of use, their faces fading until even memory felt like a betrayal.

The orphanage never spoke of those returns, or of the homes that had sent them back. It was another silence layered on top of so many others. But the children noticed. Children always notice.

Norma Jeane noticed most of all.

The clock, of course, did not care who left or who returned. It counted only hours. But in her mind, she gave it motives. The clock was the thing you had to outlast. If you could endure enough of its chimes and ticks, if you could keep breathing through its commands, one day it might be forced to let you walk away alive.

The winter she turned 10, the storm came.

Rain had battered Los Angeles all afternoon, turning the streets below the hill into shining black ribbons. The orphanage windows rattled in their frames. The heaters clanged and hissed, doing their best to stand between the children and the damp. The sisters in the kitchen brewed huge urns of weak cocoa for themselves and pretended not to notice the way the children stared at the steam.

That night, the wind rose. It howled around the corners of the building like something shut out and offended by it. The younger children whimpered in their sleep; the older ones, who should have been too tough for fear, stared at the shifting shadows on the ceiling.

Then, without warning, the lights went out.

Darkness dropped into the dormitory like a stone into a still pond. There was a collective intake of breath, then a chorus of frightened cries. Somewhere down the hall, a matron shouted for calm, her voice thin without her usual authority of light and order.

For the first time since she had arrived, the soft green numerals of the electric clock on the far wall were gone. Its face, usually a steady glow, was blind. The ticking fell silent. In that sudden quiet, the absence was almost brutal.

No ticking. No chime. No measured, merciless division of the night.

For a moment, she felt the sharp edge of terror. Time had vanished. Without the clock, how would morning come? How would anything come? If the hands stopped moving, what if nothing ever changed again and they were trapped in this dark forever?

And then, as her eyes adjusted, the terror shifted.

The dormitory began to reveal itself in shapes: the dull shine of metal bedframes, the pale smudges of faces turned toward her, the glimmer of streetlight bleeding through the high, narrow windows. Over everything lay a strange new softness. Without the clock's tick, without its little electric hum, the night seemed unpinned. Borderless.

She was used to being trapped in other people's time—her mother's breakdowns, the social worker's schedule, the orphanage routine. This was different. This felt like floating outside of time altogether.

In the bed beside her, a girl began to sob. Someone else hissed for her to hush before the matrons came and assigned punishments in the dark. The girl choked on her own crying, swallowing it like something she would be blamed for wasting.

Norma Jeane could have reached out and taken her hand. Instead, she did the one thing she had practiced more than perhaps anything else in her short life: she told a story.

Her voice was barely more than a breath, but across the narrow gap between their beds it carried.

"Once upon a time," she whispered, "there was a princess locked in a tower."

The girl sniffed, the crying catching mid-sob. Another head lifted on another pillow. Fingers curled over the metal bars of the nearest cot. Someone said, "Shh, listen," and for once they weren't talking about the clock.

"The tower was tall," she went on, "so tall it scraped the clouds. And there was a wall around it and another wall around that wall, and a forest, and a moat, and everybody said: No one gets out of there. Not ever. Not the princess, not anyone."

"Like us," breathed a voice to her left.

"Exactly like us," she said. "Only the princess had something nobody knew about."

"What?" someone demanded, in the impatient tone of a child who has been denied everything except curiosity.

"She had wings," said Norma Jeane. "But she didn't know it yet."

She spun the story longer, pulling threads from every fairy tale she'd ever half-remembered and weaving them together with scraps of movies, scraps of wish. Outside, the storm battered the roof. Inside, the girls huddled in their beds, invisible to anyone who might have cared, and listened to a girl with no family describe a princess discovering that she could fly.

In the story, the tower began to crumble. In the story, the walls shrank. In the story, the princess ran to the edge of the highest parapet, spread the wings she hadn't known were there, and launched herself into the night.

"She flew away from the tower," murmured Norma Jeane, half-hypnotized by the world she was making. "She flew so far that even the clocks couldn't find her."

The girl beside her gave a small, triumphant sigh. "Tell it again tomorrow," she said drowsily, as the storm's fury began to ebb.

"I will," she promised.

And she did. Night after night, piece by piece, she added to the saga of the princess in the tower. The story lengthened the way a child tries to lengthen cake by taking the smallest possible bites. It wasn't just entertainment; it was survival. For an hour each night, they were not orphans in regimented beds under a merciless clock. They were co-conspirators in an escape.

The power came back the next morning. The clock resumed its reign, its face lit, its hands marching. But something had shifted. She had felt the world without its ticking. She had learned, in that one blackout, that even the most permanent-seeming rules could fail.

The knowledge lodged inside her like a seed.

There were other small rebellions.

On the playground swing she chased that feeling of the blackout—of being unmoored from schedule and command. In the laundry room, where steam rose like ghosts, she let a few quiet tears flow and counted it as a luxury. At the inspection line she polished her shoes so well the leather reflected her face; she liked seeing herself there, small but undeniable, as if she were signing each day with her own image: I was here. I existed.

And in front of the bathroom mirror, she rehearsed.

It began almost as a game. After one of the rare movie outings the orphanage arranged—a cheap matinee for which they'd marched in two-by-two, scrubbed and stiff—she shuffled back into the dormitory trailing the images behind her like a train. The screen had been full of women whose lives were nothing like hers: sparkling gowns, glamorous tears, the kind of sorrow that made men lean in tenderly instead of backing away. They were abandoned, sometimes, or misunderstood, but always in a way that made them luminous.

In the warped mirror, she tried on their expressions the way other girls might try on dresses. A half-smile, full of mischief. A tragic gaze, a little up and to the side. A sudden, delighted laugh that made it seem as though the world had surprised her kindly.

The other girls teased her—"Look at our movie star"—but their voices held a streak of longing. They tried the faces too when they thought no one was looking.

She discovered that she liked holding her own gaze. In a place where she was one among dozens, one more mouth, one more cot, her reflection was a private audience. She talked to that girl in the glass the way she talked to the invented father in the magazine photographs.

"One day we'll get out," she would murmur. "One day we'll walk right past that clock and it won't be able to stop us."

Years later, when the flashbulbs popped and directors asked her to turn her head just so, to give them something "no one could look away from," she wasn't inventing from nothing. She was drawing on all those stolen minutes in the orphanage lavatory, all those nights of making other children forget where they were. She had been rehearsing for fame in a dress that smelled of lye and hung on a nail.

Holidays at the orphanage were exercises in almost.

At Christmas, a tree appeared in the main hall, its branches hung with paper stars and a few tired strands of tinsel that had seen more winters than most of the children. The girls and boys were given "gifts"—castoffs from charity drives, toys that had already had their first lives with other, luckier kids. A doll missing an arm. A book scribbled in. A scarf someone's aunt had knit in the wrong color and decided to feel virtuous by donating.

Norma Jeane accepted each offering with a smile that was half politeness, half hunger. Later, sitting on her cot, she ran her fingers over the cheap fabric, the chipped paint, the scribbled margins. The objects were supposed to stand in for love. They never quite did.

Once, there was cake.

It arrived on chipped plates, a thin sheet cut into exact rectangles cunningly arranged to look more generous than they were. In each slice was a single raisin, pressed carefully into the crust. The other children swallowed theirs in three bites, eager for the rare sweetness. She held hers on her tongue as long as she could and pretended it was rich with frosting, with cream, with every dessert she had ever seen in a movie.

She was not pretending it was cake. She was pretending it was being cherished made edible.

Childhood, she would one day say, was something she didn't have. What she meant was: she did not have anyone to share it with. Childhood is not simply a set of years; it is a set of witnesses. Someone to remember the cake with you. Someone to laugh about how small the pieces were. Someone to say: yes, you were there, and I saw you.

At the orphanage, the witnesses kept leaving. The clock saw everything and remembered nothing.

Once, there was a Christmas pageant. The staff decided the girls should put on a nativity play. Someone needed to be Mary, someone Joseph, someone shepherds and wise men. A few others would be angels.

They pinned a white sheet over her dress and fastened cardboard wings to her shoulders with string that bit into her skin. A tinsel halo, gone slightly rusty with age, perched on her curls. The whole thing might have been ridiculous, but when she stepped onto the makeshift stage in the multipurpose room, a strange stillness came over her.

Every eye in the orphanage was on her.

The clock on the wall behind the audience ticked, but for once she couldn't hear it. She lifted her arms—not to fly, not this time, but to bless the sad little gathering with their paper crowns and crooked staffs. It was a play, nothing more. Yet when the staff and children clapped, polite and brief, she felt the applause run through her like current.

They saw me, she thought. For one minute, they all saw me.

The costume went back in the box afterward. The wings were folded, flattened, forgotten. But the memory stayed. The girl who told princess stories in the dark, who flew on rusty swings, who marked time under a merciless clock had discovered something serious: applause was proof you existed.

In later years, interviewers would ask her about the orphanage. Sometimes she would tell them there was no childhood to speak of, that she had started out as a grown woman in a little girl's body. Other times she would say nothing at all. What could she explain? That her strongest memory was not of a single event, but of a sound—the relentless ticking of a clock that belonged to everyone and no one?

What she rarely said, even to herself, was that the orphanage had given her two gifts it never intended.

First, it gave her a hunger so vast it could never be filled by one person's love. Only a world's would do. The absence of being chosen carved out a hollow that later millions of eyes could only half-fill. Every camera, every crowd, every adoring letter felt like one more tick against the old, indifferent metronome.

Second, it taught her how to turn invisibility into performance. She learned to read faces the way the matron read ledgers: who could be charmed, who could be defied. She learned to smile when she was breaking inside, to cry on cue, to sweeten her voice just enough to draw a little warmth in a cold place. Those were not tricks she picked up in acting class. They were habits acquired in survival.

The night the clock went dark was, in the grand sweep of things, a tiny incident in a city full of bigger dramas. The storm passed. The power returned. Breakfast was served at the usual hour. Chores resumed. The matron scolded the girls for their "carryings-on" during the blackout and docked them playtime for the next day.

But for a girl with no one to claim her memories, it was a kind of private genesis.

She had seen the institution without its spine. She had felt time falter. She had discovered that when the official voice of the world fell silent, another voice could rise—a small one, a child's, spinning tales of wings and escape.

The orphanage thought it was teaching her discipline. It thought it was teaching her gratitude and humility and the art of not asking for more than what was given. What it actually taught her was how to live under a clock and dream past it. How to let the tick-tock of neglect become the backbeat to a performance that would, one day, drown it out.

And so the hands turned, and the bell rang, and the children lined up, and the world went on. In a narrow bed under the high windows, a girl lay awake, listening. Not to the clock not anymore—but to the faint echo of imagined wings.

15

School Pictures and Secondhand Shoes

She always smiled in school pictures. Chin tilted just so, eyes widened to catch the light, a smile stretched beyond the measure of her mood. The teacher would dab at her forehead with a paper towel, hand her a comb with missing teeth, and murmur, *You're photogenic.* Norma Jeane didn't know the word, not at first, but she learned its meaning in the way the teacher's voice softened, the way the other children looked over, half-envious, half-mocking. Photogenic meant she looked like someone worth looking at. It meant she could step out of the blur of ordinary children, if only for a heartbeat.

Her shoes betrayed her, though. The camera never caught the scuffed toes, the mismatched buckles, the way leather pulled apart from soles like tired lips. Sometimes they were too small, biting into her feet until red crescents marked her skin. Other times they flopped too loose, as if she were wearing someone else's life. Dresses came from donation bins or the charity of neighbors—fabric already thinned from too many washings, hems awkwardly raised or lowered to make them fit. But she wore them like they were silk. She had learned early that dignity was an act you performed until others believed it was real. Walk tall, swing your arms, and the world might not notice the seams.

In the classroom, the other girls whispered. They shared secrets in pairs, giggling behind their palms, glancing at her with sidelong looks that cut more sharply than words. Boys tried to trip her in the hallway, tugged at her braids, made jokes about the orphanage. Yet when the camera clicked, none of that mattered. In those moments she was untouchable. The lens didn't know second-hand shoes. It didn't care about charity hems. It only knew the tilt of her chin, the spark in her eye, the way her smile refused to collapse under the weight of her life.

The flash was a baptism. Harsh, sudden, transforming. Each photograph became proof that she was more than the girl who went hungry, more than the one who lay awake in fear of being moved again. In photographs she was someone permanent, someone framed, someone who could not be forgotten as easily as a foster child's name could be lost in the shuffle of papers.

At recess she walked alone, balancing along the chalk lines of hopscotch squares long after the other children had run off. Sometimes she would swing herself higher and higher, so high the chains rattled like a warning, and close her eyes against the sky. In those private flights, she imagined a life where she belonged—where shoes were bought new, where dresses smelled of lavender drawers instead of mothballs. She would picture a mother waiting for her at home, brushing her hair, saying the words she most longed to hear: *You are mine. You are enough.*

Even then, she understood the power of appearances. She had little control over who came and went in her life, but she could control how she held herself. She studied the older girls, copied the sway of their hips, the way they laughed with their heads tossed back as if they didn't care who was watching. She practiced in front of the mirror—when there was one—her smile, her posture, the tilt of her face. Sometimes she caught herself staring at her reflection until it blurred, until she wasn't sure which girl was real: the one with the tattered shoes or the one who looked like she belonged in a magazine.

The cruelty of children could be sharp, but their attention, even cruel, meant she wasn't invisible. That was her greatest fear—not pain, not hunger, but vanishing. So she endured the whispers and the stares. Better to be noticed and mocked than not noticed at all. Better to be "photogenic" than faceless.

She learned to see the world as a stage, and herself as a performer on it. A tilt of the head here, a widening of the eyes there. Her classmates didn't know it, but she was rehearsing for something bigger. The camera was not just a machine that captured her image; it was a promise, a portal. If she could shine for a fraction of a second, then perhaps she could shine longer, brighter, until the whole world saw her.

At school, the rhythm of bells and chalk dust carried on as if no one noticed the girl who tried so hard to blend in. Norma Jeane slipped into her desk with the practiced quiet of someone who knew that attention could sting as much as it could soothe. Her pencil was always sharpened, her handwriting neat, her smile ready. It was the smile, she was beginning to realize, that could change the air around her. Teachers softened. Boys leaned closer. Even the girls who rolled their eyes found themselves watching, if only to figure out how she did it.

The smile didn't cost her anything—except that it did. Holding it too long made her cheeks ache. At night, lying in bed, she sometimes pressed her palms to her face as if to remind herself there was a girl beneath the performance. But in daylight, she wore it like armor. It was easier than explaining the truth: the shoes that pinched, the dresses that never quite fit, the way hunger gnawed louder than the lessons.

She knew the other children could see. They saw the scuffed leather at her toes, the hemline that had been let down one too many times. In photographs, though, the camera never asked questions. The flash did not care about worn soles. It captured only the tilt of her chin, the glow in her eyes, the dream that hovered just out of reach but shone in her anyway. The camera didn't see lack—it saw possibility. And that gave her courage.

On picture day, the classroom transformed into a small theater. Girls lined up with ribbons in their hair, boys tugged at collars, and the air filled with nervous giggles. Norma Jeane stood among them, clutching her comb like a talisman. When her turn came, she stepped onto the little platform and let the photographer guide her chin, her shoulders, her gaze. The moment the shutter clicked, she felt it—the strange alchemy of being chosen, even if only for an instant. Later, when the black-and-white prints came back, she stared at her own image as if it were proof that another version of her existed, a girl who was radiant, assured, untouchable.

That photograph became her secret companion. She traced the outline of her face with her fingertip, learning herself as if she were a stranger she longed to know. Maybe this was the girl she could become. Maybe the picture knew more than she did.

At recess, she sat on the edge of the schoolyard while the other children played. The kickball smacked against the dirt, the jump ropes slapped the pavement, but she let her mind wander elsewhere. She imagined herself in a dress that wasn't borrowed, shoes that didn't blister her feet. She imagined walking into a room and hearing silence fall, not because she was odd or poor, but because she was dazzling. She rehearsed it in her head until it almost felt real.

Some afternoons, she lingered in front of store windows, gazing at mannequins draped in silk dresses and patent leather pumps. The glass became another mirror, reflecting the gap between what she was and what she longed to be. But she didn't turn away. She studied, memorized, tried to imprint elegance onto herself through sheer will. It wasn't envy exactly—it was practice. She was learning how to be seen.

At night, after the long walk home from school, she would sit cross-legged on the floor with her shoes in her lap. They were rarely hers to begin with, always passed down through cousins or donated by neighbors who had children just a size older. The soles curled, the stitching frayed, but she polished them anyway, rubbing at the leather until it caught the weak light of the single bulb in the kitchen. She worked like a girl trying to erase proof of her poverty, as if shine could stand in for newness.

Ida would sometimes watch from the table, folding laundry with the same repetitive devotion. "Keep them clean," she'd say without looking up, "the Lord helps those who help themselves." And Norma Jeane would nod, swallowing the ache that came with knowing no amount of polish could turn them into what she dreamed of—gleaming white shoes like the ones the rich girls wore on Sundays.

She learned to sew too, her fingers pricked from needles, reattaching buttons or taking in a waist so that a too-big dress didn't hang like a curtain. She studied herself in the mirror afterward, tilting her head, tucking in her stomach, trying poses that made the dress seem intentional rather than borrowed. Sometimes she would strike a dramatic stance—one hip out, a hand behind her hair—and then laugh at her own foolishness. But behind the laughter was a question that never left her: could she make herself into someone who wasn't invisible?

The city around her offered answers she only half-believed. Billboards with Rita Hayworth's smile, posters promising new films at the Fox or the Pantages, magazine covers lined in the drugstore window—glamour like a religion, demanding belief. On the walk to school she lingered by them, whispering the names like prayers: Carole Lombard, Jean Harlow, Claudette Colbert. She studied their eyes, their lips, the tilt of their heads. She practiced those same expressions in the bathroom mirror with her toothbrush still in hand, foam around her mouth like a clumsy disguise.

The other children never knew about her rehearsals, about the small theater she built each evening in front of that cracked mirror. They only saw the girl who smiled too brightly on picture day, the girl whose dresses carried the faint scent of another house. But inside, she was already crafting an armor made of gestures, a self she could step into when the laughter of her classmates grew too sharp.

Once, she found a discarded copy of *Photoplay* left on a bus seat, its pages wrinkled from someone else's rain. She carried it home like treasure. That night she lay awake, tracing the faces of women who looked like they owned the world. The captions told her what they wore, who they loved, how they were discovered. It was a map, she thought—a secret map that might lead her out of the life she knew. She folded the magazine under her pillow and dreamed herself into its pages.

The photographs mattered more than the lessons. Arithmetic blurred on the blackboard, geography shrank to meaningless maps, but the moment the teacher announced picture day, the classroom transformed into a stage. Children fidgeted, tugging at collars, flattening skirts. Norma Jeane watched them with a quiet intensity, studying every gesture, every nervous laugh, as if they were all characters in a play she needed to memorize.

She prepared differently. She did not have the luxury of new ribbons or polished shoes that still smelled of leather. Her shoes came scuffed, sometimes a size too big, sometimes patched so carefully by Ida's needle that the stitches themselves looked like scars. Her dresses were chosen from donation bins, fabric softened thin by other girls' lives, carrying perfumes that weren't hers. She wore them anyway, smoothing her hands down the seams as if she could rub someone else's story into her own skin.

The mirror at home was cracked, its reflection jagged, but she knew how to find the angle that showed her whole. She practiced the tilt of her chin, the opening of her eyes, the careful balance between wide innocence and knowing poise. It was the first armor she ever wore: a smile that looked effortless but was built from hours of rehearsal.

The teachers always praised her. Photogenic, they said, as if the camera itself conspired with her, making her brighter, softer, easier to love. She didn't know the word's full meaning, but she felt it like sunlight on her skin. Photogenic meant she had a secret advantage, one thing that made her special when everything else marked her as ordinary—or worse, less than ordinary.

She began to understand the difference between how she felt and how she appeared. Inside, there was the girl who counted every penny, who blushed when her shoes squeaked, who dreaded the whispers when classmates noticed her hems riding too high. But in the photographs, that girl vanished. The camera caught only the tilted chin, the sparkle of eyes, the smile that suggested she belonged in magazines instead of on the edges of charity.

When the prints arrived, passed out in stiff envelopes, the other children flipped theirs carelessly, laughing, trading, mocking their own faces. Norma

Jeane held hers like a fragile treasure. She studied herself, not with vanity but with wonder, as though meeting a version of herself who had slipped free of hunger, free of shame. The girl in the picture looked like she was meant for more.

Even then, she understood the power of illusion. A photograph could hide holes in stockings, turn poverty into poise, transform the overlooked into the unforgettable. And though she was too young to name it, she was already learning the art of survival through performance—the subtle alchemy of turning pain into beauty, of smiling wide enough to blind the world to the truth.

At night, she tucked the pictures under her pillow, as if they could guard her dreams. When loneliness pressed close, she whispered to the frozen smile, asking it to remind her that she was more than the girl in hand-me-downs. That somewhere beyond the orphanage walls, beyond the classrooms and the borrowed shoes, a future waited where the world would not just glance at her, but stop and stare.

The streets of Los Angeles in those years were a patchwork quilt of dust and neon, stitched together by trolleys, gas stations, and storefronts where mannequins seemed to smirk through their glass prisons. Norma Jeane often lingered in front of those windows, pressing her nose close enough to fog the pane, staring at shoes that gleamed with polish, shoes that matched each other, shoes that had never been worn by someone else first. The shopgirls inside barely glanced at her. They had the kind of lipstick smiles that made little girls shrink and dream harder.

Her own shoes told other people's stories before they ever told her own. Some bore the creases of another girl's steps, grooves molded to feet longer or shorter than hers. Some pinched. Some flopped. But Norma Jeane carried herself as if they fit, head high, walk steady, pretending the blisters were badges of endurance. She had already learned that pretending often got her farther than complaining.

School was its own battlefield. Girls whispered about her behind open palms, the kind of cruel laughter that seemed harmless to teachers but landed like stones in the chest of a lonely child. The boys were rougher, tugging at her hair ribbons, tripping her in hallways polished to a dull shine. Yet when picture day came, when the folding chairs were dragged into neat rows and the photographer set up his tripod, the world tilted in her favor.

"Chin up, just a little," the man behind the camera would murmur. She obeyed. "Smile. There, that's it."

And in that click of a shutter, something strange happened. The room stilled. The boys who mocked her were out of frame. The girls with polished shoes and newer dresses no longer mattered. The camera liked her. She could feel it. The lens didn't ask who her father was. It didn't care about hand-me-down hems. It simply recorded her face, and in the black-and-white echo that came back a week later, she looked—different. Better. Chosen.

Those photographs became talismans. When she studied them in secret, she saw not only the girl she was, but the one she could become. She smoothed her hair in the mirror and tried to hold the same tilt of her smile. She imagined the flashbulb as a spotlight.

She loved movies for the same reason. Inside the dark hush of a theater, she could shed the shoes that pinched and slip into anyone else's life. The women on screen—Garbo, Harlow, Dietrich—had shoes that matched, dresses that clung, men who adored them. They lit cigarettes with fingers that trembled not from hunger but from practiced allure. Norma Jeane memorized them. The arch of an eyebrow. The sway of a hip. The way they turned their loneliness into gold, spun from celluloid.

When the house lights came back up, reality rushed in like cold air. She filed out with the rest of the crowd, clutching the stub of her ticket, half-believing it was a passport. On the street, her shoes scuffed against the pavement, but in her mind, she walked in silver heels.

At school, when other children jeered, she would think of those actresses, their eyes unbothered by gossip. She began to practice her own little performances—not grand gestures, but subtle ones. A tilt of the head that softened an insult. A laugh that made cruelty sound like background noise. The world was telling her she was poor, odd, unworthy. But she was already rehearsing for a world that might someday tell her she was radiant.

Her foster mother scolded her once for spending too long in front of the bathroom mirror. "Vanity's a sin," she snapped. But Norma Jeane wasn't gazing at herself in vanity. She was trying to learn who she was becoming. The reflection was both stranger and friend, and if she looked long enough, she could almost see past the bruises of childhood into the light of something waiting.

And always, in the photos—school portraits, snapshots from church picnics, a neighbor's camera borrowed for a birthday—she smiled. That smile became her shield. It said: *I belong here.* It said: *You can't see how hungry I am.* It said: *Look at me now, and just maybe, you'll remember me later.*

16

The Mirror Girl

She leaned toward the mirror, breath fogging the glass, as if her reflection might be hiding a secret she had to coax into speaking. The bathroom bulb flickered overhead, buzzing like a tired insect, and the cracked pane threw back her image in fractured lines. She didn't mind the crack. Sometimes it felt right—as if the mirror knew her better than the people who told her she was pretty, or sweet, or photogenic. Sometimes it felt like the mirror alone knew she was more than the face she wore for others.

At first it had been just a game, a child's ritual of pulling faces when no one else was looking. She could be serious, then sly, then cross-eyed and ridiculous, laughing at the strange stranger who copied her every move. But as the years pressed in, the game turned heavier, the rehearsals longer. She no longer looked at the mirror for entertainment. She looked at it for answers.

What was beauty? Did she have it? Could it save her?

She pursed her lips, dabbed at them with drugstore rouge that smelled faintly of wax and dust. The color was too loud for her pale skin, but under the mirror's spell, she could almost believe it belonged there. She tilted her chin. She lowered her eyelids. She parted her lips just enough to let a secret hover unspoken.

There—there she was.

The girl in the mirror wasn't the foster child who polished borrowed shoes until her knuckles hurt. She wasn't the girl whose dress seams itched from being let out and taken in too many times. She wasn't the daughter of a woman who showed up at doorsteps with trembling hands and eyes that saw things no one else could see. She wasn't the child left behind in orphanages where the sound of the dinner bell was the only music.

The girl in the mirror was someone else entirely.

She was radiant. She was composed. She was chosen.

And yet, if she stared too long, the glamour thinned. The rouge smeared at the edges, the powder showed its chalk, the curl in her hair loosened, and behind it all the barefaced child blinked back at her. The one with the bruised silences. The one who slept with her arms wrapped tight around a pillow as if it might turn against her. The one who believed too much in Sundays and their false promises.

That girl haunted her more than any ghost. She wanted to leave her behind, but the mirror was merciless—it showed both versions, one layered atop the other, like film reels spliced imperfectly together.

And so she worked harder.

She borrowed a spoon from the kitchen to curl her lashes, pressing the metal edge gently against her eyelid until the lashes bent upward, wide and startled. She dusted talcum powder along her collarbone, pretending it was the shimmer she saw in the magazines. She brushed her hair in long strokes, counting each pass, whispering the names of actresses she'd memorized: Garbo, Harlow, Dietrich. She practiced their gazes until she could almost feel their shadows inside her, as if beauty were a language she might learn if she rehearsed long enough.

The bathroom became her theater. The mirror, her only audience.

At school, she wore the mask she had perfected: the modest smile, the quick laugh, the slight tilt of the head that suggested she wasn't just listening but waiting for you to adore her. Teachers remarked on her brightness. Boys leaned in closer. Girls rolled their eyes, but even they sometimes studied her, trying to understand what made her stand out when her shoes and dresses gave away nothing but poverty.

What they couldn't see was the discipline behind the act. She was learning how to wield herself the way others wielded money or family name. If she could master the reflection, she could master the gaze of others. If she could master the gaze of others, she could make them forget what they thought they knew about her—the foster homes, the absence of parents, the hunger that pressed her ribs.

She was her own invention, hammered out with powder and rouge, with poses borrowed from women in magazines, with hours of staring until the stranger in the mirror felt familiar enough to carry into the world.

But invention had its price.

Late at night, after the rehearsals, she would sometimes crawl into bed still painted with powder, her lips still tinged red, and stare at the ceiling as if afraid to wash the illusion away. She wanted the reflection to last, to follow her into dreams. Sleep was treacherous—it had betrayed her before, filling her nights with the rustle of footsteps in darkened halls, with the weight of a pillow pressed against her face, with the whispers of men who told her she was special while they stole from her. Awake, she could fight with performance. Asleep, she was only a child again.

So she clung to the mirror's promises.

Each morning, she returned to it as if it were scripture. She adjusted her hair, smoothed her dress, tested her smile. She carried herself differently once the ritual was complete, straighter, taller, with a confidence that seemed to come from nowhere but the glass.

The other children thought it was natural, that she simply glowed. They didn't see the hours of rehearsal, the aching jaw from practicing smiles, the careful choreography of glances and gestures. They didn't know that the girl they mocked for her second-hand shoes was already constructing a version of herself that might one day dazzle the world.

And sometimes, in the privacy of her thoughts, she believed it too. She whispered it to herself like a prayer: You are not what they think. You are not invisible. You are becoming.

The mirror girl knew. The mirror girl had always known.

At night the mirror became her truest confidante. She would sit cross-legged on the floor, clutching a compact salvaged from some forgotten purse, the glass chipped but still able to hold her reflection. Sometimes she whispered to it, half-prayers, half-secrets, the kind of things children usually tell mothers. She would ask if she looked older, if her smile could fool them, if she was already halfway to becoming someone the world might want. The mirror, indifferent but reliable, always gave her back the same girl—hungry, restless, full of longing—but lit by a spark that no cruelty seemed able to extinguish.

She learned how to make herself beautiful with the simplest of tools. A bit of Vaseline rubbed onto her eyelids gave them a shine that looked like movie-star glamour. A stub of pencil smudged into her brows gave them definition. She borrowed tips from magazines left behind in waiting rooms or from older girls at school who whispered about rouge and mascara as if they were contraband. Each experiment was like a rehearsal for a role she hadn't been cast in yet but believed was coming.

The mirror showed her not only who she was but who she might be. She tilted her head, lowered her lashes, and imagined a marquee with her name spelled out in lights that blinked against the Los Angeles night. She pictured herself stepping onto a soundstage, cameras swiveling, voices calling her name. The fantasy filled the silence of the foster houses, lifting her out of the loneliness. If the Bolenders offered her a hymn, the mirror offered her a prophecy.

But every reflection had a shadow. Sometimes she lingered too long, staring into the glass until the girl looking back seemed like a stranger. Her own eyes unsettled her—the way they seemed both innocent and knowing, both wide with wonder and heavy with secrets. There were nights she pressed her palms against the mirror, begging it to show her someone else, someone free of the weight she already carried. Instead, the mirror showed her the truth: beauty alone could not heal the fractures. Behind the painted lips and practiced smiles, there was still the child who remembered the pillow, the orphanage, the betrayals.

Still, she persisted. She knew instinctively that the world rewarded surfaces, that a well-timed smile could soften a blow, that a perfect curl could distract from hunger. Each small success in the mirror gave her courage to face the day. When the children at school whispered, she reminded herself of the reflection that belonged only to her. When adults overlooked her, she practiced an expression that demanded notice. She would not disappear—not into foster homes, not into anonymity.

The mirror also became her first stage. She posed with a borrowed scarf draped across her shoulders, imagined she was Jean Harlow leaning against a grand piano, or Claudette Colbert peeking over her shoulder in some Parisian boudoir. She mimicked the way the women in magazines lifted their chins or parted their lips in suggestion. These were not childish games. They were lessons in survival. Each pose was a shield, each gesture a weapon against invisibility.

Sometimes she caught herself laughing at her own dramatics, twirling before the cracked glass with a broom handle balanced on her shoulder as if it were an ermine stole. But even the laughter held a kind of defiance. If she could laugh at herself, she could endure the world laughing at her. And if she could believe in the performance, maybe others would too.

What she did not know yet was that the mirror was both an ally and a tyrant. It gave her hope but also fed her restlessness. It reminded her of what she was not as much as what she could be. She would stare at her reflection and wonder: will anyone ever see me the way I see myself here, in this secret place? Will anyone recognize the star already glowing inside this poor girl's frame?

The mirror girl was not yet Marilyn. She was still Norma Jeane, piecing together fragments of identity like a patchwork quilt—some squares stitched from charity, some from fantasy, some from sheer will. But with each night of practice, with each glance that lingered longer than it should, the transformation edged closer. The girl in the glass was learning to command herself, and soon, she would learn to command everyone else.

At school, the mirror girl became something else. Teachers saw a quiet, diligent child who colored inside the lines and never caused trouble. Classmates saw a strange, half-pretty girl with thrift-store clothes and an eagerness that made her easy to tease. But no one saw the secret girl in the mirror—the one who rehearsed glances that lingered and smiles that turned shadows into spotlight. It was as if Norma Jeane was living two lives already: the visible one and the one waiting to break through.

The bathroom at school became her second studio. Between classes, she'd sneak a few moments to splash water on her face, flatten a cowlick, practice her smile in the warped tin mirror nailed above the sink. Sometimes other girls caught her and giggled, but she didn't care. She had seen the magazines. She had studied the way Rita Hayworth leaned into the camera, the way Jean Harlow's lips curved just enough to make you wonder what she wasn't saying. These weren't accidents; they were craft. And Norma Jeane was determined to learn the craft, even if her stage was a cracked mirror with rust along the edges.

At home, the mirror told different stories. She leaned close enough to fog the glass with her breath, whispering questions: Who are you? Will anyone ever stay? She was beginning to recognize the woman she might become, but she also saw the child who had been abandoned too many times, who still flinched when footsteps came down the hall. The mirror held both girls at once, refusing to choose. And maybe that was the lesson—she didn't have to choose. She could be both: fragile and powerful, wounded and dazzling.

One night, she painted her lips with beet juice, the only "makeup" she could find, and stood in front of the mirror for nearly an hour. She practiced a laugh, a sigh, a mysterious glance over her shoulder. When she finally pulled away, her reflection haunted her. She had begun to look less like herself and more like someone else entirely. A ghost of the woman she would one day be.

But the mirror could be cruel, too. On days when the laughter at school was sharpest, or when Ida scolded her for daydreaming, she saw only the flaws: ears that stuck out too far, hair that refused to lie flat, teeth she thought too big for her mouth. The mirror girl mocked her, daring her to believe she could ever be more than the foster child in hand-me-down shoes. She pressed her palms against the glass as if to push that reflection away, only to find her own skin pressing back.

Still, she returned to the mirror, night after night. It became her first audience, her first confidante, her first confessor. She learned to hold eye contact with herself, to stare until she almost believed her own performance. And in the silence of those rehearsals, she discovered the dangerous truth: if you practiced long enough, the performance became real.

By the time she was a teenager, the mirror girl had grown bolder. Norma Jeane experimented with hairstyles, copying what she saw in movie stills and fan magazines borrowed from neighbors. She teased her curls into waves, dabbed talcum on her chest to mimic the powdered glow of screen idols. She watched herself move in fragments—an arm brushing back hair, a hip angled just so. She began to understand her body not only as her own but as an instrument, a vessel that could draw attention, that could command a room even if she had no power to command her own life.

The mirror became her prophecy. It told her that the girl in hand-me-down dresses could transform. That beauty could be armor. That a smile could be survival. And though she sometimes cried into that same glass, pressing her forehead against its cool surface, she never stopped returning. Each night, the mirror swallowed her sorrow and reflected back possibility.

Years later, when cameras flashed in studios and directors shouted her name, she would remember those evenings in front of the cracked glass. She would remember how the mirror girl had been her first teacher, her first stage, her first audience. And she would understand that she had been performing long before Hollywood ever found her.

Because it was never just about makeup or curls or lipstick stolen from a drugstore shelf. It was about survival. The mirror girl was not vanity—it was vision. A vision of who she could be, of who she had to become, in order to outlast the loneliness.

And so the girl in second-hand shoes, the orphan with too many addresses, the daughter of a mother lost to shadows—she built herself, piece by piece, in the looking glass. She rehearsed the woman who would one day be known to the world. But in the quiet hours, when the house slept and the mirror stared back unblinking, she knew the truth: no matter how perfect the performance, the girl beneath still whispered, still waited, still asked the question that would haunt her forever—Do you love me?

17

The Radio and the Dream

The radio in the Silver Lake house was older than she was, a wooden box with a cracked dial and a faint hum that seemed to seep from its seams even when it wasn't tuned to anything. It had traveled with one of her foster families through years of moves, its varnish scarred, its grill cloth frayed, but to Norma Jeane it was a living thing. At night, when the house quieted and even the crickets seemed tired, she would lie on her narrow bed and turn the knob until voices and music rose out of the static like ghosts called back into the world.

The radio was her secret cathedral. She knelt before it in spirit, if not in body, letting the songs wash over her like hymns. Sometimes it was the lush swell of violins, sometimes the bright chatter of announcers describing faraway places, sometimes a torch singer's voice curling through the dark like smoke. Each sound felt like a lifeline thrown across the chasm of her loneliness. She imagined the women whose voices glided so effortlessly over the airwaves—draped in gowns, their lips painted in crimson, their laughter tinkling against champagne glasses. She whispered their names to herself as though summoning saints: Judy, Jeanette, Dinah, Billie. They seemed both impossibly distant and intimately hers, secret companions who never tired of her listening.

On evenings after school, she sometimes pressed close to the radio with a stub of a pencil and a sheet of paper, scribbling down lyrics she half-heard, words she thought she might one day sing herself. She wasn't sure if she had a voice worth hearing, but she had the hunger, and hunger was its own kind of talent. The radio told her that the world was wider than Los Angeles streets and wider even than the disappointments she carried like shadows.

It was during one of those nights, the radio whispering faint strains of a film score, that she began her game of names. She lay on her back, the ceiling cracked and yellowing above her, and mouthed syllables into the dark as though testing costumes. Dolores. Lana. Hedy. She tried them on like dresses borrowed from another girl's closet—too long in the hem, a little loose in the waist, but shimmering with possibility. Each name glittered with promise. None fit perfectly, but each one edged her closer to someone she could imagine becoming.

Her own name felt heavy in her mouth. Norma Jeane Mortenson. She repeated it silently, then aloud. It clattered against her teeth. Mortenson was a name that already seemed to belong to someone absent, someone who had never been a father in her life except as a rumor. Baker, the name of her stepfather, felt borrowed too, like one of her mismatched shoes—serviceable, but never hers. Norma Jeane: sweet, girlish, unremarkable. It belonged to the girl with second-hand dresses and foster homes. But she was beginning to suspect that a new life required a new name, just as it required a new face, a new smile, a new self.

The magazines she devoured—*Photoplay*, *Screenland*, *Modern Screen*—were full of women who had been renamed, remade. Harlean Carpenter had become Jean Harlow. Lucille LeSueur had been transformed into Joan Crawford. Frances Gumm had turned into Judy Garland. Names were spells, she realized, and the right one could open doors where none had existed before.

It was in one of those fan magazines that she found Marilyn. Marilyn Miller, the Broadway star who had danced across the Ziegfeld stage and then died too young, leaving only a name that glittered like a jewel snatched from the dark. Marilyn: the syllables curled and uncurled like a ribbon, light yet commanding. It was girlish and womanly at once, a name that could belong to a goddess or to the girl next door. She whispered it again and again until it seemed to float above her like a halo: Marilyn.

The surname would come later, handed to her by a publicist as casually as a cigarette, but in that moment on her narrow bed, it was enough to hold the first half of the dream. She rolled the name in her mouth until it became sweet. She whispered it into the crook of her arm, then into the stale air of the room, as though daring the universe to answer back.

She did not stop being Norma Jeane overnight. The world still knew her as the girl with scuffed shoes and a hesitant smile. But in secret, with the radio as her confessor, she practiced being Marilyn. She adjusted her posture when she passed the mirror. She softened her smile into something slower, more deliberate. She lowered her gaze and then lifted it again, trying to master that trick of looking both innocent and knowing. The radio taught her this too: that performance could be woven into the ordinary, that even while washing dishes or sewing a hem, she could rehearse for a life that was not yet hers.

Jim Dougherty, the quiet neighbor boy who had become her husband, would sometimes find her humming along with the radio while she ironed his shirts. "You should sing at church," he said once, half-amused, half-proud. She smiled and shook her head. She couldn't tell him that the hymns she sang were not for church, but for a stage she carried inside her head. He wanted a wife who cooked beans and folded socks. She wanted a name that could stop time.

The war pressed in on every corner of life then. Posters shouted from walls, newspapers reported lists of the dead, and radios carried grave voices about battles on islands she couldn't pronounce. Jim was bound to go, like so many boys. She lay awake at night, listening to the radio recount the march of armies, and wondered what would happen to her when he was gone. Would she be sent back to Grace, back to another foster home, back to being no one's responsibility? The thought was unbearable. The radio, with its voices of actresses and singers, became not just a comfort but a roadmap. If she could step through that invisible door, she might never again be lost.

One evening, when the announcer's voice gave way to a lush orchestral piece, she closed her eyes and saw herself not in her cramped bedroom but on a stage. She wore a dress that shimmered, though she could not name the fabric, only the way it caught the light. She sang into a microphone shaped like the radio's silver dial. The audience leaned forward, caught by her voice, her presence. For the length of the song, she was not Norma Jeane. She was Marilyn, radiant, untouchable, adored.

She startled herself with the intensity of the dream. She sat up in bed, clutching her knees, the name on her lips like a prayer. Marilyn. If she believed hard enough, maybe it would believe in her too.

The Silver Lake nights grew longer, and with them her rehearsals. The mirror became her partner, the radio her director. She no longer looked into the glass to check for stray hairs or crooked collars. She looked to find Marilyn. She tilted her head one way, then another, lowering her lashes until the girl staring back at her seemed both familiar and strange. Sometimes she startled herself—was that really her? That curve of the lip, that half-shadow in her eyes? Other times she laughed aloud at the absurdity of it, and the girl in the mirror laughed back, a conspirator in her secret ambition.

What she wanted was not just to be pretty. Pretty was for classmates who married young and disappeared into kitchens. Pretty was for the neighbor boys who whistled and then forgot your name. She wanted something more elusive—an aura, a shimmer, a way of being that made the world stop. The magazines taught her that this could be manufactured. A dress cut on the bias, a tilt of the hip, a well-placed glance. But the radio taught her something deeper: that timing, tone, rhythm, even silence could seduce. She studied the pauses between words, the way a singer let a note quiver at the edge of breaking, the way a dramatic reading slowed at just the right moment. Performance was less about what you said than how you said it.

During the day, life remained stubbornly ordinary. She scrubbed linoleum, folded laundry, stirred pots of beans, clipped coupons from newspapers. Jim brought home his paycheck and kissed her forehead like a brother. She drew little floor plans of their modest home and wrote to Grace about curtains and recipes, as though domestic life had satisfied her. But when the sun went down and the radio hummed to life, her real education began.

She filled notebooks with scribbles—snatches of dialogue overheard from radio plays, descriptions of gowns advertised in velvet voices, lists of names that might one day belong to her. The names multiplied like characters in a novel: Marilena, Arlene, Marise, Carol. But always she returned to Marilyn, as if the word itself glowed on the page. She practiced writing it in cursive, looping the M larger each time until it filled the paper. Marilyn. Marilyn. Sometimes she added "Mortenson," sometimes "Baker," sometimes no last name at all, as though she were already famous enough to need only one.

The war accelerated everything. Factories churned, men shipped out, women tied scarves around their hair and stepped into jobs once reserved for husbands and brothers. Norma Jeane joined them, working long shifts among machines that thundered and spat sparks. Her hands grew calloused, her body stronger, but her mind never left the dream. At lunch breaks she perched on a bench with her sandwich and listened to the rhythm of voices on the radio carried in from an open window. Even in the din of the factory, the music found her.

It was there, one afternoon, that a photographer appeared, his camera swinging casually from his neck as though it were a part of him. He had been sent to capture images of war work—girls in coveralls, hair tied up, grease on their cheeks. The government needed these pictures to prove that America's women were holding up the home front. Norma Jeane, bent over her station, didn't notice him until he asked her to look up. The click of the shutter startled her. She blinked, smiled faintly, and returned to her work. But the photographer lingered, sensing something. He asked for another pose, then another. Something about the way her smile lit against the machinery, the way her eyes carried both innocence and depth.

Later, when she saw the photographs, she barely recognized herself. This was no longer the girl in second-hand shoes. This was someone with the beginnings of presence, someone who might belong in the magazines she hid beneath her pillow. The radio and the dream had prepared her for this moment. The camera confirmed it.

At night, when Jim sat absorbed in the newspaper, she stared at the pictures again and again. She traced the curve of her cheek with her fingertip. Marilyn. Could this be her first step? She tucked the photos under her mattress like secret currency, proof that the dream was not entirely imagined.

Still, she was cautious. To want too much was dangerous; she had learned that as a child when she longed for permanence and received abandonment instead. And yet the hunger grew. The radio whispered possibilities, the photographs teased her with glimpses of what might be. She could not say it aloud to anyone, not even Grace, but the truth pulsed in her chest: she was not meant to stay invisible.

Sometimes, in the quietest hours, she turned the radio dial until it hummed with static and closed her eyes. In the static, she heard the ocean, the crowd of a theater, the applause she had never yet received. She let the sound wash through her until she almost believed she could step into it, vanish into the dream, and emerge as someone else.

The house smelled of starch and soap, the walls thin enough to hear neighbors argue or laugh. She moved through its rooms with the careful grace of a girl trying not to disturb the silence. Yet inside she burned with restlessness. Every advertisement on the radio, every announcement of a new film, every melody that lingered at the edge of her hearing seemed like an invitation addressed to her. She answered in secret, in her mirror, in the scribbled loops of her imagined name.

The transformation was slow, but she felt it gathering momentum. She began to fix her hair differently, to experiment with lipstick shades, to walk with a rhythm that echoed the swing of actresses she adored. The neighbors might have seen only a shy young wife, but inside the cocoon of her imagination, the butterfly was stirring.

Marilyn was no longer just a name. She was becoming a voice, a posture, a possibility. She was the echo in the radio static, the gleam in the photographer's lens, the figure she glimpsed in the mirror when she tilted her head just right. Norma Jeane still cooked and cleaned and smiled politely, but Marilyn waited beneath the surface, ready for the moment when the world would look her way and never look away again.

The nights became a kind of double life. By day, she was Mrs. Dougherty, folding laundry, burning her fingers on hot irons, waiting for Jim to come home. By night, when the radio glowed like a small sun in the darkened living room, she was someone else—someone rehearsing for a stage that hadn't yet appeared.

She began to keep little rituals. Before turning the dial, she would light the stub of a candle and set it near the window, as if summoning unseen witnesses. She'd comb her hair, apply a dab of borrowed rouge, and sit cross-legged on the floor, listening as if she were in a private theater. She practiced her diction along with the actresses whose voices poured from the speakers, repeating their lines until she could mimic every cadence. Sometimes she invented whole conversations with them, imagining herself cast beside them in dramas of love and betrayal.

Neighbors might have thought she was a lonely wife talking to herself. In truth, she was teaching herself how to exist in a world where being ordinary was not an option.

One evening, a broadcast played the soundtrack from *Camille*. Garbo's voice trembled, sorrow and beauty braided together in every word. Norma Jeane sat frozen, hugging her knees. She whispered the lines back, but not in imitation—she gave them her own inflection, her own softness, as though testing how they might sound if spoken by a girl from the orphanage with second-hand shoes. And in that moment she realized that imitation was not the point. Transformation was. She could take any sorrow, any hunger, and turn it into performance.

That thought gave her power.

Jim noticed only in passing. "You sure spend a lot of time with that radio," he said one night, flipping his paper without looking at her. She smiled, said something light, and let it drop. How could she explain that the radio was not entertainment but a lifeline? That it was teaching her how to become someone larger than herself?

The first time she heard her name in connection with photographs outside the factory, she felt the ground tilt. A neighbor's cousin had seen one of the pictures published in a small magazine devoted to war work. "That's you, isn't it?" the cousin asked, half in awe. Norma Jeane laughed it off, cheeks burning, but inside she carried the news like fire. Proof again that the camera had singled her out. Proof that Marilyn—this shimmering, half-invented self—was stepping closer to daylight.

She clipped the page and hid it in her drawer. When she was alone, she touched it as if it were holy. She whispered to it in the dark.

The dream was no longer a whisper. It was a pulse, steady and insistent. She could feel it even when she washed dishes or scrubbed the floor. Fame was still far away, but recognition—the smallest spark of it—had entered her life. And once it entered, it refused to leave.

Some nights she would lie awake imagining a marquee, her name spelled out in bulbs: *Marilyn Monroe*. She pictured people lining up, ticket stubs in their hands, leaning forward in their seats as the screen glowed. She imagined applause so loud it drowned out the memory of every cruel whisper in every classroom. She imagined the mother who had come and gone like fog sitting in the darkened theater, eyes wide with astonishment, finally seeing her daughter as someone the whole world loved.

The more she imagined it, the more it felt inevitable.

And yet, even as the dream grew, she carried the ache of uncertainty. Would becoming Marilyn mean killing off Norma Jeane? Would the little girl with mismatched shoes and a hunger for love be buried beneath the performance? She did not know. She only knew that she could not stay where she was.

The radio's music rose, the candle guttered low, and she pressed her palms together as if in prayer. Not for safety, not for permanence. For transformation. For the chance to step into the dream and make it flesh.

When the broadcast ended and silence reclaimed the room, she whispered the name once more—Marilyn—and felt the world lean closer to listen.

18

The Proposition

Grace's voice carried the weight of finality when she told Norma Jeane the truth. Her husband had been transferred to the East Coast. There was no room for the girl, no way to keep her. At 16, the threat of the orphanage returned like a ghost—cold corridors, metal cots, the sound of crying children who never stopped. Norma Jeane's stomach clenched at the thought. She had tasted too much of the world to go back to that silence.

Grace leaned across the kitchen table, her fingers tapping the wood, her eyes darting toward the window as if she couldn't bear to meet the girl's gaze. "There's another way," she said softly. "You could marry."

The word landed like a foreign object. Marriage. It wasn't romance, not even affection—it was paperwork, a signature that meant she would belong somewhere, to someone. Grace said the name: James Dougherty. Twenty-one, quiet, reliable. He worked at the Lockheed plant, brought home steady wages, and had already shown interest. He could give her what the courts would not: stability.

Norma Jeane sat in silence, her mind racing. Marriage was a door with no key, a room she wasn't sure she wanted to enter. Yet the alternative—returning to the orphanage—felt worse. She thought of the scratchy sheets, the endless rules, the feeling of being unclaimed. Better a husband than no one at all.

The proposal was made. Jimmy wasn't a bad choice. He was kind in his way, with a shy smile and hands that bore the calluses of honest work. He liked baseball, liked to talk about cars, liked to tell her about the future he imagined—one with a small house and children running in the yard. He didn't frighten her. He simply didn't stir her either. But at 16, safety outweighed longing.

The wedding came quickly. No lace veil trailing down the aisle of a grand church, no organ echoing through vaulted ceilings. Just a small ceremony, a borrowed dress, a handful of flowers bought at the corner market. She posed for photographs that day the same way she had at school—chin tilted, smile practiced, eyes searching for proof that this was really her life now. Grace stood to the side, relief etched on her face, as if the burden of responsibility had finally lifted.

Afterward, Norma Jeane signed her name—Mrs. James Dougherty—and felt the letters wobble under her hand. The ink dried faster than the reality sank in. Sixteen and already a wife. Sixteen and someone's responsibility, someone's property. Sixteen and no longer a girl in the eyes of the law.

The house she moved into was plain, a little box of stucco and wood, with a kitchen that smelled of onions and soap. She set about making it hers: scrubbing the floors until her knees ached, ironing shirts until the creases stood sharp enough to cut. She learned to cook meatloaf, to wash socks without shrinking them, to clip coupons from the newspaper. She drew little sketches of the rooms, rearranged furniture in her mind when she couldn't move it herself. These small acts gave her a sense of control, a fragile illusion that she belonged in the life she had been handed.

Yet at night, when Jimmy read the newspaper or drifted off in his chair, she felt the ache of something missing. Marriage had solved the problem of where she would sleep, but not the deeper hunger for a family, for a mother's arms, for permanence that wasn't dependent on the kindness of a man. She was grateful, yes, but gratitude could not quiet the voice that whispered: is this all?

She wrote to Grace often, filling her letters with cheerful details. She described the meals she cooked, the way she kept the house tidy, the little garden she wanted to start. The letters read like the diary of a girl determined to be good, to prove herself worthy of this new arrangement. Between the lines, though, the ache leaked through. Marriage was a performance too, and she was still learning her lines.

Jimmy was patient, but he was a man with the easy expectations of someone who had never been abandoned, never been passed from house to house. He did not understand the tremor in her voice when she asked if he would always be there. He thought she was being sweet. She thought she was begging for survival.

The nights were the hardest. The silence pressed too close, and the bed felt like both safety and a trap. She stared at the ceiling and wondered if this was what adulthood meant: trading one dependency for another. She was no longer a foster child, but she had not yet become her own woman. She was tethered, bound by vows she barely understood.

And yet, she smiled. She wore the ring even when it slipped on her finger, too loose for her narrow hands. She smiled in the photographs they took, the ones where she leaned against Jimmy's arm, her face glowing with a brightness that was part hope, part illusion. The camera still caught her best self—the one who seemed assured, radiant, ready. The camera didn't know the truth. The camera didn't care.

She settled into routines because they were the safest thing she knew. Routines meant predictability, and predictability meant she might not be uprooted again. The mornings began with the whistle of the kettle, the smell of coffee, the scratch of Jimmy's razor against his chin. He'd leave for work with a kiss on the cheek, and she would stand at the door watching him go, already calculating the hours until he returned. She filled the empty space with chores. Laundry flapping on the line became her chorus. The iron hissed like a warning snake. The scrub brush in the sink sang its own rough hymn.

Neighbors peered in on her sometimes, curious about the pretty young bride. They'd comment on her hair, on the freshness of her cheeks, on her diligence with housework. They assumed she was happy, because she looked happy, because that was what young wives were supposed to be. She returned their smiles, offered them tea, and never let slip the fear that still curled in her stomach.

When she walked through the market, she noticed the glances. Men turning their heads just a beat too long, women whispering to one another as she passed. She felt their eyes more than she saw them. At first it unsettled her, then it became a kind of secret power. She smoothed her dress, tilted her head just so, and pretended she didn't notice. But she did. She noticed everything.

Jimmy liked to take her to the movies. They'd sit in the dark, his hand heavy over hers, while she studied the screen with an intensity that bordered on hunger. The women there glowed, luminous and untouchable. She copied their gestures in her mind, memorized the sway of their hips, the softness of their laughter, the way light seemed to cling to their faces. Back home, standing in the small bathroom with its cracked mirror, she would practice. The curve of a smile. The arch of an eyebrow. The tilt of her head at just the right angle. She was rehearsing for a role she couldn't yet name.

Sometimes she wrote lists in her notebook—dreams disguised as chores. Learn to bake better pies. Save money for a sewing machine. Take a beauty class. Visit the ocean more often. The lists looked ordinary, but between the lines she was sketching the possibility of another self. One who wasn't bound to laundry and meatloaf, one who might find her face not only in school portraits or wedding snapshots but in magazines, on billboards, on screens 10 feet tall.

And yet the ache persisted. Marriage had given her a roof, a surname, a sense of belonging in the eyes of the law. But it hadn't given her what she most longed for: a place where she could stop performing, stop smiling, stop proving herself worthy of being kept. In bed at night, she would turn her wedding ring round and round, watching the metal catch the moonlight. It was too loose, forever threatening to slip off. She worried that if it did, she might disappear with it.

She kept her silence about those fears. Jimmy was good, kind in his steady way, but he was not someone she could confess to. He wanted a cheerful wife, not a girl haunted by shadows. So she swallowed the words, smiled through the ache, and made sure the house gleamed when he returned.

But the restlessness wouldn't be contained. One afternoon, alone in the house, she found herself dancing barefoot across the kitchen linoleum, the radio turned up loud, the hem of her skirt swirling around her knees. For those few minutes, she wasn't Mrs. Dougherty. She was someone freer, brighter, unnamed but radiant. The music ended, the moment vanished, and she stood panting in the silence, suddenly aware of how small the room was, how low the ceiling pressed.

The proposition that had saved her from the orphanage had become its own kind of confinement. The walls were painted a soft cream, but they closed in all the same. She was safe, yes. But safety, she was beginning to understand, was not the same as living.

She remembered how quickly it had been arranged. Grace had sat her down, voice gentle but eyes firm, and explained the choice that wasn't really a choice at all. "You'll marry Jimmy," she'd said. "He's a good boy, and he'll take care of you." Norma Jeane had nodded because nodding was easier than crying, easier than admitting she wanted something else entirely. At 16, wanting something for herself felt dangerous.

The wedding was as brief as a signature. A borrowed dress, a small gathering, the scent of gardenias that wilted in the afternoon heat. She smiled for the photographs, because smiling was her only constant. Inside she felt like she was standing on the edge of a cliff, not sure whether the ground beneath her would hold.

In the weeks that followed, she tried hard to be the wife she thought the world expected. She ironed Jimmy's shirts until the fabric was as stiff as armor. She cooked meals by the book, scribbling notes to herself about how much salt to use, how to keep beans from burning. She dusted every corner of the house, polished the wooden chairs until they shone. It was all performance, each act a line in the script of "Mrs. Dougherty," a role she hadn't auditioned for but had been cast in anyway.

And yet there were moments—tiny fissures—when her real self slipped through. When she leaned too close to the radio and whispered along with the singers, imagining her own voice rising through the static. When she caught her reflection in the window at dusk and tilted her chin, just so, pretending she was someone being photographed, not someone folding laundry. When the neighbor down the street, a woman with lipstick always fresh and heels that clicked like applause, smiled at her knowingly, as if she saw through the costume.

The nights were harder. Jimmy's breathing heavy beside her, the silence pressing in, the ache in her chest louder than the clock ticking in the kitchen. She turned her wedding band in slow circles, feeling its cool looseness on her finger. The ring didn't fit, not quite, just as the marriage didn't fit, not quite. It spun when she moved, reminding her that permanence could still slip away.

Letters to Grace became her outlet. She filled them with domestic details—recipes tried, curtains sewn, how Jimmy liked his coffee. But between the lines, the truth seeped out. Words like "sometimes lonely" and "learning still" appeared like stains she couldn't quite scrub away. Grace wrote back with encouragement, advice, the tone of someone who believed she'd given Norma Jeane a gift. And perhaps she had. The alternative would have been worse. But survival was not the same thing as love.

One Sunday afternoon, she found herself at the beach, walking alone while Jimmy played ball with friends. The Pacific stretched out before her like an unfinished sentence. Children shrieked in the surf, gulls dove and screamed, the sun glared mercilessly. She stood with her feet in the sand, letting the waves lap at her ankles, and thought: I could be anyone here. The ocean didn't know her name. The sky didn't care who she belonged to. For a fleeting moment, she believed in the possibility of escape.

Back home, she hung laundry and tried to chase the salt air from her hair. Jimmy asked about her walk, and she said it was fine, nothing more. She couldn't tell him that the ocean had felt like a doorway. He wouldn't understand. He wanted steadiness. She wanted a horizon.

In the quiet hours, when the chores were done and the house hummed with stillness, she would take out a pencil and sketch dresses she'd seen in magazines. Silhouettes of gowns with nipped waists and flowing skirts, shoes with perfect straps, hats tilted at daring angles. She traced them carefully, shading with the side of the lead, creating a paper wardrobe for the girl she wanted to be. Sometimes she drew faces too—eyes wide, lips painted, hair curled in soft waves. The faces looked like hers, but not exactly. They looked like the woman she was becoming in secret.

Jimmy never asked about the sketches. He was content with the surface: the tidy house, the warm meals, the sweet young wife who smiled when company came. He didn't see the girl rehearsing in mirrors, the one whispering her name to herself in the dark, trying on futures like costumes.

It was Grace who understood, if only partly. She'd written once, "You've always had a light about you. Don't let anyone put it out." Norma Jeane read those words again and again, tucking them away as if they were scripture. A light. Yes, she wanted to believe in that. Even if the world had only ever given her second-hand shoes and borrowed names, she wanted to believe she carried something inside that could not be extinguished.

And so the days passed. Laundry and meatloaf, letters and sketches, laughter that sounded rehearsed. She wore the ring. She played the part. But beneath the surface, a quiet rebellion grew, fragile and determined as a seed pushing through concrete.

The wedding day itself arrived without fanfare, as if it had been penciled into the calendar by a careful hand that didn't want to draw attention. The air smelled faintly of hot pavement and wilting blossoms. She wore a simple dress borrowed from a neighbor—white, not because anyone had insisted on purity, but because it was the one that fit after Ida took in the seams. The hem tickled her shins when she breathed. A pair of low heels, scuffed at the toes, clicked softly on the floor like a polite request to be noticed. She'd pinned her hair back with bobby pins that tugged, smoothing flyaways into submission with a damp comb. Lipstick was a thin, brave line.

The ceremony was over almost before it began. A small room, a desk with papers, the smell of ink and floor polish. Two witnesses who spoke kindly because kindness costs little. Jimmy's hand was warm and dry. He cleared his throat once, twice, as if he were about to deliver a speech he hadn't prepared and then thought better of it. When the vows came, they sounded practical, like instructions: to have and to hold, for better or worse. She repeated them carefully, each word placed where it was asked to go, like forks on a set table.

Afterward there was coffee in cups that didn't match and a plate of cookies that crumbled too easily. Someone made a joke about young love and rationing sugar. Someone else asked where they would live. She smiled at all the right moments, letting laughter bubble up from a place that had learned to produce it on command. When they stepped outside, the sun startled her. The light felt too loud.

In photographs taken that afternoon—just a few, snapped by a friend who liked to pretend he was a professional—her smile is perfect, steady, convincing. You can't see the bobby pins. You can't see the way the ring sits slightly loose, as if time itself might still wriggle free. You only see the girl who refuses to blink.

Jimmy looked proud in a decent, ordinary way. That was his gift: the ordinary made sturdy. He had the posture of a man who had been told to stand up straight and had never stopped obeying. He admired her beauty without quite knowing what it meant or what it might cost. When he glanced at her, there was affection and a blink of astonishment, as if he'd found a delicate glass ornament in a box of tools and wasn't sure where to put it so it wouldn't break.

They began their life together in a neighborhood that smelled of cut grass and hot tar, where porch steps sagged in friendly ways and children chalked hopscotch squares that survived until the next hard rain. The evenings held the familiar chorus—radios murmuring through open windows, screen doors slapping, a dog complaining at a distant fence. She learned the creaks of the house the way other girls learned the notes of a piano: this board near the bedroom sighs; the hinge on the pantry sings; the faucet in the bathroom stutters before it flows.

She learned Jimmy's sounds too. The clink of coins into a dish by the door. The soft grunt when he lowered himself into his chair after work. The newspaper rattle, steady as a metronome. He liked his shirts crisp, his dinners hot, his plans plain. He would talk, sometimes, about saving for a car with seats that didn't squeak, about planting a lemon tree in the backyard. She listened with her chin in her hand, nodding in the right places, trying to locate herself inside these small futures.

During the day, she wrote to Grace. The letters were bright, filled with domestic detail: "I tried meatloaf again, and it didn't fall apart," or "I moved the lamp by the chair so Jimmy won't squint when he reads." She drew little rectangles for rooms, arrows for where the couch might go if they ever got a second one. On the backs of envelopes, she sketched curtains the way a child sketches clouds: hopeful outlines of softness. If a sentence came out too honest—*sometimes the quiet is so loud my heart hurts*—she would scratch it away and write instead about the weather.

She learned shortcuts in the kitchen. How to butter the pan just enough that eggs didn't cling to the bottom. How to stretch a stew with a potato and a story about how it tasted better this way. She learned stitches: blind hems, ladder stitches, the tug that means the thread has caught. Once, while pressing a pleat, she burned the tip of her finger and pressed it to her mouth, tasting iron. She laughed a little at herself, then laughed again because her laughter sounded like a stranger's.

On good afternoons, she walked. She liked the stretch of street where the jacarandas threw down purple flowers as if the sky had decided to decorate the ground. She liked the way store windows caught her reflection in pieces—now the curve of a cheek, now the glint of an eye—so she could assemble herself from fragments. The shoe store always slowed her, even when there was no money for shoes. She memorized the elegant slope of a pump, the neat bow on a sandal, the way leather gleamed like a promise. Once, a salesgirl asked if she wanted to try a pair "just for size." She slipped her feet in and felt the shock of something that fit so perfectly it felt like permission. She walked two careful steps on the carpet, thanked the girl, and returned them. On the way home, her own shoes seemed to clatter louder than usual, as if protesting their demotion.

Neighbors noticed her in their small ways. A woman two doors down told her she had "movie-star lips," then giggled and asked if she'd ever thought about entering a beauty contest. A boy on a bicycle circled twice to tell her she had the nicest smile on the block. Compliments were little coins people flicked at her, curious to see what sound they made when they landed. She stored them without looking at them too closely, small proof that the world was sometimes willing to be kind.

At twilight she found the window where the light made her face soft and golden. There, with the radio low, she practiced the trick of looking up through her lashes, then away, then back again—an eyelid's choreography that promised something and its refusal. It wasn't vanity. It was study. She watched, adjusted, learned which angles made her look like the girl she felt trembling under her skin. If a neighbor walked by and saw her reflected in the glass, they'd think she was daydreaming. She was. But the dreams were not idle. They were drills, the quiet training of a soldier who suspects a different war is coming.

Jimmy would sometimes brush her shoulder with the back of his hand and say, "You're the prettiest thing on this street." He meant it sweetly, and she accepted it sweetly, and between their sweetness lay a distance neither of them knew how to cross. He loved the version of her that made sense in his life—a lovely wife in a clean house. She longed for a life that made sense to whatever unnamed force had kept her smiling through foster homes and orphanage bells. They were both sincere. Sincerity can still be a wall.

On Sundays, after church, she stood in the kitchen with her sleeves rolled, washing dishes while the sermon's phrases echoed in her mind—mercy, covenant, redemption—words that sounded like they belonged in a larger story than the one she was living. She stacked plates in neat towers and thought of covenants she had never been offered, redemptions no one could grant. Water ran over her hands, warm, relentless. In the next room, the radio counted measures between songs. She matched its rhythm without meaning to.

There were nights when the wind lifted the curtains and the house seemed to inhale. On those nights, when Jimmy slept and the street was a hush of tires on distant pavement, she would sit at the little table with a stub of pencil and write her name again and again on a scrap of paper, testing how it felt—how she felt—wearing it. Sometimes *Mrs. James Dougherty* in loops that tried to look confident. Sometimes just *Norma Jeane*, stubborn, girlish. And sometimes—only sometimes, and then quickly folded away—another name that tasted like a secret and a dare. She didn't show that one to anyone. She kept it under the plate that wobbled, the one she had to steady with a matchbook when company came.

In the dim, she listened for the future. Not words, not even a tune. More like a pressure behind the walls, a faint electricity under the skin. She could feel it gather when she walked past the jacarandas, when she slipped her feet into shoes that fit and then slipped them out again, when a stranger's gaze lingered a second longer than it should, when the radio crooned and she found herself answering, in her own soft key. It was coming from far away and from inside her, both at once. The proposition had saved her from the orphanage; the proposition had built her a room. She was grateful for the room. She was learning where the door was.

And on a particular evening, as the last of the sun laid its hand along the kitchen floor and the radio found a violin that could ache the way a body aches, she dried her hands on a towel and stood very still, as if she'd heard someone call her name. Not the one she wore in public. The other one. The secret one. She didn't answer out loud. She didn't need to. The answering was already happening, molecule by molecule, in the way she held her head, the way she breathed, the way she refused—quietly, stubbornly—to disappear.

19

A Ring to Stop the Clock

The wedding was small, as if it were afraid to be noticed. A rented hall with whitewashed walls, folding chairs that creaked under the weight of relatives and neighbors, and a minister whose voice was more practical than poetic. There were no violins, no cathedral bells, no throngs of guests. Just a handful of people and the girl who had been moved from house to house like a parcel suddenly expected to stand still forever.

Norma Jeane wore a simple dress sewn by hands more used to mending than creating finery. Its hemline skimmed awkwardly above her ankles, her shoes pinched, and her hair—cropped shorter than she liked—refused to lie flat. She was 16, still growing into herself, and yet on this day she was meant to appear finished, ready, a bride. Her groom, Jim Dougherty, was 21, sturdy, broad-shouldered, employed at the Lockheed plant. To most eyes, he was the picture of stability. To Norma Jeane, he was not a love story but a doorway. A way out of the orphanage. A way into something resembling permanence.

She smiled for the pictures, tilting her chin just so, the way she had practiced. The camera always liked her better than she liked herself. Behind her smile, though, was a different truth: she was too young to promise forever, too desperate to refuse it. The ring Jim slid onto her finger spun loose, almost comically, as though her body knew it did not belong there. She turned the band around with her thumb, trying to will it into significance.

Later, she would write letters to Grace, her guardian and orchestrator of the marriage, detailing the rhythms of her new life. She described floor plans, recipes she had mastered, the small victories of keeping house. She made it sound like a dream realized. But even in her neat handwriting, there was a restlessness between the lines. This was not the permanence she had longed for. It was a pause button, pressed hard enough to hold back the chaos of her childhood—but not strong enough to stop time itself.

The first weeks of marriage unfolded like an apprenticeship. Jim showed her how to fold his shirts, how to press trousers with a sharp crease, how to cook beans in a way that stretched the flavor through the week. She learned quickly, eager to please, eager to make the role fit. But in the quiet hours, when the dishes were stacked and Jim's snores filled the small rooms, she sat awake, staring at her hands. They were still the hands of a child, nails bitten to the quick, knuckles scarred from housework. The ring glinted back at her like a stranger's possession.

The neighbors thought them charming. "Such a sweet young wife," they said when she waved from the porch, apron tied neatly at her waist. She knew how to smile on cue, how to nod at the right moment, how to perform happiness. It was not so different from picture day at school. Only now the stakes were higher. She was not just hiding poverty but trying to conjure a whole life from scratch.

Sometimes, while Jim read the evening newspaper, she would let her eyes wander to the mirror on the far wall. There she saw not Mrs. Dougherty but a girl rehearsing the part. The reflection blinked back at her with curiosity, as though asking, Who are you, really? Was she the dutiful wife with polished shoes and beans simmering on the stove? Or was she still the girl who whispered prayers into photographs and dreamed of being seen by the whole world?

At 16, she had not yet learned how to bridge those selves. Instead, she let them take turns—Mrs. Dougherty during the day, and at night, when the house fell silent, the dreaming girl returned. She whispered names she had read in movie magazines, rolled them across her tongue like candy: Carole, Jean, Hedy. Names that shimmered with possibility, names that belonged to women who had clawed their way out of obscurity and into the glow of a marquee. She wondered what it would feel like to be called by a name like that, instead of the clumsy, hand-me-down "Mrs. Dougherty."

Jim was kind, but kindness was not enough to erase the absence in her life. He was a provider, not a dreamer. He looked at her and saw a wife who should be content with beans and pressed shirts. She looked at him and saw the walls of a house closing in. She wanted to be grateful—after all, he had rescued her from the orphanage. But gratitude is not love, and a wedding band is not an anchor when the tide inside you is pulling you toward something larger.

And so, each night, after the lights were out, she traced the outline of the ring on her finger and listened to the clock ticking in the kitchen. She thought of her childhood—the endless moves, the orphanage bell, the revolving doors of mothers who weren't hers—and she told herself this was different. This would last. But deep down, the tick of the clock reminded her: nothing lasted. Not mothers, not homes, not even promises made under whitewashed ceilings.

The ring was supposed to stop the clock. Instead, it only made her hear it louder.

She began to measure time differently after the wedding. Before, it had been counted in Sundays, in the hope of her mother's perfume at the door, in the school bells that marked each uncertain season. Now, time was measured in beans soaking in a pot, in the thud of Jim's boots by the door, in the careful folding of bed sheets still warm from the line. She told herself this was stability. This was permanence. But permanence, she discovered, could also be a kind of silence.

The little house they rented in Van Nuys had a porch just wide enough for two chairs, though Jim rarely sat there. He was often at work or reading the paper. Norma Jeane would sit alone in the evenings, watching the sun slide down behind the rows of eucalyptus trees, listening to children's laughter rise and fall in the neighborhood. She longed for someone to laugh with her, someone to share the quiet ache that filled her chest. But Jim, though decent, was not that kind of companion. He was steady in the way a locked door is steady—reassuring, protective, but also confining.

She tried to fill the space with industry. She scrubbed the floors until her knees burned. She clipped recipes from magazines and practiced them with near-religious devotion, as though learning to make a perfect meatloaf could consecrate the marriage. She ironed Jim's shirts until the creases were sharp enough to cut. In her letters to Grace, she described all of this as if it were joy. She drew floor plans of the house, carefully sketching the kitchen, the living room, even the little patch of yard. She made it sound like a home she loved. But underneath the ink, the words trembled. What she wanted was not floor plans but blueprints for a life she couldn't yet name.

The neighbors noticed her prettiness, even before she did. Women commented on her skin, her smile, the way her hair caught the sun. Men looked a little too long. She felt it—both the flattery and the danger of it. At 16, her body was betraying her with curves she didn't yet know how to command. She laughed too quickly at compliments, blushed too easily, and then went home and stared at herself in the mirror, trying to reconcile the girl she saw with the woman others seemed to glimpse.

It was in those mirrors that something began to stir. She would stand in the bathroom after Jim had gone to bed, brushing her hair until it crackled with static, tilting her head this way and that, watching the light slide across her face. Sometimes she whispered lines from magazines, mimicking the stars she admired. "Hello, darling," she would say to her reflection, her voice low and playful. Then she would giggle at her own foolishness, only to try again the next night, a little bolder, a little closer to someone she didn't yet recognize but couldn't stop chasing.

Jim never asked about these late-night rituals. He wanted a wife, not a dreamer. He was proud when she kept the house neat, when she cooked well, when she smiled at the right times in public. But he didn't see the flicker in her eyes when she caught sight of a movie poster, the way her breath caught at the glamour of women in magazines. He didn't notice how she lingered over photographs of actresses, memorizing the way they held themselves, the way they seemed to command attention without asking.

The ring on her finger grew looser as the months passed, spinning easily when she twisted it with her thumb. She began to think of it less as a promise and more as a reminder of the trade she had made. The orphanage was behind her, yes. She no longer feared being uprooted, passed along like a borrowed coat. But in exchange, she had bound herself to a life that didn't fit, a role that pinched worse than second-hand shoes.

She wasn't unhappy, exactly. Jim was not cruel. He didn't raise his hand, didn't shout. He was gentle in his way, proud to have a young wife, proud to be seen as a man who could provide. But for Norma Jeane, kindness was not enough. She craved recognition—not just as Mrs. Dougherty, but as someone singular. Someone luminous. She wanted to be looked at the way cameras looked at her, the way strangers sometimes did on the street. She wanted a gaze that said: you are more than this.

The nights stretched long. Sometimes she would sit by the window, listening to the hum of cars on the boulevard, dreaming of other lives. She thought of the movies she had seen—the women in silk gowns, their voices confident, their faces lit by something more than lamps. She whispered their names again: Carole, Jean, Lana. Each name was a possibility, a lifeline thrown out to her from the darkness. She didn't know yet that one day she would choose her own new name, that she would slip out of Norma Jeane as easily as stepping out of a borrowed dress. For now, she just let the syllables hover on her tongue like a secret.

The marriage gave her a pause, nothing more. A fragile stillness in which she could begin to imagine who she might become. But the clock ticked on, louder than ever. Every time she looked at the ring, she felt it: time wasn't stopping. It was running. And if she stayed too long in this role, it might run out before she had the chance to claim what she had been rehearsing for all her life.

She tried to memorize the sound of her name as Mrs. Dougherty, but it always caught in her throat. Jim used it in jest sometimes, calling from the porch, "Mrs. Dougherty, supper ready yet?" and she would laugh, but the laugh felt like it belonged to someone else. Sixteen-year-olds weren't supposed to be called "Mrs." Anything. When the neighbors nodded politely, when they waved at her with knowing smiles, she wondered what they saw—a girl playing house or a woman already worn into her role?

Her hands smelled of starch and soap. She ironed Jim's shirts until the sleeves were stiff, pressed creases into trousers with the concentration of a student hoping to earn top marks. Every chore was a test: did she measure up? Did she seem old enough, woman enough, to keep the life she had been given instead of being sent back to the orphanage?

She listened for Jim's footsteps the way she once listened for her mother's knock on a Sunday. A door opening could mean safety, or it could mean loss. He was kind, steady, gentle enough. But his presence reminded her that she was no longer simply Norma Jeane. She was tied by law and promise to someone else, and every night she lay beside him she felt the strangeness of it—like wearing a dress too big, the fabric slipping off her shoulders no matter how tightly she tried to fasten it.

She filled the silence with letters to Grace. Long, looping handwriting across thin paper, telling of beans simmering on the stove, of sweeping the porch, of fixing curtains that let in too much sun. The details were a disguise. What she really meant was: I'm trying, I'm learning, I'm good, please don't take this from me. Grace wrote back, warm and encouraging, but always with the authority of someone reminding her that this was her choice, her safety net. Marriage was better than the orphanage. Marriage was her chance.

She smiled at Jim, leaned her head against his shoulder, kissed him goodnight because that's what wives were supposed to do. But afterward she lay awake, staring at the ceiling, whispering names into the dark. Rita. Jean. Carole. Marilyn. The radio hummed softly from the kitchen, a torch song floating across the linoleum. She mouthed the lyrics like prayers.

In the mornings, sunlight slanted through the thin curtains and painted stripes across her skin. She studied herself in the mirror before Jim stirred awake. The girl who stared back was both child and woman, caught in the in-between. She traced her lips with the tip of her finger, imagining them painted in crimson. She tucked her hair behind her ears, wondering how it would look platinum. She tilted her chin the way the magazines showed the stars did, and for a moment she could almost believe.

But the day always pulled her back: laundry on the line, neighbors' gossip drifting through windows, the sound of Jim's laughter as he read the sports page. He didn't notice the longing in her eyes when she lingered over a photograph in Photoplay. He didn't hear the quickened beat of her heart when she tried a pose in the bathroom mirror. To him, she was his young wife, dependable, pretty, waiting at home. To her, she was a shadow rehearsing for a role the world had not yet offered.

And yet, there were moments of tenderness, brief but real. When Jim brushed her cheek with his hand and said she was lovely. When he praised her cooking, even if the roast was dry. When he looked at her with pride as if to say, we've made it, we're doing fine. She held onto those moments, not because they satisfied her, but because they steadied her. He was not her dream, but he was her harbor—for now.

The ring turned loosely on her finger, a constant reminder that permanence was never really hers. She wore it like a charm against disappearance, the way she once held photographs under her pillow. If the ring was there, she could not be returned, could not be cast aside. It was her anchor, even as it spun like a restless clock.

In quiet hours, she began to wonder if love was supposed to feel this way—like endurance, like pretending. Perhaps love was a kind of script, too, something you practiced until it became believable. If so, she was already rehearsing. And rehearsing was something she had always been good at.

20

A Girl on the Pier

The factory smelled of oil and hot metal, the air thick with the musk of machines that never slept. Norma Jeane tied a kerchief over her hair, rolled up the sleeves of a borrowed blouse, and stepped into the rhythm of the war. The clang of hammers and the whine of drills filled her ears, a kind of music that had no melody but demanded endurance. It was 1944, and Los Angeles hummed with war work. Every corner of the city pulsed with men and women bent over rivet guns, wrenches, welding torches.

She was 16 but looked older in her overalls, grease streaked on her cheek. The supervisors liked her—"a cheerful worker," one of them said—but they didn't see the hunger that gnawed at her, or the ache that lived in her shoulders after ten hours on her feet. They didn't see the girl who still dreamed of mothers that returned and fathers who stayed.

Her husband, Jim Dougherty, was already gone to sea, training with the Merchant Marine. She wrote letters to him in the evenings, neat little reports about cooking beans, mending shirts, and keeping the tiny house in order. She made it sound like a romance, though the truth was closer to loneliness disguised as routine. By day she was Mrs. Dougherty, war worker, steady and reliable. By night she was Norma Jeane again, curling in bed with a book or staring at the ceiling, whispering prayers to a God who didn't always answer.

The other girls at the factory talked about boyfriends, soldiers, ration stamps. Some painted their lips crimson on breaks, standing in front of dented bathroom mirrors as if to remind themselves they were still women, not just parts in a machine. Norma Jeane joined them sometimes, watching their rituals, studying how powder could hide fatigue, how a smile could turn the drab into the glamorous. She borrowed their rouge now and then, dabbing it lightly, then wiping it off before returning to the floor. But something stirred in her each time—an inkling that beauty might be its own kind of currency.

On her lunch breaks she walked to the edge of the Santa Monica Pier, where gulls screamed and the ocean stretched farther than her imagination. The pier was weathered, its boards worn smooth by years of footsteps, but to her it felt like a stage. She leaned on the railing, letting the salt wind whip her hair loose from its kerchief. She stared at the horizon, not looking for ships but for answers.

People noticed her there. A fisherman tipped his cap. A mother with two children glanced twice. And once, a photographer passing through stopped to watch her silhouette against the sea. He didn't approach, not yet. But his eyes lingered, as though he saw something more than a war worker on her lunch break.

Norma Jeane loved those moments on the pier. The waves spoke in a language she almost understood, promising that everything changed, always. The tide never stayed. The gulls never circled forever. The sea both gave and took away. It felt like her life—always moving, always uncertain, yet dazzling in its restlessness.

When she returned to the factory, her hands blackened by grease, she carried the ocean inside her, a reminder that she was not just another girl punching a timecard. She was someone on the edge of becoming, though she couldn't yet name what.

The factory floor rattled with noise that became a kind of second heartbeat. Norma Jeane learned to live inside that racket, her body moving almost automatically: lift, press, fasten, pass along. She joked with the other girls when she could, but mostly she listened. She heard the way they spoke about husbands gone off to war, the fear and pride tangled in their voices. She watched how they tucked photographs into shirt pockets—boys in uniform, smiling stiffly, their futures uncertain.

She had her own photograph folded in her wallet: Jim in his merchant seaman's cap, his expression more dutiful than affectionate. She looked at it sometimes when the whistle blew, when exhaustion threatened to blur the edges of her determination. The picture steadied her, though not in the way people might have imagined. It wasn't longing she felt—it was obligation, the reminder that she was tied to a man, to a home, to a life she had not fully chosen.

After her shift, she would step out into the twilight, the clang of the machines still ringing in her ears. She often headed toward the pier instead of straight home. Something about the water called to her. The ocean didn't care who she was married to. It didn't care if her shoes pinched or her dress was patched. It rolled and roared, untamed and eternal, and in its presence she felt less small.

The pier carried its own life after dark. Couples strolled, laughing softly, arms entwined. Sailors on leave swaggered, their uniforms bright even under the dim pier lamps. Street musicians played guitars and sang half-forgotten ballads. Norma Jeane walked among them quietly, her eyes wide, her heart tugging toward something she couldn't name.

Sometimes she leaned over the rail and studied her reflection trembling in the dark water. The girl who looked back seemed older, as if the sea itself had painted shadows under her eyes. She whispered questions to that reflection: Who are you becoming? Who will believe in you? Who will love you without leaving?

One evening, a man with a camera approached her. He wasn't the first to look, but he was the first to see. He asked if he could take her picture. She hesitated, then nodded. The flash startled her, a small burst of light against the vast dark sea. Later, when he showed her the photograph, she caught her breath. There she was—chin lifted, hair caught by the wind, eyes shining like someone who belonged on the cover of a magazine.

It was only a snapshot, a moment. But for Norma Jeane, it was a revelation. The pier had become more than a refuge. It was a threshold.

The first photograph was passed around like gossip. One of the factory girls whistled when she saw it. "You look like somebody," she said, though she couldn't decide who. Another teased her, "Hollywood'll come for you if you're not careful." Norma Jeane laughed, embarrassed, but she slipped the photograph into her bag and carried it home like a fragile secret.

At night she studied it under the weak light of the kitchen bulb. The face in the picture was hers, but it wasn't. The smile was shy, but the eyes—there was something restless in them, as if they were waiting for a world that hadn't yet arrived. She touched the edges of the photograph, her fingertips trembling, and wondered if this was the beginning of something or just another cruel tease, like so many promises in her life that had never lasted.

The war demanded its sacrifices, but it also created odd opportunities. With so many men gone, women stepped into roles they had never been allowed to hold. They carried rivet guns, they measured steel, they packed munitions. Some days, Norma Jeane felt powerful in her coveralls, her hair tied up in a scarf to keep out the grease. She worked with a precision that startled even herself, as though all the years of trying to be careful, invisible, had trained her for this. And yet, when the day ended, when the grease clung to her skin and the ache set into her shoulders, she dreamed of other work—of the click of the shutter, the soundless applause of film advancing through a camera.

The pier became her classroom. She watched how couples posed for quick pictures snapped by wandering photographers. She noticed how women angled their shoulders, how men tilted their hats. She practiced when no one was looking, her body moving just slightly, shifting weight, turning her chin to catch the light. It was play at first, but then it became more—an apprenticeship in visibility.

On Sundays, she sometimes rode the trolley into Hollywood, just to walk among the theaters. Posters loomed like stained glass windows, worshipping starlets with painted lips and impossible eyes. She studied them the way another girl might study saints. Jean Harlow with her white-blonde hair. Rita Hayworth, lush and untouchable. Lana Turner, discovered at a soda fountain. Each one seemed to whisper a promise: It could be you.

But the whisper was followed by a warning. Could be. Not would be. Hollywood had a way of dangling dreams like fruit just out of reach. She knew this. She wasn't foolish. Still, when she looked again at that photograph taken on the pier, she felt the tiniest spark of defiance. Why not her?

The sea answered with its endless rhythm. It told her she was small, but not insignificant. It told her that tides could lift anything, even a girl with second-hand shoes and a name too long to fit in lights.

The days at the factory blurred into a rhythm of metal and sweat. The air smelled of grease and hot steel, of oil thick enough to coat the back of her throat. Machines pounded like iron hearts, steady and relentless, each thump a reminder that the war was still raging across the ocean. Norma Jeane tied back her hair with a rag, the curls catching stray wisps of dust, and pressed her body into the work. Rivets, bolts, casings—she learned them all by touch, her hands moving with a mechanical grace that belied the boredom gnawing at her mind.

The other girls worked beside her, sleeves rolled to their elbows, chatter rising over the din. They shared stories about sweethearts in uniform, about movie stars whose posters were tacked above their beds, about ration coupons and the latest dances at the USO. Norma Jeane listened, smiled when expected, even joined in their laughter. But inside she was elsewhere—her thoughts floating to the pier, to the sea, to the photographs already beginning to whisper promises she barely dared to believe.

She received letters from Jimmy, written in a neat, earnest hand. They smelled faintly of salt and foreign paper, like the trace of another world. He wrote about the Navy, about the camaraderie of the men, about longing for home. She read them carefully, holding each one as if it might tether her to the life she had sworn to live. But more and more, the words felt distant, like echoes from a hallway she had already walked down. Jimmy's letters reminded her of loyalty, but not of destiny. She wanted something bigger than loyalty. She wanted to be seen, not only remembered.

On her breaks, she wandered down to the pier. It was her sanctuary, her mirror, her stage. Children shrieked as they chased kites; couples strolled with arms entwined, the women in dresses that swished like promises. Sailors crowded the boardwalk, flirting with girls who laughed too loudly, their shoes clattering on the planks. Vendors sold popcorn, hot dogs, candy apples. The smell of saltwater clung to everything, sweet and sharp, as if the ocean itself had secrets to tell.

Norma Jeane leaned against the railing, watching the waves roll in with their endless insistence. Sometimes she closed her eyes and imagined the sea carrying her name farther than she could ever walk. Not Norma Jeane Dougherty, not even Norma Jeane Mortenson, but something new. A name that shimmered. A name that held her whole story without giving it away. She tried them on silently, savoring syllables like dresses pulled from a rack. Dolores. Jeanette. Marilyn.

One afternoon, a man with a camera approached her on the pier. He wasn't the first, but he carried himself differently—confident, certain that he could see something others had missed. He asked if she'd ever considered modeling. The question wasn't new, but the way he asked it was. His lens was a promise, his gaze both professional and electric. He snapped a few shots, just for practice, he said. When she saw them later, she almost didn't recognize herself. Her eyes caught the light, her mouth hinted at secrets, her whole body radiated possibility.

That night she couldn't sleep. She stared at the photographs under her lamp, running her fingertips over the gloss as if touching proof of another life. She felt the tension sharp in her chest: Jimmy's ring on her finger, the letters folded in her drawer, the vows that had bound her to permanence. And yet—here was evidence of another fate, one that glittered just out of reach.

At the factory the next morning, the machines seemed louder, the work heavier. Every clang of metal echoed against the images she had seen of herself. She moved more slowly, her hands aching, her shoulders stiff. It was as if her body had already begun rejecting the life of rivets and grease. When the foreman barked at her to hurry, she bit back a smile. If only he knew. If only he could see the girl in the photographs.

The pier called to her again and again. She found herself drifting there even when she had no time, as if the sea could steady the storm inside her. She watched young couples kiss, their shadows stretching long in the setting sun, and she felt the loneliness press against her ribs. She longed for a love that wasn't arranged, that wasn't survival, that didn't come with conditions written in someone else's hand. She wanted a love that saw her—truly saw her—the way the camera did.

And so the transformation deepened. She bleached her hair lighter, brighter, letting the curls soften into a halo that caught every sliver of light. She bought cheap lipstick and painted her mouth into a new language. She practiced her walk in front of the mirror, a rhythm of sway and pause, as if each step declared a secret. Slowly, Norma Jeane dissolved into a figure she barely recognized but could not stop becoming.

The ocean knew. The ocean always knew. It lapped at the pier, eternal, indifferent, yet strangely affirming. Each wave seemed to whisper: go farther, go brighter, don't turn back. She breathed it in, salty and raw, and felt the girl she had been recede like the tide.

By the time the war neared its end, the factory no longer felt like a prison. It felt like a stepping stone. The pier was no longer just a refuge. It was a launching pad. And the photographs—those images caught in a square of paper—were no longer dreams. They were instructions. She followed them without hesitation, each pose a prophecy, each glance a map to the life that awaited her.

The factory was its own strange theater, louder than any orchestra pit. The girls worked shoulder to shoulder, hair tied up in scarves, overalls stained with oil, fingers nicked by the sharp edges of metal parts. Some whistled along with the radio, belting out war songs off-key, others muttered about paychecks or sweethearts gone overseas. Norma Jeane fit in and stood apart all at once. She was eager, cheerful, quick to laugh when a drill bit slipped or a wrench clattered to the floor. But beneath her bandanna, a few loose curls glowed like embers, and when she leaned into the light, even the grease on her cheek couldn't hide the glow in her eyes.

At lunch breaks, the women gathered in noisy clusters, swapping sandwiches and lipstick tips. Norma Jeane sometimes sat on the edge of the group, chewing slowly, listening more than she spoke. Once, a girl named Frances leaned across and said, "You ever notice the foreman watches you more than the rest of us?" The others giggled, teasing her until her cheeks burned. She shook her head, smiling nervously, and muttered something about not noticing. But she had noticed. She always noticed when eyes lingered. It was the same sensation she'd known in school when a photographer's lens found her face. A mix of dread and delight. Attention was dangerous, but it was also the only proof she existed.

When her shift ended, she often wandered to the pier before catching the trolley home. In daylight, the boardwalk was a noisy carnival of hawkers, saltwater taffy stands, and sailors with their caps tilted just so. But at night, the neon lights pulsed like veins against the dark, the Ferris wheel turned slow and solemn above the surf, and the laughter of strangers carried over the water. Norma Jeane walked alone, clutching the rail, letting the wind whip through her curls. She studied the couples arm in arm, the sailors leaning too close to girls with painted lips. She watched, memorized, wondered if she would ever be one of them—not a shadow on the pier but a star glowing above it all.

Sometimes she dropped a nickel into the fortune machine, watching the card spit out with its promise of luck or love. She tucked them into her pocket like evidence of another life waiting just ahead. Once the machine declared: "A new name will bring you fortune." She laughed, but the words haunted her long after, as if even the tin machine could sense the tug-of-war inside her. Mrs. Dougherty on one side, Marilyn Monroe stirring on the other.

At home, she unfolded Jimmy's letters carefully, smoothing the creases as if the paper itself might bruise. He wrote about barracks life, about drills and mess hall food, about missing her cooking and the way she hummed when she washed dishes. His words were steady, kind, ordinary. She answered in the same tone—descriptions of the weather, of her chores, of how she longed for his safe return. But after sealing the envelope, she sometimes sat at the table staring at her hands, imagining them holding not just a pen but something more—perhaps a script, perhaps a bouquet of flowers from a stranger who adored her without knowing her story.

The factory photographer had been back more than once. He liked her look, he said. The light loved her. She laughed it off, pretending she didn't care, but when she got home, she slipped into the bathroom, stared at herself in the mirror, and whispered the names she was trying on: Dolores. Jean. Marilyn. Each one felt like a garment too big or too small, none fitting yet, but each suggesting a possibility. The reflection staring back seemed to shimmer between them, never fully settled, as if waiting for permission to step forward.

Nights at the pier, mornings at the factory, afternoons with grease under her fingernails—it was all ordinary and not ordinary at once. She was Mrs.

Dougherty on paper, but inside, something larger hummed. The war had given women work, had given her a paycheck, but it had also given her a glimpse of herself outside the confines of wife and ward. She could be more. She could be seen. That thought terrified her. That thought kept her awake long after the whistle blew and the lights went dark.

21

The Golden Chosen

The war had a way of swallowing men whole. Jim Dougherty shipped out with a crisp uniform and steady handshakes, leaving his young bride behind with promises that bent like reeds in the wind. Letters would come, he said. He would write about the sea, about the ports, about the faraway days that would pass until they were back in each other's arms. Norma Jeane clung to those words as if they were made of oak, but the truth was paper—thin, fragile, and already yellowing around the edges.

In the absence of Jim, the house became something else. It echoed differently, emptier, the walls more brittle. Norma Jeane scrubbed them anyway, as if polishing wood could fill silence. She prepared dinners for one, sat at the small table with her fork and knife carefully placed as if she were expecting company. The radio hummed through the evenings, pulling her from loneliness into the voices of strangers who crooned, promised, and sometimes lied. War made liars of many men, and women left behind had to make peace with silence.

She was 16 and then 17, balanced on the edge of adulthood with no one to steady her. The war pulled young women into factories, and she was no exception. The munitions plant was a place of clang and roar, machines pounding like steel hearts. She tied a kerchief over her hair, slipped into coveralls, and became one more Rosie among the rivets. Grease stained her hands, and the air smelled of oil, sweat, and something acrid that clung to her skin long after she washed. Yet even there, amid the thunder of industry, she carried herself with a grace that startled the men who passed by her station.

It was there—on one of those long, loud days—that fate wandered by in the form of a man with a camera. He was documenting the war effort, capturing the faces of women who had stepped into men's roles while their husbands and brothers fought overseas. Most of the girls looked away or laughed shyly, caught off guard by the lens. Norma Jeane looked directly into it. The camera looked back. Something happened between them—an exchange, a recognition. In that instant, she wasn't a factory girl. She was possibility itself.

The photograph made its rounds, first through the company bulletin, then into the hands of someone who saw more than a dutiful worker. She was invited to pose again, properly this time, not beside roaring machines but in the soft light that made her skin glow like milk. She had no training, no idea how to stand or tilt her chin. But when the flash went off, she felt that same baptism she had known in school pictures: the transformation from invisible girl to chosen one. Each click was a door opening, and she stepped through willingly.

Her hair darkened by factory soot seemed heavy in the photographs, so one photographer suggested lightening it. Just a shade, he said. A touch of gold. She agreed. The dye stung her scalp, smelled like chemicals, and left her dizzy, but when she looked in the mirror, she saw something electric. The girl from orphanages and borrowed shoes was fading. In her place was someone brighter, someone who shimmered under lights. It wasn't yet Marilyn, not quite, but it was no longer only Norma Jeane.

The first modeling jobs were modest: ads for soap, for stockings, for small magazines that promised beauty on a dime. She posed with a practiced smile, one hand on her hip, the other cradling a box of detergent or smoothing a hemline. Yet there was something in her that refused to stay modest. The camera caught more than she offered. It pulled from her a light she hadn't known she carried. Men in the studio leaned in. Photographers adjusted their lenses as if she had changed the laws of exposure. The photographs spoke louder than she did, and they said: here is someone meant to be seen.

The checks came small at first, but even coins felt like liberation. She bought her own shoes—shoes that fit, shoes that gleamed without polish, shoes that carried her like she belonged on every sidewalk. She bought a dress not from a donation bin but from a store where the clerk folded tissue paper around it as though handling treasure. She wore it home under her coat, bursting with the secret knowledge that she was building herself piece by piece.

Still, the ache of absence lingered. She wrote letters to Jim with dutiful affection, describing her days at the plant, her cooking, her walks along the beach. She left out the photographs, the small triumphs, the quickening of her pulse when she stepped in front of a lens. She knew those details belonged to her alone. To confess them would be to risk losing them. Jim was kind, steady, practical—everything she was not. Their marriage had been born from necessity, not fire. He was the answer to a problem, not the question she burned to ask.

At night, when the radio whispered songs through the static, she lay awake imagining herself on a screen. She practiced the names again: Dolores, Lana, Hedy, Marilyn. The sound of them soothed her like a lullaby. She whispered them until sleep took her, and even then, she dreamed of lights brighter than day and applause louder than war.

Her modeling caught more eyes. A photographer named David Conover saw in her not just a subject but a star in embryo. He coaxed expressions from her that startled even her own reflection. "The camera loves you," he told her. She blushed, not out of modesty but because it felt like prophecy. Each photograph he took seemed to erase the years of silence, the times she had been left behind, the bruises, the hunger, the endless goodbyes. In their place was an image of a girl who might someday walk into a room and silence it with nothing more than her presence.

She began clipping her own pictures from magazines, tucking them into a box beneath her bed. It was her secret shrine. Each page smelled faintly of ink and hope. She wasn't just in them—she was becoming them. She studied the angles of her face, the curl of her smile, the way light loved her. It wasn't vanity. It was survival. The girl who had once hidden behind borrowed dresses was learning to step into a body the world wanted to see.

And yet, every time she folded a letter to Jim and signed it "Yours, Norma Jeane," she felt a tremor. Whose name belonged to her now? The girl in the letters or the girl in the photographs? Could they both survive? Or was one destined to vanish so the other could be born?

The war gave her cover. With men overseas and women stepping into their places, no one questioned why a young wife sought work beyond her kitchen. Factories were full of faces like hers, women in kerchiefs with sleeves rolled up, carrying wrenches and rivet guns. But she was not like the others, not exactly. Where most wore fatigue like armor, she wore it like costume. Her smile, even beneath the grime, was theater. Her laugh carried through the din of machinery. Supervisors noticed. Photographers noticed. Even her fellow workers noticed, though they sometimes covered their envy with barbed remarks: "She thinks she's a movie star."

Perhaps she did. Perhaps she always had.

The pier became her refuge. During breaks she would walk to the edge, let the salt wind lick her face, and stare at the Pacific. The waves folded over one another endlessly, like a script written and rewritten by a restless hand.

She thought of her mother, somewhere behind hospital walls. She thought of her absent father, a shadow whose name still burned. And she thought of herself—was she Norma Jeane, the girl with second-hand shoes, or someone else entirely, someone the tide had washed clean?

On some afternoons, sailors strolled the boardwalk. They leaned against the railings, laughed too loudly, bought peanuts from vendors. A few tipped their caps at her, whistled when she passed. She smiled politely, but inside she wondered what it might feel like to belong to that kind of gaze—not as prey, but as prize. The ocean roared behind her, eternal and indifferent, as if mocking her small human hunger to be remembered.

Her letters to Grace betrayed none of this inner turmoil. She wrote of beans on the stove, of ironing shirts, of sweeping sand from the doorstep. She drew floor plans of the house she shared with Jim, careful sketches that suggested order and permanence. But between the lines was a truth she couldn't yet name: she had built herself into a wife, and it fit her no better than the too-loose shoes she had once polished to a shine.

The photographs, however, told another story. Each one was a step further from the girl who had cowered in dormitory beds or clutched her pillow in fear. Each pose was an argument with her past: look, I am not invisible. Look, I am worth keeping. Look, I can be beautiful. And in those pictures, she was.

The first time she saw her face on a small poster for a local shop, she stood frozen on the sidewalk, staring as if at a ghost. Passersby brushed past, but she couldn't move. The girl in the poster smiled back, her hair curling at her cheek, her eyes glimmering with a light she barely recognized. Was that her? Or had she already become someone else?

The world was beginning to conspire in her favor. A studio scout mentioned her name. A stylist offered to lighten her hair. "Blondes sell," he said, and though she laughed, she understood. To be seen, she might have to let go of the last traces of the girl she had been. To rise, she might have to disappear.

The ring on her finger spun loosely, as if it too knew she was slipping. Jim was still away, his letters dutiful but uninspired. He wrote of ship routines, of weather, of the monotony of service. She replied with careful affection, but her heart no longer lived in the words. It lived in the photographs, in the pier, in the mirror where she rehearsed smiles meant for larger stages. The marriage had given her shelter, yes—but now the shelter felt like a cage.

She walked home from the pier one evening, the last light of day painting the sky bruised purple. She clutched her coat around her shoulders and whispered to herself the name she had tried on in secret. Marilyn. It felt dangerous on her tongue, like a spark that might ignite if spoken too loudly. Marilyn. The ocean swallowed the word whole, but she knew she had said it. And once said, it could not be unsaid.

Evenings were the hardest. The factory day left her hands raw, her hair coated with a fine dust that never seemed to rinse out completely. Other women trudged home, arms full of groceries, babies tugging at their skirts. She envied them, though she knew better. Their lives were no fairy tale—ration books, long lines, nights alone with radios whispering bad news from overseas. Yet they had a rhythm, a claim on normalcy. She had only the silence of the little house, the loose ring on her finger, and the letters that came like clockwork from Jim.

She read his words aloud sometimes, trying to hear affection in their stiff syllables. "Dearest Norma Jeane . . ." followed by weather reports, mentions of chow, of poker games with the other sailors. She underlined the endearments, as if ink could make them more true. Then she folded the letters carefully and tucked them away, where they would not betray how empty they made her feel. Jim was faithful, steady, everything a husband was supposed to be. But she was already drifting away, her mind crowded with flashes of light bulbs and shutter clicks, with the dizzying possibility that someone else might want her—not as wife, but as vision.

On nights when sleep refused her, she walked back to the pier. The boardwalk smelled of salt and fried food, of popcorn gone stale and the oil of carnival rides. She watched couples leaning against the railing, watched the shadows of soldiers with their girls, watched the carousel spin with its painted horses chasing eternity. The lights of Santa Monica blurred into the horizon, and she imagined her face among them, 10 feet high, impossible to ignore. She whispered again the name she had only dared to try in solitude. Marilyn. Each time, it felt less like fantasy and more like destiny.

Neighbors began to notice. The girl who posed for photographs was no longer just Jim's young wife; she was the one photographers called "a natural." Some looked at her with suspicion—who did she think she was, grinning for strangers? Others with admiration, as if her ascent might sprinkle light on their own dim lives. She walked between those gazes with the practiced smile she had perfected since childhood, balancing on the edge between ridicule and adoration.

The modeling money was small, but it shimmered with promise. Each check felt like a ticket out of invisibility, like a signal that the camera saw something permanent in her. With each assignment, her confidence grew. She learned how to angle her face, how to lift her chin to elongate the neck, how to let her eyes carry both innocence and hunger. The men behind the cameras praised her, their voices thick with approval, and though she flushed under their attention, she also thrived on it. The camera didn't ask about her mother's illness, didn't pry into her childhood. It wanted only her face, her smile, her light. For once, that was enough.

But in the quiet afterward, doubt crept in. She would peel off her lipstick in front of the mirror, watching the girl beneath reappear—Norma Jeane, plain, tired, uncertain. Who was real? The wife who cooked beans and ironed Jim's shirts, or the dreamer who leaned into the lens as if it could hold her forever? She pressed her palms to the mirror, as if trying to fuse the two selves into one, but the glass only chilled her skin.

One afternoon, a photographer mentioned platinum. "You'd be dynamite as a blonde," he said, and though she laughed it off, the suggestion lodged itself in her imagination. Platinum. A color not of this world, a transformation that would banish Norma Jeane's shadow for good. She pictured herself emerging from the beauty parlor, light bouncing off her hair like a halo, strangers turning to look, whispering, Who is she? Already the girl with scuffed shoes and second-hand dresses was fading. Already Marilyn was stirring.

The factory never truly slept. Even when the machines wound down at night, their echoes hung in the rafters like restless spirits. The smell of oil and metal clung to her skin long after she had scrubbed her hands raw. For Norma Jeane, it was a world of thunder and sparks, a place where the hum of labor drowned out loneliness—at least for a while. She walked past rows of women in overalls, their faces streaked with grease, their hair wrapped in scarves, and she felt, for the first time, a strange sense of belonging. They were all here because someone needed them, because men had gone overseas, because war had left gaps that women were asked to fill.

She worked quickly, careful to prove herself capable. At lunch she sat with girls who smoked cigarettes down to the filter and swapped stories about boyfriends in the Pacific, husbands in Europe, brothers who might never return. They teased her for being quiet, for blushing when one of them told a bawdy joke, but they pulled her into their circle anyway. She laughed along, even when the laughter didn't reach her bones. When the bell rang, they went back to their stations, shoulders squared against fatigue, eyes fixed on the task at hand.

And yet, in the quieter moments, her thoughts returned to Jim. His letters arrived on pale blue stationery, the handwriting steady but distant. He wrote of the weather, of meals eaten in mess halls, of drills that left him sore. He never wrote of longing, not the way she wished. She read the words under her breath at night, folding the paper back into neat creases, and wondered if marriage was supposed to feel like this: an obligation more than a promise. She tried to love him, tried to summon the warmth she thought a wife should feel, but the effort left her hollow.

The pier became her refuge. On breaks, she walked to the end of the boardwalk where the ocean stretched into forever. The salt air filled her lungs, the gulls wheeled above, and she let the sound of the waves wash away the noise of the factory. Children ran past her with sticky fingers and paper kites, couples leaned into each other with the easy certainty of belonging, and Norma Jeane stood alone, watching, imagining. She whispered names to the wind—hers, but also the ones she had begun to try on in secret. Marilyn. Monroe. The words carried differently in the air, lighter, freer, like sails catching wind.

She was still the girl with second-hand shoes, still the foster child who had begged for permanence, but now there was something else, something quickening. When a photographer paused at the factory floor to take pictures of the women at work, she felt the flash strike her like lightning. Later, when she saw the print, she barely recognized herself. The girl in the photograph looked strong, almost radiant, as if she belonged to the world and not just to a factory line.

It frightened her as much as it thrilled her. The attention was intoxicating, but it also whispered of danger—because once you were seen, you could no longer hide. Fame was still a shadow on the horizon, not yet within reach, but she felt its pull already. At the pier, she leaned against the railing and closed her eyes, imagining a life beyond the machines, beyond the letters, beyond the limits of a girl who had once been told she was only temporary.

She stayed there until the gulls settled, until the neon lights blinked awake along the boardwalk, until she could almost believe the dream waiting for her was not just a dream at all.

22

Winning the War

She was no longer just Norma Jeane Dougherty, the girl in scuffed shoes and hand-me-down dresses. But she was not yet Marilyn Monroe either, not yet the woman whose face would cover the gloss of magazines stacked at newsstands from Broadway to Sunset. She lived suspended between those names, inhabiting a strange, uncharted country of self-invention.

The war had made everything feel provisional, temporary, like stage scenery that could be torn down overnight. Jimmy was overseas, his letters full of clipped sentences and assurances that he was fine, that she should take care of herself. He wrote of the sea, the monotony of drills, the boredom of nights spent playing cards. His letters read like reports from another planet, and though she answered dutifully, she could not help feeling like their marriage belonged more to Grace's imagination than to her own heart. She had been promised as a kind of bargain, a girl traded into security, and now security itself was an ocean away.

She worked at the Radio Plane factory in Van Nuys, the clang of machinery and the sharp scent of varnish filling her days. She sanded fuselage panels until her arms ached, ran drills into aluminum, painted the edges of wings. Grease stained her nails, her hair was tied back with kerchiefs, and the air was so thick with dust that it clung to her throat. It was grueling, repetitive work, but it was steady, and in those years steady was everything.

And yet—something was shifting. The factory was crawling with photographers, newspapermen, propagandists eager to showcase the fresh-faced women who had replaced men in overalls. It was supposed to be patriotic—the American girl stepping in to build the weapons of war—but sometimes the men behind the cameras lingered too long, their lenses focused less on the rivets than on the curve of a smile.

One day, when the factory floor was buzzing with the drone of drills, a photographer from *Yank* magazine spotted her. She was crouched beside a plane wing, hair tucked back, coveralls rolled up at the ankles. She looked up, squinting into the light, and something in her face caught him. He asked her to pose, to look this way, that way. She laughed nervously, brushing dust from her cheeks. For once, the camera didn't demand a schoolgirl smile—it seemed to want her, exactly as she was.

When the pictures came back, they circulated fast. Men on the floor whistled, nudged each other. "That's Dougherty's wife," one said, holding up the magazine like proof. She stared at the image in disbelief. Was that her? The tilt of the chin, the flash in the eyes—she looked confident, luminous, nothing like the girl who had stared into cracked mirrors in Hawthorne. That photograph didn't show grease under her nails, didn't reveal the rent notices pinned to the wall. It suggested something else, something she could become if she dared to believe it.

Soon, other photographers came sniffing around. They saw not just a worker in coveralls but a girl who glowed even in bad light. They asked her to sit for more pictures, offered a few dollars, promised introductions. At first, she hesitated. She was still married, still supposed to be Mrs. Dougherty, keeping house and waiting for her husband's return. But the lens called to her with a voice louder than duty. Every click of the shutter was like a note in a new song, a song she hadn't yet learned the words to but already knew by heart.

At night, she practiced poses in the mirror, studying the angles of her face, the ways she could widen her eyes or part her lips to suggest mystery. She copied what she saw in movie magazines—Greta Garbo's inscrutable stare, Jean Harlow's brazen tilt of the head. But she added something of her own: vulnerability, a hint of tremor behind the smile, as though she were asking the viewer to look closer, to notice the ache beneath the glamour. Even then, before the world knew her name, she was inventing the alchemy that would one day make her unforgettable.

Jimmy did not understand. When he came home on brief leave, she showed him a photograph clipped from a newspaper. He looked at it, then at her, then shrugged. "It's nice," he said, his voice flat. She waited for more, for admiration, for jealousy, for anything that suggested he grasped what was happening. But he only asked whether she'd remembered to send his shoes to the cobbler. She realized then how far apart they already were, living not just in different places but in different stories.

Still, she pressed on. She signed with the Blue Book Model Agency, where the agents taught her how to stand, how to walk, how to look at a camera as though it were a lover across a crowded room. They told her to bleach her hair, to trade the soft brown curls for something brighter, more electric. She hesitated—her mother's hair had been auburn, her own childhood photographs marked by the natural softness of her waves. But the stylists insisted: blonde was the ticket. Blonde was a golden passport.

The first time she saw herself in the mirror after the peroxide, she almost didn't recognize the girl staring back. The hair was platinum, the skin luminous, the eyes somehow wider. She touched the strands, half-ashamed, half-thrilled. She felt like an imposter and a queen all at once. She walked out of the salon into the Los Angeles sun, and the city seemed to notice her in a new way. Men turned their heads. Women glanced twice. The world had shifted by a shade, and she was at its center.

Her modeling career quickened. She appeared in catalogs, advertisements, small spreads in magazines. Sometimes she modeled sweaters, sometimes swimsuits. She learned how to smile without showing too much tooth, how to arch her back to lengthen her figure, how to let a photographer's command wash over her without flinching. And she began to sense the double edge of visibility: how easily admiration slid into objectification, how quickly praise became possession.

But she also felt something else—power. For the first time in her life, she could shape how she was seen. Poverty, orphanages, hand-me-down shoes—those did not matter in the gloss of a photograph. She could choose the angle, the expression, the impression. She could be someone else entirely.

The studio men noticed. Casting agents drifted into the modeling shoots, slipping her their cards, suggesting screen tests. She wasn't ready yet, not fully, but she listened. She listened the way a thirsty person listens to the promise of water. The name "Marilyn Monroe" began to circulate, first as a whisper, then as a suggestion. Norma Jeane Mortenson had never meant much to anyone. Marilyn Monroe sounded like destiny.

And yet, even as she was remade in peroxide and flashbulbs, loneliness clung to her. At night, after a day of being posed and praised, she returned to the small apartments where she lived with borrowed furniture and silence. She thought of her mother, locked away, and wondered if Gladys would even recognize her now. She thought of Jimmy, so far away, and realized she barely remembered the sound of his voice. She thought of herself—this self, this blonde apparition—and tried to believe she was real.

It was a precarious magic, and she knew it. Fame was beginning to stretch its fingers toward her, but she also knew how easily things slipped away. Shoes wore out. Families fractured. Mothers vanished. Husbands sailed off and didn't look back. She clutched the photographs to her chest, not because she believed they told the truth, but because they promised a future. A future where she would not be erased, where her smile would outlast the loneliness that had shadowed her since birth.

The girl in the second-hand shoes was almost gone. In her place stood a woman rehearsing for eternity.

The war years blurred, a calendar torn into pages of factory shifts, ration cards, blackout curtains, and letters folded into careful squares. For other wives, it was sacrifice. For Norma Jeane, it was a strange kind of cocoon. Jimmy was far away, his presence reduced to ink on paper, and she was left to grow in his absence. The world saw her as Mrs. Dougherty, but the mirror saw someone else emerging—someone who stood a little straighter each time a camera caught her.

The munitions factory hardened her hands. Splinters from wooden crates lodged in her palms, grease stained her cuticles until no amount of scrubbing restored them. She wore the bandanna high across her forehead, the way the magazines showed Rosie the Riveter, but even when she tried to mimic that sturdy pride, she never quite felt it was her costume. She was still too soft, too fragile, too full of longing to be satisfied by the clang of machinery. Yet she worked without complaint. She knew how quickly complaints were punished. The orphanage had taught her that gratitude was safer than honesty.

On her breaks she scribbled notes in the margins of envelopes—half-formed lines about how the light struck the ocean, or how the smell of the pier reminded her of freedom. She didn't know she was keeping a diary. She only knew that when she wrote, she could hold herself together, pin her life down with ink the way a photographer pinned it with film.

Sometimes, after the shift, she wandered toward the pier still wearing her grease-stained dress, the scarf slipping from her hair. She would lean on the railing, letting the sea wind lift her curls into disarray, and watch the sun dissolve into the horizon. The waves glittered like sequins, endless and unreachable. Lovers strolled arm in arm past her, their laughter mixing with the cries of the gulls. She watched them the way a child watches the closed door of a party, aching to be let in. The pier reminded her that she was both part of the world and apart from it—a girl on the edge, waiting to be called inside.

The call came not from a mother, not from a husband, but from the camera. The more she posed, the more she learned the alchemy of transformation. Tilt the chin, soften the eyes, let the lips part slightly as if caught mid-breath. She became a study in illusion. Each click of the shutter was a rehearsal for a life she had not yet claimed. The men behind the lenses murmured praise—"beautiful," "perfect," "a natural"—and she drank their words as if they were water in a desert. For the first time, someone wanted her not out of duty but desire. She was chosen. That mattered more than she dared admit.

But the attention frightened her too. She had learned that what was given could be taken, and faster than the blink of a flash. At night she lay awake staring at the ceiling, wondering if her brief spark would vanish, if she would return to being invisible. She touched her face, her hair, as if checking that she still existed. Sometimes she whispered her new name, Marilyn, into the dark, to test if it belonged to her yet. The sound startled her—it was both foreign and familiar, like a melody she half-remembered. She clung to it the way children cling to lullabies.

Jimmy's letters reminded her of the other life, the one she was supposed to be living. He asked after her days, after meals, after the little house they would share when he returned. She answered dutifully, drawing sketches of floor plans, describing casseroles she hadn't cooked, pretending to relish the role of housewife she was already outgrowing. The lies tasted like chalk on her tongue, but she sent them anyway. She didn't want to wound him, not while he was serving, not while death brushed so close to the men around him. But with each letter, the distance widened. She was becoming someone he had never met, someone who might not wait for him at the station when the war ended.

The pier became her confession booth. She whispered her fears into the salt wind, as if the sea could absolve her. Some nights she imagined walking into the water and letting it carry her away, washing off the grease, the lies, the weight of being unwanted. Other nights she imagined the ocean lifting her up, turning her reflection into a starry marquee. Both visions felt possible, and both terrified her.

The more she modeled, the more she tasted the strangeness of being seen. Photographers urged her to arch her back, to pout, to widen her eyes. They dressed her in clothes she had never touched before—silk blouses, pencil skirts, even a swimsuit that felt like both armor and exposure. When she saw the proofs, she barely recognized herself. The girl staring back was polished, glamorous, almost untouchable. Yet inside she still felt the sting of old shoes, the hollowness of going hungry, the ache of a mother's absence. The pictures told one story; her heart told another. She wondered which story the world would believe.

The war made it easier to explain her new life. With Jimmy overseas, she was free to pose, to travel to shoots, to reinvent herself without the scrutiny of a husband's eyes. She wrote to Grace, spinning cheerful details about her work, about how much she was learning, about how proud Jimmy would be. But she knew Grace understood the subtext. Grace had always known she was destined for something beyond small kitchens and mended dresses. Grace had been the first to call her pretty, to suggest she could be more. Now, in the quiet between letters, Grace was proved right.

The pier lights blinked on at dusk, each bulb a tiny star strung across the boardwalk. Norma Jeane—or Marilyn, as she practiced calling herself—sat on the benches and let the glow wash over her. She imagined an audience watching her silhouette against the ocean, waiting for her to step onto a stage. The applause was not yet real, but she heard it anyway. It carried her home, carried her through the factory doors the next morning, carried her into the arms of the camera that never stopped asking for more.

She was beginning to understand the cost of being seen. Once the world noticed you, it never stopped looking. And once you learned to shine, it was impossible to return to the shadows without grief. Still, she chose it. Again and again, she chose the light. Because light, even borrowed, even cruel, was better than the darkness of being forgotten.

The nights grew longer, and with them her sense of waiting—waiting for Jimmy, waiting for a letter that might steady her, waiting for a chance that seemed always just out of reach. At the factory gates, the foreman tipped his hat and called her "kid." At the pier, sailors on leave whistled and called her "doll." But no one called her home.

She began to measure her days in photographs. A smile here, a glance there, the click of a shutter that seemed to hold more truth than any diary. Photographers compared her to Lana Turner, to Betty Grable, even to Jean Harlow, whose platinum hair haunted her. Norma Jeane pretended to laugh at the comparisons, but inside she trembled. If they could see her as those women, maybe she could become them. Maybe she could step through the frame and into a life where shoes matched, and nobody forgot her name.

And yet, when she walked home through the dim streets, the war still pressed close. Families taped windows against bomb blasts that never came, neighbors collected rubber and tin, mothers clipped ration stamps with hands that shook. Every radio broadcast brought the crackle of news, and in the pauses between words she heard the silence of Jimmy's absence. His ring still circled her finger, but it felt like a borrowed prop now, heavy with promises that belonged to another girl, a younger one who had not yet been kissed by flashbulbs.

Some evenings she stopped before a mirror in a drugstore window, her reflection blurred by neon. The woman who stared back looked older than 16. The scarf slipping from her curls, the lipstick bright against her tired face, the faint ache in her eyes—she didn't look like a child playing house anymore. She looked like someone standing at the edge of a stage, waiting for the curtain to rise.

What she didn't know, not fully, was that she was already changing. Each pose, each photograph, each whisper of "Marilyn" under her breath—these were the first rehearsals for the myth. The ocean, the factory, the borrowed dresses, the long nights of waiting—they were her stage wings. And when she finally stepped forward, when the world turned its gaze to her, she would remember the salt wind of the pier and the flashbulbs of the factory floor as the places where she first learned to be seen.

23

The Ghost in the Mirror

The war droned on relentless as the tide. Factories thundered, headlines screamed victories and losses in equal measure, and telegram boys rode their bicycles through neighborhoods like omens. Every knock on a door could undo a family. Every shadow held both fear and longing. Norma Jeane moved through it all with the quiet focus of someone who had already survived too much to be undone by waiting.

Jimmy was away, swallowed by the war's machinery. His letters came steady, filled with plain words about rations and routines, about the ship that carried him across dark waters, about the hope of coming home. She read them carefully, tracing each line with her finger, but they never quite reached her heart. His words were like fences—meant to reassure, meant to enclose—but they left her outside in the wind, staring through the slats at a life she had agreed to but did not live in.

She worked, she posed, she smiled. The factory became its own strange stage: the hiss of steam, the clang of steel, the smell of oil in the air. She tied her hair up in a kerchief, smeared her face with grease, and laughed with the other girls who called themselves "Rosies." But inside she was different. Every time a photographer passed, she straightened her back, lifted her chin, and let her eyes hold a secret. She wasn't just another girl doing her part. She was already rehearsing for a future they couldn't imagine.

The camera adored her. Even when she was caught unaware, even when the light was wrong, even when her dress was wrinkled, there was something that drew the eye. Photographers began to ask her name, to tell her to stand closer, to look left, to look right, to laugh, to pout. She gave them all of it—eager, hesitant, hungry—because in those moments she felt alive in a way that scrubbing floors and making meatloaf never could.

But the nights told a different story. Alone in the small house, she sometimes caught her reflection in the mirror and did not recognize it. The curls falling over her forehead, the powder on her cheeks, the practiced smile—it was a mask. Beneath it was a girl who still dreamed of a mother arriving at the door with cookies, who still remembered the weight of shame when shoes didn't fit, who still feared the silence of being forgotten.

She whispered to the mirror sometimes, asking it questions she could not put in letters. Who am I becoming? Who do you see? The reflection answered only with her own gaze, soft and haunted, as if another presence lingered just behind the glass. She thought of Jean Harlow again, the star who had died too young, her ghost rumored to haunt Hollywood boulevards. Was that the face she glimpsed in the mirror—some spirit of glamour, some promise of transformation that demanded her surrender?

When she walked the streets of Los Angeles, she felt the city shifting beneath her feet. Billboards announced the latest stars, neon lights flickered above nightclubs, radios poured jazz into the air. Men in uniforms leaned against lampposts, cigarettes glowing like fireflies. Women in fur collars hurried past, perfume trailing after them like smoke. She studied them all, memorizing gestures, tilts of the head, the way laughter could hide hunger. She was learning her lines without a script, improvising her way toward a stage she had not yet seen.

The truth was, marriage had already become another orphanage. Not cruel, not cold, not loveless—but confining. A safehouse disguised as home. Jim had given her his name, but not the belonging she craved. She wore the ring like a hand-me-down dress, aware it was useful, aware it was protection, but never convinced it was hers. She was grateful, she was dutiful, she was careful. But inside she was restless.

She turned to the radio at night, letting music carry her away. Bing Crosby, Glenn Miller, the Andrews Sisters—they filled the silence, gave her room to dream. Sometimes she would stand in the living room and dance alone, her shadow flickering on the walls. She imagined an audience, imagined applause, imagined the world opening its arms. She was no longer just Norma Jeane, the girl with the second-hand shoes. She was becoming someone else. The name still hovered on her tongue—Marilyn Monroe—like a secret waiting to burst free.

One evening, after a long shift, she stopped at the pier again. The ocean roared like a restless crowd, the lights shimmered across the water, and she felt, for just a moment, that she was standing between two lives. Behind her was the girl who had survived orphanages, foster homes, betrayals, and loneliness. Ahead of her was the woman who would be asked to give everything she had, who would be adored, devoured, remembered, and mourned.

She wrapped her arms around herself against the wind, and for the first time, she didn't feel afraid of the choice. She felt ready. Whatever the cost, whatever the loss, she would not go back. She would not be forgotten.

The ghost in the mirror was no longer haunting her. It was guiding her.

She found herself daydreaming during the smallest of tasks—washing dishes, folding laundry, hanging Jim's shirts in the closet as if he might return any minute. The shirts looked like ghostly silhouettes lined in a row, sleeves swaying with the draft, waiting for arms that were thousands of miles away. Sometimes she pressed her cheek against them, breathing in the faint smell of starch and soap, and wondered what it would feel like to have a life filled with certainty, a life where nothing and no one disappeared.

At the factory, she worked among women who carried the same kind of weariness. They were wives, mothers, daughters, all pressed into service by the demands of the war. Their hands grew calloused, their backs ached, their laughter carried a note of defiance. But Norma Jeane always seemed to glow in a way the others didn't. Even beneath the fluorescent lights, even with grime smudged across her forehead, there was something luminous about her. When a photographer asked to take her picture for the company newsletter, she said yes, though her cheeks burned with nerves.

The photograph circulated quickly. "Who's that girl?" the men asked. "She looks like she belongs in pictures." Soon others came, cameras clicking, and Norma Jeane realized the world had just opened a small door. She peeked through it, afraid and thrilled all at once.

She did not tell Jim about the photographs. His letters were full of requests for loyalty, for steadiness, for the promise that she would wait for him. She wanted to wait. But how could she explain the way the camera made her feel? It wasn't vanity. It was survival in another form. Just as she had once learned to smile through hunger, she now learned to pose through longing. The shutter froze her in moments when she could believe she was destined for more.

At night, lying in bed with the radio humming low, she practiced names under her breath. Marilyn. Jean. Lana. Rita. She tried them on like veils, letting each alter the shape of her mouth, the rhythm of her breath. She whispered "Marilyn Monroe" into the darkness and felt her chest tighten with a strange kind of certainty. It wasn't just a name. It was an incantation.

She thought often of Gladys, of her mother's laughter that could turn to silence without warning. Did her mother dream of other names? Did she too imagine a different life in the quiet hours? Sometimes Norma Jeane worried that she was chasing illusions, the same way her mother had chased happiness through men, through movies, through the shifting haze of her own mind. But then she would see her photograph in print—her smile, her bright eyes—and she knew this wasn't madness. It was possibility.

Walking through Los Angeles, she began to feel the city responding to her. Not with recognition, not yet, but with attention. Men at newsstands let their gazes linger. Women glanced twice, sometimes with curiosity, sometimes with suspicion. Even children seemed to stare. She wore simple dresses, the same scuffed shoes, but she held herself differently now. It wasn't pretense anymore. It was the beginning of belief.

And yet, in the quietest hours, doubt still curled inside her like a hidden bruise. She feared she was betraying Jim. She feared she was betraying the fragile girl who once clutched photographs beneath her pillow and begged for permanence. She feared that every smile she gave to the camera was another step away from the people who had tried, however imperfectly, to keep her.

But when she stood in front of the mirror, she saw more than fear. She saw the faint outline of a destiny that seemed to shimmer just out of reach. She didn't know if she could grasp it. She only knew she had to try.

The ghost in the mirror was no longer only Jean Harlow, no longer only an echo of the stars who came before. It was herself, unformed, waiting to be born.

The days blurred into each other at the factory, each shift beginning with the shriek of the whistle and ending with the ache of her shoulders. The women lined up at their machines, scarves tied tight over their hair, hands blackened by grease and powder. Some sang to keep time, voices rising above the roar of presses and grinders, turning the place into a strange choir of survival. Norma Jeane joined in when she dared, her voice soft but sure, carrying a melody she wasn't certain she knew until it left her mouth.

The air was thick with oil and dust. Sparks flew. Shoes scuffed against concrete. She often looked around and wondered if anyone else felt the same—the sensation of being swallowed up by the work, disappearing into the anonymity of the crowd. Yet now and then, one of the foremen or even a fellow worker's gaze lingered a little too long. She was just another girl in coveralls, but somehow, she wasn't.

In stolen moments, she caught sight of herself reflected in the gloss of metal. The distortion was always strange, a funhouse version of her face, but it gave her ideas. What if someone were to catch her properly, with a real camera, with real light? Would she still look like this—half-child, half-woman—or would she become someone else entirely? The question haunted her, and thrilled her, and terrified her too.

On her breaks, she wandered outside to the open air. The war made everything tense, but the pier remained a place of possibility. She loved the sound of gulls fighting over scraps, the slap of waves against pylons, the laughter of children who were too young to know what headlines meant. Sailors strolled by in pairs, uniforms pressed sharp, their futures uncertain. She imagined them watching her, the way their eyes might shift as she passed, even if she kept her gaze steady on the horizon. The pier was a place of dreams for many people, but for her, it became a stage.

She practiced her walk there, alone, back straight, shoulders squared, just enough swing in her hips to suggest she belonged to no one but herself. She wondered if passersby could tell she was rehearsing, that each step was as intentional as a line in a script. Sometimes she smiled just to see if they'd smile back. Sometimes she lowered her eyes to practice mystery. The pier gave her space to pretend, and pretending was often the only thing that kept her alive.

Letters from Jim arrived sporadically, words scrawled on paper that smelled faintly of ship oil and sea air. He wrote of duties, of mess halls, of long watches under foreign skies. He called her "honey" and "sweetheart," words that should have warmed her but instead pressed on her like a weight. She answered dutifully, describing dinners she cooked and errands she ran, omitting the loneliness that clung to her like a second skin. The distance between them stretched further with each letter, an ocean made wider not by miles but by silence.

And then came the photographer. He was older, not unkind, with an eye that saw what most overlooked. He asked if she'd mind posing during her lunch break, right there on the factory floor, sunlight streaming through the high windows, dust swirling like golden confetti. She hesitated—then agreed. The camera clicked, and in that instant something shifted. The way he looked at her was not the way the boys at school had looked, nor the way Jim had, nor even the way strangers on the pier had. His gaze was intent, professional, as though he were capturing a secret she hadn't yet told herself.

When she saw the picture weeks later, her breath caught. There she was—coveralls, scarf, grease smudge across her cheek—and yet luminous, as though the camera had caught the light inside her rather than merely what was on the surface. It was the first time she understood that the camera did not just take, it transformed. She carried that photograph like a charm, tucked in a drawer, but in her mind it burned brighter than any jewel.

At night, lying alone, she traced her finger along the invisible outline of the name she hadn't yet fully claimed. Marilyn. The sound of it swelled in her chest. It was still only a whisper, a secret rehearsal like the ones she practiced on the pier. But each day, she felt the line blur a little more between the girl she had been and the woman she was becoming. And though she was still Norma Jeane on paper, in photographs, in letters from Jim, something else had already begun to bloom.

Sleep was no refuge. Dreams brought her back to places she wanted to forget—rooms where doors slammed, whispers curled like smoke, hands reached for her in the dark. But alongside those shadows came flashes of the new image: herself lit up like the women on magazine covers, her face suspended in brilliance. She woke torn between dread and hope, her heart pounding as though she'd lived two lives overnight.

Sometimes she would sit at the kitchen table long after the dishes were done, staring at the single bulb that swayed faintly with each draft of air. The silence pressed heavy, broken only by the occasional bark of a dog in the alley or the hum of a passing car. In that silence, she practiced lines she invented for herself, dialogue from films she hadn't yet been offered. She played both parts, shifting her voice, raising an eyebrow, imagining the audience laughing, sighing, leaning forward in their seats. It was theater performed for no one, yet it kept her alive.

When neighbors stopped by, she slipped into another role entirely. She was Mrs. Dougherty, the cheerful young wife, apron tied tight, voice polite. They'd compliment her biscuits or her tidy curtains, and she'd thank them sweetly, smiling as though her heart weren't aching for something nameless. She knew they saw her as settled, safe, ordinary. What none of them knew was that she was already living a double life—Norma Jeane who folded laundry and clipped coupons, and another self who was rehearsing her escape.

The war rumbled on, and with it came stories of men lost at sea, of telegrams that turned mothers into widows and wives into ghosts. She wondered if such a telegram might come to her. She pictured the knock at the door, the folded flag. Would she grieve? Would she feel freed? The thought filled her with shame, but she could not deny it. Marriage had never been the dream—it was the bargain she had struck with life to avoid the orphanage. And bargains, she was beginning to learn, always came with fine print.

The factory picture circulated more than she expected. Someone knew someone, and suddenly she was asked if she'd consider posing again. A different photographer this time, one with connections to modeling agencies. She said yes before her fear could catch up. The second set of photos was less accidental, more deliberate: her scarf tied carefully, the angle of her jaw adjusted, her eyes asked to linger on the lens as though it were a lover. The results startled her. She looked older, yes, but also bolder, as though the camera had coaxed out a woman who had been hiding inside all along.

She began receiving small checks. Five dollars, ten dollars. Not much, but more than she'd ever earned outside of the factory. More importantly, each photograph was a kind of proof—a mirror in which she glimpsed the life she wanted. She hid the checks in a jar and the photographs in a box under her bed, treasures too fragile to show anyone yet. Jim wrote letters about the monotony of military life, and she wrote back about the monotony of housework, never mentioning the photographs. How could she? How could she explain that she had started to believe in another destiny, one that had nothing to do with beans simmering on the stove or shirts pressed smooth under an iron?

One evening, walking home from the pier, she paused before a movie poster pasted to the wall of a corner store. The face of Lana Turner gazed down at her, luminous, untouchable. The crowd bustled around her, but she stood still, staring until the paper blurred. She whispered to herself, "That could be me." The words startled her, but once spoken, they could not be unsaid. She walked the rest of the way home with her shoulders a little higher, her steps a little quicker, carrying the dangerous weight of possibility.

The world around her did not change overnight. The streets were still rough, the factory still loud, her shoes still pinched. But inside, something had shifted. Each day she carried a small spark, a secret that no one could extinguish. She was not just Norma Jeane Dougherty, wife of a man at sea. She was also someone else, someone waiting for her moment. Someone who would one day walk into a room and change it just by being there.

And though she could not name it yet, she knew the truth as surely as she knew the rhythm of the factory whistle or the roll of waves against the pier: she was becoming Marilyn.

24

Cedars of Lebanon

The rain had fallen all night, rinsing the streets of Laurel Canyon until they glistened like dark mirrors. Los Angeles was a city in love with its illusions, but rain had a way of washing them thin, showing cracks beneath the neon. Norma Jeane was just another girl riding in a borrowed car, lipstick borrowed too, her laughter spilling into the wet night like coins tossed into a fountain. She was 16, still half-child, half-woman, her heart eager to be anywhere but the rooms that smelled of starch and sermons.

The crash came without warning. Tires screeched, a horn cut short, and then the shriek of metal folding in on itself like paper. The world tilted, glass burst, and the night swallowed her scream. When she opened her eyes, the windshield was a spiderweb, the steering wheel twisted at a cruel angle, and the boy beside her was slumped against the seat, his face slick with blood. For a moment, she thought he was dead. For a moment, she thought she was.

The ambulance smelled of rain-soaked leather and gasoline. She lay still, her arm bent at an awkward angle, her head throbbing. Sirens wailed, their pitch rising and falling as if in mourning. She tried to ask about the boy, but her voice was drowned out, first by the siren, then by the rush of doors opening into a flood of light.

Cedars of Lebanon Hospital loomed at the edge of Hollywood, its name a promise of Biblical healing, though the reality was less poetic. Inside, the corridors reeked of iodine and carbolic soap, a smell that clung to her skin even through the morphine haze. Nurses moved briskly, their white shoes squeaking across linoleum, their faces unreadable behind the discipline of training.

She was placed on a cot beneath a light that flickered as though unsure of its own endurance. A doctor bent over her, his breath a mixture of coffee and cigarettes, his questions quick and precise. "Name?" he asked, and when she whispered it, *Norma Jeane*, it sounded unfamiliar, like she was trying on someone else's dress. He noted her age, her injuries, the abrasion across her temple. She stared past him, to the corner of the room where shadows thickened.

That was where she saw her. A woman, blonde hair shining like a halo, eyes soft as candlelight, lips parted in a half-smile she had seen before—on the screen, in magazines, everywhere dreams were printed. Jean Harlow, the platinum saint of Hollywood, dead just three years but already myth. She stood there shimmering like moonlight caught in glass, looking at Norma Jeane with recognition, as if she had been waiting.

"Not your time yet," the ghost whispered, her voice like bubbles rising in champagne. "You're going to be me. Better."

The morphine hummed through her veins, making the room sway, and she could not tell if she had heard it or dreamed it. But when the nurse returned, adjusting the sling on her arm, Norma Jeane smiled with blood still on her teeth. Something inside her had shifted. Whether it was fever or fate, she believed it. She had been chosen—by ghosts, by destiny, by something larger than the ordinary life she had been handed.

For the first time, pain felt like a passage.

The days blurred into one another inside Cedars of Lebanon. The light through the high hospital windows shifted from dawn's pale blue to the syrupy gold of afternoon and then into a dark that felt bottomless. Nurses in white uniforms glided past like ghosts of efficiency, the starch of their skirts whispering against one another, their shoes squeaking on the polished floor. To Norma Jeane, the hours felt like a film spliced wrong—frames missing, scenes looping, conversations repeating until she wasn't sure what she had lived and what she had imagined.

Her arm throbbed under the sling, a dull, insistent reminder of the crash, but the deeper ache was in her chest. She was 16, and the boy who had been beside her had stopped moving in a pool of broken glass and twisted metal. They said he hadn't survived. She replayed it in her mind: the lipstick she had carefully painted before the drive, the way she'd laughed too loudly at one of his jokes, the sudden lurch of the car as if the earth itself had tilted. And then nothing but shattering sound.

At night, when the ward fell quiet except for the occasional cough or the faraway moan of a patient in pain, she drifted on the edge of sleep. That was when the vision came. A shimmer in the corner of her eye, then a figure made of light and powder and perfume. The blonde curls, the wide eyes, the sensuous mouth—Jean Harlow, Hollywood's platinum ghost, dead before her time. Norma Jeane had seen her in magazines, pressed her nose to posters in the lobby of the neighborhood theater, memorized her tilted poses. And here she was, floating at the edge of a hospital cot.

"Not yet," Harlow whispered, her voice both gentle and commanding. "It's not your time. You have things to do. You'll be me. Better."

The words sank into her like scripture. Better. She clutched at them like rosary beads, turning them over in her mind as the morphine swirled through her veins. She woke one morning with her pillow damp from tears, unsure if she had been crying or sweating. The other patients talked of pain, of relatives visiting, of insurance bills. She talked to no one. She kept the ghost for herself.

The nurses said she was lucky. She heard them whisper it outside her door: "That girl's a survivor." They meant the crash, but she knew it was larger than that. She had survived her mother's breakdown, the orphanage, the foster homes, the cold kitchens where shoes didn't fit. She had survived loneliness so sharp it cut into her bones. This was just another test. Another near miss.

When she was finally allowed to walk the corridor, her sling pressed tight against her ribs, she shuffled past the other patients and wondered what they saw when they looked at her. Did they see a girl nearly broken? Or did they see the ghostlight already burning in her, the strange shimmer that the camera had once caught and would catch again?

Every step down that corridor felt like rehearsal. She imagined herself in a costume, hospital gown exchanged for satin, slippers replaced with heels. The other patients became an audience. She walked slower, straighter, and though her body ached, she lifted her chin. The performance began there, in the antiseptic halls of Cedars of Lebanon.

The doctors signed her release weeks later. She stepped outside, the California sun harsh and real, and for a moment she blinked, unsure whether she was truly alive or still floating in the dream where Jean Harlow had touched her shoulder and promised her a destiny. She breathed in the smoggy air, clutched the paper bag of medicine they gave her, and smiled—a small, secret smile that no one else understood.

For the rest of her life, Norma Jeane would talk about that night as though it had been the hinge of everything. Not in public—never for the magazines, never for the studio's neat little biographies. But privately, to friends who pressed close in darkened rooms, she spoke of it. The crash, the hospital, the ghost of a movie star long dead. She told them she believed she had been chosen. That the crash was not an ending, but an anointing. That the morphine and the moonlight had mixed to christen her for something larger than herself.

And maybe she was right. Maybe in that hospital, bruised and bandaged, Norma Jeane began her true metamorphosis—not because of hair dye or contracts, but because she had glimpsed death and heard it say: not yet.

The days at Cedars blurred, stitched together by morphine drips and the rhythm of nurses' shoes clicking across the tiled floor. Norma Jeane drifted in and out of consciousness, the ceiling above her a vast blank page where her fears and fantasies played like silent films. At first, she kept waiting for Gladys to appear, but the door never opened with her mother's perfume. Instead, the people who came were strangers with white coats and clipped voices, measuring her pulse, checking her pupils, whispering to one another about the girl who had been lucky. Lucky to survive. Lucky to walk again. Lucky not to have been thrown through the windshield like the boy.

She didn't feel lucky. She felt marked. Each bandage was like a question she couldn't answer. When she closed her eyes, she saw headlights splitting the rain, the world spinning, the red smear of lipstick against broken glass. And then she saw Harlow. Always Harlow, standing just out of reach in her shimmering gown, pale and luminous as moonlight. Sometimes she smiled. Sometimes she shook her head as if to warn her. Sometimes her mouth formed words Norma Jeane couldn't hear, and that silence haunted more than the crash itself.

The nurses noticed the way the girl stared into corners, smiling at nothing. They assumed it was the medicine. One said quietly that the girl had "that look"—fragile, otherworldly, as if her mind were a half-step away from drifting out the window with the city's night air. But when the doctor leaned over her bed and asked how she felt, she straightened, summoned her practiced smile, and said, "Better, thank you." The performance had begun even there, in the antiseptic halls of Cedars, before any camera or contract.

Visitors came in trickles. A neighbor from Hawthorne. A school friend who stood awkwardly at the end of the bed, clutching a get-well card. Grace Goddard, her guardian, whose face softened when she saw the girl alive and whole, and who brought magazines and told her gently that everything would be all right. Grace did not mention the boy who had been driving. She did not mention his silence, his stillness, the way his absence clung to the hospital room like a draft.

In the quiet hours, Norma Jeane began to imagine that her survival was no accident. How else could she explain the ghostly figure who had appeared at her bedside? Jean Harlow had died when Norma Jeane was only 9, but she remembered the photographs: the platinum hair, the gowns, the way men looked at her as if she were light itself. And now here she was, rising from the shimmer of morphine dreams, telling her it wasn't her time. The idea took root like ivy. Maybe she was chosen. Maybe she was meant to carry on where Harlow left off. Maybe the crash had been less a tragedy than an anointing.

When she was discharged, her arm still tender in its sling, the city looked different. The rain-slick streets glowed brighter, the billboards seemed to call her name. Passing a movie theater, she saw Harlow's face again on an old poster, and she stopped in her tracks. It felt less like coincidence than confirmation. She wasn't just another foster child, another forgotten girl. She was being prepared. Tested. Shaped by fire and glass into something larger than herself.

Back home, she told almost no one about the visions. To mention it aloud was to risk ridicule, and she already knew how laughter could wound. But in her secret heart, she replayed the words she thought she had heard, the ones Harlow might have spoken: *Not yet. You're going to be me. Better.* It was enough to stiffen her spine when the nights grew long and the loneliness pressed close. It was enough to turn every mirror into a stage, every smile into rehearsal.

Years later, when she was Marilyn Monroe, she would still speak of that crash, hinting that she had glimpsed something beyond herself that night. She never named Harlow directly—some things were too delicate, too precious—but she carried the ghost with her into every role, every photograph. The crash at Laurel Canyon was her private prologue, the secret chapter in which Norma Jeane was nearly erased but instead reborn.

And if the photographs afterward seemed to catch more light in her eyes, if her smile looked sharper, almost defiant, it was because she knew what it meant to come close to the edge and walk back. Cedars of Lebanon was her first audition for destiny, and she had passed.

When she was discharged from Cedars, the sunlight looked different. It was too sharp, too white, as if the world had been scrubbed raw in her absence. She cradled her injured arm against her body, the bandages scratching her skin, and walked carefully out of the hospital doors. The city roared around her—streetcars grinding their rails, newsboys calling out the day's disasters—but she heard it all through the muffled hush of someone who had brushed too close to silence.

People who visited her afterward told the story in quick, casual tones. "Lucky you weren't killed," they said, as if luck were a coin she had flipped. They told her she'd heal. That she'd put it behind her. No one asked about the dream in the hospital bed. No one asked about the woman with the platinum halo and the whisper that still clung to her ribs. To them, the accident was an event, a fact to be filed away. To Norma Jeane, it was a doorway she had stumbled through, and the world on the other side would never look the same.

At night, she dreamt of headlights. They burst through her sleep like twin suns, searing and unstoppable, until they dissolved into Harlow's smile. In those dreams, the blonde ghost reached out a gloved hand and said, "Stand taller. They'll see you if you stand taller." She woke with the sheets twisted around her legs and her mouth full of words she hadn't spoken. Sometimes she laughed at herself. Sometimes she pressed her hand against her chest and whispered, *Thank you*, as if the dead star could hear her.

The scar on her arm remained faint but real, a line of memory stitched into her flesh. She touched it often, tracing it as if it were a signature. A reminder. Not everyone carried proof that destiny had bent down to brush against them. She wore hers like an invisible jewel.

Back at Grace's, life returned to its ordinary rhythms. Chores, school, the quiet shuffle of foster siblings. But something inside her had shifted. She began to see herself differently, as if her reflection in the mirror were an understudy waiting for her cue. The plain brown hair, the too-wide smile, the hand-me-down dresses—these were costumes, temporary. The girl in the photograph, the one with the tilted chin and the light in her eyes, was closer to the truth. The accident had told her so.

When neighbors asked how she was doing, she told them she was fine, better, almost herself again. But in private, she rehearsed. She tried new ways of walking, slower and smoother, as though the crash had pressed glamour into her bones. She studied the magazines more closely, tracing not just the poses but the way the women seemed to belong to the page. She clipped out Jean Harlow's picture and taped it inside a drawer where Ida would not find it. "Not your time yet," the ghost had said. That meant she still had time to prepare.

The world wanted her to forget. She refused. Instead, she built the crash into her secret mythology. Just as other girls dreamed of guardian angels or fairy godmothers, Norma Jeane believed she had been visited by Harlow's ghost, chosen by fate. She wasn't foolish enough to speak it aloud—people laughed at that kind of talk, and she'd had enough of laughter at her expense. But in her heart, she held it close. When the house was quiet, when the laundry was done, when the rest of the children had gone to bed, she would close her eyes and see that shimmering figure in the hospital ward, see the smile that said she belonged to something larger than herself.

And so the accident did not end with the crash. It rippled through every day afterward, a reminder that she had been spared, that she carried a responsibility with her now. To be more. To become the girl the camera saw. To keep walking toward the woman the ghost had promised.

The Cedars of Lebanon hospital was more than just a medical ward in those days. It was a cathedral of Hollywood's fragile flesh, where screen idols limped in under cover of night and were stitched together under fluorescent light. The lobby smelled of antiseptic and wilted roses left behind from visitors. Somewhere in those halls Clara Bow had wept after a nervous collapse, and countless starlets had been quietly patched up from botched studio diets, car wrecks, or nights when the glamour could no longer hold.

For Norma Jeane, barely on the cusp of becoming someone else, the hospital felt like a stage set stripped bare. No sequins, no light—just the raw machinery of survival. She noticed the clatter of metal trays, the hiss of oxygen tanks, the pale blue curtains that shielded one cot from another like half-drawn veils. Every sound imprinted itself on her memory. Later, when she became Marilyn, she would still wake some nights hearing those hospital wheels squeak down the linoleum, rolling endlessly toward nowhere.

It was there, in that blur of chloroform and sutures, that the vision came: Jean Harlow, blonde ghost of an earlier Hollywood. Some called Harlow the Platinum Venus, others the Baby, but to Norma Jeane she was a dream made flesh, a girl who had also started poor, who had also been renamed, remade, consumed by the very dream she embodied. Harlow had died young at Cedars, not far from where Norma Jeane now lay. It was no wonder her presence haunted the corridors like perfume lingering after the woman is gone.

In her feverish half-sleep, Norma Jeane heard Harlow's whisper as if it floated through the drip of rain outside the hospital windows: *Not yet. Not you. You'll carry me forward.* She clutched at that ghostly blessing. She had no mother who could steady her hand, no father who had ever claimed her, but here was an inheritance of another kind—the mantle of stardom passed from one fractured girl to another.

When she was discharged, her arm stiff in its sling, she did not walk out of Cedars as the same girl who had been carried in. Something of Norma Jeane's fear had been burned away, cauterized in the wreckage. In its place was a strange conviction: that she had been chosen, marked. The city had not swallowed her whole. Fate had paused, allowed her to rise again. She walked into the drizzle of the hospital's parking lot with a crooked smile and the faint taste of blood still in her mouth, and she told herself it was lipstick.

Years later, when reporters asked her about Jean Harlow—how she had adored her, studied her films, modeled herself after her—Marilyn never mentioned Cedars of Lebanon, never confessed the spectral encounter she believed had occurred that night. Some truths were too fragile for print. But in her diaries and in her silences, she held it close: the night the ghost of Harlow whispered across the gulf of death and promised her that she, too, would be unforgettable.

25

Becoming Marilyn

The day they mixed the bleach, the room filled with the sharp tang of peroxide and possibility. Norma Jeane sat in the chair, a cape tied snug around her shoulders, and tried not to squirm as the stylist sectioned her chestnut hair into careful strands. She had been warned: the process stung, it burned, it could strip more than just color. But she wanted it. Needed it. Every tug of the comb felt like a step away from the foster homes, the cracked mirrors, the name that no one had ever bothered to say with pride.

The dye foamed white, frothing at the roots, hissing faintly as if secrets were being dissolved. "Hold still," the stylist said, painting each lock with reverence, as if he were gilding a statue instead of a girl. Norma Jeane inhaled the acrid scent and closed her eyes. She imagined the old self draining away, each strand surrendering its history, until only light remained.

When it was done, when the towel was whisked away and the curls dried to a golden halo, she opened her eyes and gasped. A stranger looked back at her from the mirror—but not a stranger she feared. This girl was luminous, as if touched by moonlight. The hair caught every glint of the bulb overhead, shimmered with a promise that seemed larger than the small salon where she sat. She reached up, fingertips grazing the softness, and whispered, "Marilyn."

The name had been suggested by a studio publicist, plucked out of thin air the way men plucked flowers to pin on lapels. Norma Jeane Mortenson was too clumsy, too heavy with the syllables of a past best forgotten. Marilyn Miller had been a Broadway star once, a blonde who died too young, and perhaps some ghost of her lingered in the suggestion. "Marilyn Monroe," the publicist repeated, as though he had just minted a coin. Monroe was her mother's maiden name, polished and repurposed, stripped of all the sorrow it carried. It sparkled now, bright enough to catch on marquees.

She practiced writing it that night on a scrap of paper, looping the letters, dotting the "i" with a flourish. Norma Jeane's hand trembled, as though it knew the gravity of what it was surrendering. Each signature was both an incantation and a betrayal. She was naming herself into existence, but in doing so, she was also erasing the girl who had survived on second-hand shoes and school picture smiles.

Still, she couldn't stop. The name felt alive in her mouth. Marilyn. She said it in the mirror, lips parting in feigned surprise, as if she were already on stage. Marilyn was someone who could not be ignored, someone who belonged to the whole world. The girl in the foster homes had longed to be chosen. Marilyn was already chosen, if only by the audacity of her own reinvention.

The studio men noticed immediately. It wasn't just the hair, though the platinum gleam caught every flashbulb like fire trapped in glass. It was the way she carried herself differently now, as if the name had re-stitched her bones. She smiled brighter, her laugh fell lighter, her posture demanded attention without asking for it.

"She's got something," one of the executives said, squinting through cigarette smoke. Something. They never named it, not fully. Too mysterious to define, too precious to waste time labeling. A presence, a charge in the air, a sudden flicker of light in a dark room. Men leaned in when she entered. Women looked twice, first with envy, then with a startled kind of admiration.

But for all the sparkle of her new name, Marilyn felt the tug of Norma Jeane inside her. At home in her tiny apartment, she still cooked beans, still scrubbed the linoleum, still worried about rent. She folded laundry and whispered prayers for her mother, still locked away in the hospital. She walked streets where no one recognized her, only to step into the studio the next morning and be bathed in the hush of cameras clicking as though she were already famous.

The contradiction unsettled her. Who was she now? The girl polishing borrowed shoes at night, or the blonde apparition learning to sign autographs she hadn't yet been asked for? Sometimes she feared the transformation was a trick of the light, that if she stepped too far into darkness the dye would fade, the illusion vanish, and the world would laugh at her for believing.

But then came the photographs.

A young photographer named André de Dienes coaxed her into the desert, where the wind tangled her hair and the horizon stretched endless as her hunger for something more. She posed barefoot, wrapped in blankets, the sun kissing her skin until it glowed. He caught her laughing, caught her serious, caught her staring straight into the camera as though daring the world to turn away.

When she saw the proofs, something shifted. That wasn't Norma Jeane in those photographs. That wasn't even the in-between girl, half-wife, half-child. That was Marilyn—luminous, sensual, untouchable. She lingered over the images, tracing the lines of her own face as if trying to memorize a woman she was only just beginning to meet.

At the studio, they encouraged the illusion. More bleach, more lipstick, higher heels. They pinned her into gowns she could barely breathe in, trained her to walk like her hips belonged to the world. She obeyed. She had learned long ago that survival meant saying yes—yes to the photograph, yes to the whisper, yes to the name that now rang like a promise.

Yet at night, when she washed off the rouge and the powder, Norma Jeane stared back from the mirror, damp curls clinging to her temples. She felt both haunted and protected by the girl beneath the glamour. Marilyn was armor. Norma Jeane was the wound. Together, they made something fragile and ferocious: a star in the making.

The first screen test felt like a dare. They put her in front of a blank backdrop and asked her to be interesting while doing nothing at all. The camera whirred like a patient animal. A man with a clipboard told her to turn her head left, then right, then down, then up, as if her face were a compass they were trying to read. She swallowed, lifted her chin, and let the silence fill with breath. The light was hot on her skin. The old name trembled somewhere behind her ribs, wanting to crawl back into her mouth. She held her ground. The new one steadied her.

"Say your name," the man said without looking up.

She parted her lips, let the vowels soften. "Marilyn . . . Monroe."

The syllables seemed to glide into the air like a satin ribbon. She watched for the flinch, the sneer, the boredom—the reactions she had learned to expect when the world measured her and found her wanting. The man only nodded and wrote something down. He asked her to smile, to be serious, to laugh as if she had just heard a secret meant only for her. She gave them all three, then added a fourth expression that wasn't on their list: a kind of shy defiance, as if she were daring the camera to love her and knowing it would.

The test traveled through rooms she would never enter and onto desks where she would never sit. "There's a glow," someone said. "Find out who she is," said someone else. The words returned to her as a telephone call, as a contract thinner than a prayer but printed with a studio's letterhead. She pressed the pages flat with trembling palms, read the clauses she did not understand, and signed the name she had invented twice, slowly, to make sure the ink believed it.

The studio sent her to lessons: diction to soften the edges of the neighborhoods she had lived in; movement so her hips learned a rhythm that said runway when they had been trained for waiting lines; singing so her voice could thread itself through a melody without snagging. She devoured it all. Teachers discovered she was sponge and steel, able to listen with a hunger that flattered them and a will that frightened them a little. "Again," she would say. "Let me try it again."

She learned how to enter a room as if the air itself brightened to greet her. She learned where to find her light—quarter-turn to the left, chin down, eyes up—so the pupils flashed like ink in a glass of milk. She learned to make a pause into a promise. And she learned, perhaps most importantly, how to keep a piece of herself off the table, tucked behind the rib where no camera could follow.

Between lessons she modeled, the way girls like her learned to pay for dreams. A photographer with elegant hands positioned her at the edge of a chaise and said, "Think about something you want." She thought of a small apartment with a door that locked from the inside and a refrigerator that hummed with actual food. He pressed the shutter. Later, another photographer—older, gentler—took her to the ocean at daybreak. She wrapped herself in a sweater, hair blown salty and wild, and looked past the lens into something that existed only in her mind: a marquee with her name on it, or perhaps the ghost of a girl in a hospital whispering not yet. The photographs seemed to hold more than her body; they held the shimmer of almost.

The studio tried her on like a dress. They put her in three scenes that were mostly light—crossing a room, turning a head, letting a smile bloom and fade like a trick candle. In the rushes, that small work looked larger. She didn't steal scenes; she illuminated them, the way a mirror makes a room look twice its size. A director with a face like granite tapped ash into a paper cup and said, "She plays to the camera without pushing at it. That's rare." Another muttered, "She's a menace. The extras will disappear around her." They meant it as a warning; it sounded like a blessing.

They dyed the hair again. There was always a brighter blonde to chase, a higher wattage of light. The colorists spoke in tiny adjustments the way surgeons whisper over arteries. She endured the sting, the chemical halo itching along her scalp, and stared at the ceiling while the clock hands crawled.

What does it cost, she wondered, to glow like this? The girl she had been would have said: everything. The woman she was becoming said: whatever it takes.

At night she memorized lines she hadn't been given yet, turning sentences into breath, breath into music. She watched old films in a boardinghouse common room and copied the way Carole Lombard timed a joke so it landed without bruising, the way Garbo slow-blinked her way through heartbreak, the way Harlow made even a silence sound like a laugh. She wasn't stealing; she was learning the scale so she could improvise.

Sometimes the old life tugged at her sleeve. A letter from a friend who still worked at the factory, grease under her nails and a ribald sense of humor that made Marilyn laugh so hard she spilled tea into her lap. A note from a relative asking for five dollars, then ten, written in a script that leaned forward as if trying to outrun shame. A message from a neighbor who'd once brought soup after a fever: We saw your picture in the paper. Is that really you? She wrote back to all of them with warmth and care and the daintiest lies she knew how to tell, the kind meant to protect both sides from the distance that was already opening up.

She practiced signatures until her hand cramped, not out of vanity but as a hedge against doubt. If a woman can write her name in twenty styles, perhaps the world will choose at least one to believe. On bad days she tried to remember the orphanage clock and how she had once measured her life by bells; on good days she measured it by call times scrawled in pencil on the back of an envelope.

A publicist taught her how to enter a flashbulb storm: chin angled, eyes lit, lips parted just enough to imply welcome and withhold permission. "Don't look down," he said, "unless you want them to follow you there." Another taught her how to tell a story about herself that sounded true without setting down roots. "Give them the melody," he said. "Keep the lyrics." She nodded as if he had told her a secret. He had.

There were stumbles. A test that fell flat, a producer who liked the way she looked but not the way she existed, a script supervisor who sighed loud enough to wound. There were days when she felt like a photograph left in the sun too long, all the contrast leached out until only a faint outline remained. On those days she went home early, washed her face, and sat very still with her hands in her lap, reminding herself that she had lived through worse. The orphanage. The Sunday waiting. The pillow. The crash. This was only light, and light did not kill you—it asked to be learned.

She learned.

On a set that smelled of sawdust and sweat, a gaffer tilted a reflector until her eyes sparked like struck matches. "Hold it," the cameraman said, and she did, holding not just the look but the state of being behind it—the blend of shyness and exhibition, of wanting to be seen and wanting to never be touched. The moment deepened, widened, filled. The director glanced up from his notes as if a draft had just lifted the page. "That," he said quietly, to no one in particular. "That."

Word crept. Nothing so grand as discovery—Hollywood does not discover so much as slowly turn its head—but over weeks and months people began to use her new name without asking where it came from. Hairstylists called her Marilyn. Wardrobe tags said M. Monroe. An assistant with a box of safety pins asked, "Marilyn, honey, can you breathe?" She thought about the question a beat longer than the woman expected and answered, "I can now."

She wrote to her mother in careful sentences that kept the edges soft: working hard, keeping busy, learning every day. She did not mention the nights she woke from dreams of headlights and hospital lights braided together, Harlow's whisper tinting the dark like perfume. She did not mention the way the studio gates looked like both promise and prison. She signed the letter "Your daughter" and then, as if she were practicing for a world that might one day accept both truths, "Marilyn."

There was a small part in a small picture where she walked across a lobby in a dress the color of gossip. The scene lasted less than a minute. In the theater, men shifted forward, women elbowed each other. "Who's that?" someone asked, not loudly, but the sentence made its way like a ripple through the rows. She did nothing spectacular; she looked up from her purse as if she had just remembered someone loved her and then moved on. People talked about it afterward as though a weather system had passed through the room.

Offers did not pour in. They trickled, and each one demanded a little more. A longer scene, a brighter smile, a line of dialogue that tasted like sugar on the tongue and left her throat parched. She took them. She said yes. She understood that momentum has to be fed. She understood, too, that yes was not surrender so much as strategy. You say yes until the door is open wide enough for you to choose.

At home, she cut the tags out of the one good dress she had bought on credit and sewed the hem by hand because it fell wrong when she walked. She heated soup on a single burner and hummed through mouthfuls as if warming her voice. On the dresser, a cheap frame held a photograph from the beach: hair windblown, sweater sleeves pulled over her hands, a smile there that no one had taught her, the one that belonged to her alone. She touched the glass and told the girl inside, "Come with me."

The first time a stranger asked for her autograph on the street, she startled. The woman—middle-aged, practical shoes, a face like the neighbor who once lent her sugar—said, "I know you. You're the girl from that picture with the red dress." Pride rose, bright as fever, and then fear followed, cold at the edges. If they recognized her here, in daylight, what would happen to the pieces of her that still wanted to be anonymous? She smiled anyway, wrote the practiced name with its loop and flourish, and said thank you as if the woman had given her something rather than taken it. In a way, she had.

As the months turned into a year that felt like a breath held too long, the two selves—girl and invention—learned their duet. Norma Jeane woke her in the morning, reminded her to eat, to keep a little money tucked in a book, and to call the landlady by her first name. Marilyn took the afternoons, stood in the light, stood for the fittings, stood and stood until the soles of her feet sang with pain. At night, they met in the mirror and negotiated: this much skin, this much secrecy, this much smile, this much silence.

When doubt came—and it always came, clever in its disguises—she went back to the oldest rituals. Polishing shoes that were finally her own. Rehearsing lines until they sounded like thought. Whispering in the quiet to the woman in the hospital who had leaned out of death to tell her not yet. She never decided whether the visitation had been real. She decided it had been necessary. That was enough.

There would be agents and contracts and men who mistook her glow for vacancy. There would be pictures that used her like punctuation and others that gave her room to speak. There would be days when the studio wanted only her hair and nights when the city wanted only her loneliness. She could not control any of that. What she could control was simple and nearly holy: the way she entered light, the way she received attention without flinching, the way she turned looking into seeing.

On a morning that felt like any other—coffee bitter, sky bright, a run in her stocking repaired with a dab of clear polish—she walked through the studio gate and felt something tilt inside, a small click, like a lock turned from the other side. The guard nodded. An assistant handed her pages. A wardrobe girl said, "You're going to be late if you don't hurry," and she laughed, a sound like champagne remembering it was rain.

"Marilyn," someone called from across the lot. She turned toward the voice and found her mark as if she had been born there. The camera, waiting, seemed to blink. She smiled—not the smile she had learned for protection or the one she had practiced for persuasion, but the one that belonged to becoming. The one that said: I am here now.

The light caught. The moment held. And the girl who had once tilted her chin for school pictures so the world would not forget her learned, at last, how to bloom on cue.

BIBLIOGRAPHY

Books

Bacon, James. *Hollywood Is a Four Letter Town.* Washington, DC: Regnery, 1976.

Bacon, James. *Made in Hollywood.* Washington, DC: Regnery, 1977.

Banner, Lois W. *Marilyn: The Passion and Paradox.* New York: Bloomsbury, 2012.

Barris, George. *Marilyn: Her Life in Her Own Words.* New York: Citadel Books, 2001.

Casillo, Charles. *Marilyn Monroe: The Private Life of a Public Icon.* New York: St. Martin's Press, 2018.

Castro, Tony. *The Book of Marilyn.* New York: Prodigal Son Books, 2025.

Clark, Colin. *My Week with Marilyn.* New York: Grand Central Publishing, 2011.

Franse, Astrid, and Michelle Morgan. *Before Marilyn: The Blue Book Modeling Years.* New York: Thomas Dunne Books, 2015.

Greene, Joshua. *The Essential Marilyn Monroe: Milton H. Greene: 50 Sessions.* New York: ACC Art Books, 2019.

Guiles, Fred Lawrence. *Norma Jeane: The Life of Marilyn Monroe.* New York: McGraw-Hill Publishers, 1969.

Heymann, C. David. *Joe and Marilyn: Legends in Love.* New York: Atria/Emily Bestler Books, 2014.

Jordan, Elisa. *Hello, Norma Jeane: The Marilyn Monroe You Didn't Know.* Essex, CT: Applause Theatre & Cinema Books, 2023.

Jordan, Larry Neal. *The Real Marilyn Monroe: Debunking the Myths and Revealing Intimate New Details of Her Life and Death.* New York: Page Turner Books International, 2024.

Leaming, Barbara. *Marilyn Monroe: A Biography.* New York: Random House, 1998.

Mailer, Norman. *Marilyn.* New York: Alskog, Inc. and Normal Mailer, 1973.

Miller, Joshua John, M. A. Fortin, and Bernard Bruno. *The Marilyn Monroe Century: From Norma Jeane to Icon—A Story in Photographs.* New York: Abrams Books, 2026.

Miracle, Berniece. *My Sister Marilyn: A Memoir of Marilyn Monroe.* Bloomington, IN: Algonquin Books, 1994.

Monroe, Marilyn. *Fragments: Poems, Intimate Notes, Letters.* Edited by Bernard Comment and Stanley Buchthal. New York: Farrar, Straus and Giroux, 2010.

Patterson, James. *The Last Days of Marilyn Monroe: A True Crime Thriller.* Boston: Little, Brown and Company, 2025.

Russell, Jane. *My Path and My Detours: An Autobiography.* New York: Franklin Watts, 1985.

Schneider, Michel. *Marilyn's Last Sessions.* Translated by Will Hobson. New York: Canongate UK, 2013.

Siriano, Christian, Rachel Syme, David Wills, and Louis Conway. *Marilyn Monroe 100: The Official Centenary Book.* New York: ACC Art Books, 2026.

Spoto, Donald. *Marilyn Monroe: The Biography.* New York: HarperCollins, 1993.
Steinem, Gloria. *Marilyn.* New York: Henry Holt & Co., 1988.
Stern, Bert. *The Last Sitting.* New York: William Morrow & Co, 1982.
Strasberg, Susan. *Marilyn and Me: Sisters, Rivals, Friends.* New York: Grand Central Publishing, 1992.
Summers, Anthony. *Goddess: The Secret Lives of Marilyn Monroe.* New York: Macmillan, 1985.
Taraborrelli, J. Randy. *The Secret Life of Marilyn Monroe.* New York: Grand Central Publishing, 2009.
Willis, David. *Marilyn Monroe: Metamorphosis.* New York: It Books, 2011.

Periodicals

Allan, Rupert. "Marilyn Monroe: A Serious Blonde Who Can Act." *Look* 15, no. 22 (October 23, 1951): 40–4. Photos Earl Thiesen.
Archer, Jules. "Meet Marilyn Monroe and a New Picture Magazine." *Foto Parade,* December 1949, 8–10.
Cahn, Robert. "Marilyn Monroe Hits a New High." *Collier's,* July 9, 1954, 98.
Corliss, Richard. "Marilyn Monroe 50 Years Later: In TIME and Out of Time." *Time,* August 3, 2012. https://entertainment.time.com/2012/08/03/marilyn-monroe-50-years-later-in-time-and-out-of-time/.
Goodman, Ezra. "Marilyn Monroe—The Figure of Fantasy." *Time,* May 14, 1956.
Graham, Sheila. "Marilyn Talks About Joe and Babies." *Modern Screen,* September 1954, 28.
Hackett, John. "Screen Sensation at 19, Hollywood Has Been at 20, Charm Champ Makes Smashing Comeback at 21." *See* 10, no. 6 (November 1951): 26–8.
Heilbroner, Robert L. "The Fabulous Story of Hollywood's Biggest Buildup." *Cosmopolitan,* May 1953, 29–32.
Henagan, Jim. "The Loneliest Star in Hollywood." *Picturegoer,* August 9, 1952, 12–13.
Johnson, Grady. "The Story Behind Marilyn Monroe." *Coronet* 32, no. 6 (October 1952): 83–88.
Muir, Flora. "Whole Town's Talking About Marilyn Monroe." *Life* 32, no. 14 (April 7, 1952): 101–4.
Nelson, Elyda J. "For the First Time! The True Life of Marilyn Monroe." *Modern Screen,* December 1952, 50–4.
Rothman, Lily. "How Marilyn Monroe Became a 'Real Actress'" *Time,* June 1, 2016. https://time.com/4346417/marilyn-monroe-time-1956-cover/.

Documentaries

Dream Girl: The Making of Marilyn Monroe (2022). Director: Ian Ayres; Writer: Ian Ayres; Stars: Ian Ayres, Marilyn Monroe, Joe DiMaggio. Archive footage.

Becoming Marilyn (2022). TV Special of Marilyn during years with Blue Book Modeling Agency. Archive footage.

Reframed: Marilyn Monroe (2022). Owner, Blue Book Model Agency. Archive footage.

The Mother of Beauty 7.2 Self (2019). Archive footage.

The Myth of Marilyn. Prime Video (2022). Director: Oliver Elphick; Writer: Oliver Elphick; Stars: Sherry Carter Brownell, Mabel Ella Campbell, Suzie Kennedy.

Rare Interview With Emmeline Snively, owner, Blue Book Modeling Agency recalls Marilyn Monroe's first impression as a "girl next door," 1964.

Selected Interviews, Witnesses, and Key Testimonies

James Bacon: Hollywood columnist for the Associated Press and *Los Angeles Herald-Examiner*; knew Monroe and DiMaggio personally from the 1950s onward and wrote about her in *Hollywood Is a Four Letter Town*.

Skip E. Lowe: Cable interviewer and Hollywood nostalgist whose friendships and taped conversations with figures such as Susan Strasberg, Jean Howard, Tony Curtis, Shelley Winters, Aldo Ray, and others helped map the social web around Monroe.

Emmeline Snively/Blue Book Agency archive: Correspondence, notes, and booking records from Monroe's modelling years, later acquired and published in part by Astrid Franse and Michelle Morgan in *Before Marilyn*.

Susan Strasberg: Daughter of Lee Strasberg; her recollections of Monroe's Actors Studio years and the family's private life inform the chapters on Marilyn's training and search for seriousness.

INDEX

ABOUT THE AUTHOR

Tony Castro is an acclaimed journalist, historian, and author, recognized for his *New York Times* bestselling work that includes the literary biography *Looking for Hemingway* (NPR: Best Books of the Year), the landmark civil rights history *Chicano Power* (*Publishers Weekly*: "Brilliant . . . a valuable contribution to the understanding of our time") and his multi-volume profile of baseball icon Mickey Mantle, detailing his crucial role in shaping the place of modern sports heroes in American pop culture.

Tony and his wife, novelist Renee LaSalle, live in Southern California.